Guidebook: A Manual For St

The American Pageant
Volume II: Since 1865

FOURTEENTH EDITION

David M. Kennedy
Stanford University

Lizabeth Cohen
Harvard University

Thomas A. Bailey

Prepared by

Mel Piehl
Valparaiso University

Australia • Brazil • Japan • Korea • Mexico • Singapore • Spain • United Kingdom • United States

For product information and technology assistance, contact us at **Cengage Learning Customer & Sales Support, 1-800-354-9706**

For permission to use material from this text or product, submit all requests online at **www.cengage.com/permissions**
Further permissions questions can be emailed to **permissionrequest@cengage.com**

ISBN-13: 978-0-547-16692-6
ISBN-10: 0-547-16692-3

Wadsworth
25 Thomson Place
Boston, MA 02210
USA

Cengage Learning is a leading provider of customized learning solutions with office locations around the globe, including Singapore, the United Kingdom, Australia, Mexico, Brazil, and Japan. Locate your local office at: **international.cengage.com/region**

Cengage Learning products are represented in Canada by Nelson Education, Ltd.

For your course and learning solutions, visit **academic.cengage.com**

Purchase any of our products at your local college store or at our preferred online store **www.ichapters.com**

Printed in the United States of America
2 3 4 5 6 13 12 11 10

Contents

CHAPTER 22

The Ordeal of Reconstruction, 1865–1877

PART I: REVIEWING THE CHAPTER

A. Checklist of Learning Objectives

After mastering this chapter, you should be able to:

1. Define the major problems facing the nation and the South after the Civil War.
2. Describe the responses of both whites and African Americans to the end of slavery.
3. Analyze the differences between the presidential and congressional approaches to Reconstruction.
4. Explain how the blunders of President Johnson and the resistance of the white South opened the door to the Republicans' radical Reconstruction.
5. Describe the intentions and the actual effects of radical Reconstruction in the South.
6. Indicate how militant southern white opposition and growing northern weariness with military Reconstruction gradually undermined Republican attempt to empower Southern blacks.
7. Explain why the radical Republicans impeached Johnson but failed to convict him.
8. Explain the legacy of Reconstruction, and assess its successes and failures.

B. Glossary

To build your social science vocabulary, familiarize yourself with the following terms.

1. **treason** The crime of betrayal of one's country, involving some overt act violating an oath of allegiance or providing illegal aid to a foreign state. In the United States, treason is the only crime specified in the Constitution. "What should be done with the captured Confederate ringleaders, all of whom were liable to charges of treason?"
2. **civil disabilities** Legally imposed restrictions of a person's civil rights or liberties. "But Congress did not remove all remaining civil disabilities until thirty years later. . . ."
3. **legalistically** In accord with the exact letter of the law, sometimes with the intention of thwarting its broad intent. "Some planters resisted emancipation more legalistically. . . ." (p. 481)
4. **mutual aid societies** Nonprofit organizations designed to provide their members with financial and social benefits, often including medical aid, life insurance, funeral costs, and disaster relief. "These churches . . . gave rise to other benevolent, fraternal, and mutual aid societies."
5. **confiscation (confiscated)** Legal government seizure of private property *without* compensation, often as a penalty; under **eminent domain**, the government may take private property for public purposes, but *with* fair compensation. ". . . the bureau was authorized to settle former slaves on forty-acre tracts confiscated from the Confederates. . . ."

6. **pocket veto** The presidential act of blocking a Congressionally passed law not by direct veto but by simply refusing to sign it at the end of a session. (A president can pocket-veto ten days of a session's end.) "Lincoln 'pocket-vetoed' this bill by refusing to sign it after Congress had adjourned."

7. **lease** To enter into a contract by which one party gives another use of land, buildings, or other property for a fixed time and fee. ". . . some [codes] even barred blacks from renting or leasing land."

8. **chain gang** A group of prisoners chained together while engaged in forced labor. "A black could be punished for 'idleness' by being sentenced to work on a chain gang."

9. **sharecrop** An agricultural system in which a tenant receives land, tools, and seed on credit and pledges in return a predetermined share of the crop to the creditor. ". . . former slaves slipped into the status of sharecropper farmers. . . ."

10. **peonage** A system, once common in Latin America, in which debtors are bound, in permanent or semi-permanent servitude, to labor for their creditors. "Luckless sharecroppers gradually sank into a morass of virtual peonage. . . ."

11. **scalawag** Disparaging term for a white Southerner who supported Republican Reconstruction after the Civil War. "The so-called scalawags were Southerners, often former Unionists and Whigs."

12. **carpetbagger** Disparaging term for a Northern politician who came south to exploit the unsettled conditions after the Civil War; hence, any politician who relocates for political advantage. "The carpet-baggers, on the other hand, were supposedly sleazy Northerners. . . ." (p. 495)

13. **felony** A major crime for which severe penalties are exacted under the law. "The crimes of the Reconstruction governments were no more outrageous than the scams and felonies being perpetrated in the North at the same time. . . ."

14. **terror (terrorist)** Using violence or the threat of violence in order to create intense fear in the attempt to promote some political policy or objectives. "Such tomfoolery and terror proved partially effective."

15. **president pro tempore** In the United States Senate, the officer who presides in the absence of the vice president. "Under existing law, the president pro tempore of the Senate . . . would then become president."

PART II: CHECKING YOUR PROGRESS

A. True-False

Where the statement is true, circle **T**; where it is false, circle **F**.

1. T F Most of the aristocratic southern plantation owners lost their wealth during the Civil War.

2. T F Most white southerners recognized that secession had been a mistake and welcomed returning to the United States as American citizens.

3. T F Many newly emancipated slaves undertook travel to demonstrate their freedom or to seek separated loved ones.

4. T F The focus of black community life after emancipation became the black church.

5. T F The newly established Freedmen's Bureau proved effective as a social agency providing economic opportunity as well as food, clothing, and medical care to emancipated blacks.

6. T F Lincoln's 10 percent Reconstruction plan was designed to return the Southern states to the Union quickly and with few restrictions.

7. T F Andrew Johnson's first Reconstruction actions pleased radical Republicans by harshly punishing Southern leaders and refusing to grant them pardons.

8. T F The sharecropping system, developed during Reconstruction, trapped most blacks and many poor whites in a condition of perpetual debt to their creditors.

9. T F The Black Codes, enacted by the Johnson-established southern state governments, provided freed slaves with basic political rights but not social integration.

10. T F Congressional Republicans demanded that the Southern states ratify the Fourteenth Amendment in order to be readmitted to the Union.

11. T F Radical Republicans succeeded in their goal of redistributing land to the former slaves.

12. T F During Reconstruction, blacks controlled most of the Southern state legislatures.

13. T F Many women felt betrayed when the Fifteenth Amendment gave voting rights to black males but not to women.

14. T F The federal government made no effort to attempt to suppress the violent white supremacists in the Ku Klux Klan.

15. T F The Republicans impeached Andrew Johnson essentially because of his opposition to their Reconstruction policies and not on the basis of "high crimes and misdemeanors."

B. Multiple Choice

Select the best answer and circle the corresponding letter.

1. Which of the following was *not* among the critical questions that faced the United States during Reconstruction?
   a. Would the president, Congress, or the states direct Reconstruction?
   b. How would liberated blacks manage as free men and women?
   c. Would the South be granted some kind of regional autonomy short of independence?
   d. How would the economically and socially devastated South be rebuilt?
   e. How would the southern states be reintegrated into the Union?
2. The Freedmen's Bureau was originally established to provide
   a. land, supplies, and seed for black farmers.
   b. job registration.
   c. food, clothing, and education for emancipated slaves.
   d. political training in citizenship for black voters.
   e. transportation and assistance in reuniting separated family members.

3. Lincoln's original plan for Reconstruction in 1863 was that a state could be reintegrated into the Union when
    a. it repealed its original secession act and withdrew its soldiers from the Confederate Army.
    b. 10 percent of its voters took an oath of allegiance to the Union and pledged to abide by emancipation.
    c. it formally adopted a plan guaranteeing black political and economic rights.
    d. it ratified the Fourteenth and Fifteenth Amendments to the Constitution.
    e. it barred from office and punished those who had voted for secession or served in the Confederate government.
4. The Black Codes, passed by many of the Johnson-approved Southern state governments in late 1865, aimed to
    a. provide economic assistance to get former slaves started as sharecroppers.
    b. prohibit interracial sexual relations.
    c. permit blacks to vote if they met certain educational or economic standards.
    d. force blacks to leave the South.
    e. ensure a stable and subservient labor force under white control.
5. The congressional elections of 1866 resulted in a
    a. victory for Johnson and his pro-Southern Reconstruction plan.
    b. further political stalemate between the Republicans in Congress and Johnson.
    c. decisive defeat for Johnson and a veto-proof Republican Congress.
    d. gain for Northern Democrats and their moderate compromise plan for Reconstruction.
    e. split between moderate Republicans in the Senate and radical Republicans in the House.
6. In contrast to radical Republicans, moderate Republicans generally
    a. favored states' rights and opposed direct federal involvement in individuals' lives.
    b. favored the use of federal power to alter the Southern economic system.
    c. favored emancipation but opposed the Fourteenth Amendment.
    d. favored returning the Southern states to the Union without significant Reconstruction.
    e. supported policies favorable to poor southern whites as well as blacks.
7. Besides putting the South under the rule of federal soldiers, the Military Reconstruction Act of 1867 required that all the reconstructed southern states must
    a. give blacks the vote as a condition of readmission to the Union.
    b. give blacks and carpetbaggers majority control of Southern legislatures.
    c. provide former slaves with land and education at state expense.
    d. try former Confederate officials and military officers for treason.
    e. effectively suppress the Ku Klux Klan and other white supremacist groups.
8. Which of the following was *not* among the provisions of the Fourteenth Amendment?
    a. Disqualification from federal and state office for former Confederate officials who had violated their oaths
    b. Reduction in Congressional representation and Electoral College vote for states that did not let blacks vote
    c. Repudiation of any Confederate debts
    d. Citizenship and full civil rights (except voting) for former slaves
    e. Elimination of one senator from each southern state until Reconstruction was complete
9. The Fifteenth Amendment provided for
    a. readmitting Southern states to the Union.
    b. full citizenship and civil rights for former slaves.
    c. voting rights for former slaves.
    d. voting rights for women.
    e. racial integration of public schools and public facilities.

10. Women's-rights leaders opposed the Fourteenth and Fifteenth Amendments because
    a. they objected to racial integration in the women's movement.
    b. the amendments granted citizenship and voting rights to black and white men but not to women.
    c. they favored passage of the Equal Rights Amendment first.
    d. most of them were Democrats who would be hurt by the amendments.
    e. they feared interracial sex and marriage.
11. Achieving the right to vote encouraged southern black men to
    a. form a third political party as an alternative to the Democrats and Republicans.
    b. seek a formal apology and reparations for slavery.
    c. organize the Union League as a vehicle for political empowerment and self-defense.
    d. organize large-scale migrations out of the South to the West.
    e. demand that each southern state grant blacks "forty acres and a mule."
12. The radical Reconstruction regimes in the Southern states
    a. took away white Southerners' civil rights and voting rights.
    b. consisted almost entirely of blacks.
    c. established public education and adopted many needed reforms.
    d. were largely the pawns of white northern carpetbaggers.
    e. were almost one hundred percent honest and free from corruption.
13. The major long-term effect of white terrorist organizations like the Ku Klux Klan was to
    a. disempower blacks politically and restore white supremacy.
    b. drive the U.S. Army out of the South.
    c. create a permanent secret government of former Confederates in the southern states.
    d. make most southerners forget their nostalgia for the lost cause of the Confederacy.
    e. encourage many blacks to arm themselves for self-defense.
14. The radical Republicans' impeachment of President Andrew Johnson resulted in
    a. Johnson's acceptance of the radicals' Reconstruction plan.
    b. a revision in the impeachment clause of the Constitution to make such an action more difficult.
    c. Johnson's conviction on the charge of violating the Tenure of Office Act.
    d. Johnson's resignation and appointment of Ulysses Grant as his successor.
    e. a failure to convict and remove Johnson from the presidency by a margin of only one vote.
15. The skeptical public finally accepted Secretary of State William Seward's purchase of Alaska partly because it
    a. learned that there were extensive oil deposits in the territory.
    b. was found to be strategically vital to American defense in the northern Pacific.
    c. realized that Alaska would be the last frontier after the settling of the West.
    d. was grateful to Russia as the only great power friendly to the Union during the Civil War.
    e. became entranced by the natural beauty and wildlife of the territory.

C. Identification

Supply the correct identification for each numbered description.

1. ___________ Federal agency that greatly assisted blacks educationally but failed in other aid efforts

2. ___________ The two largest African American denominations (church bodies) by the end of Reconstruction
   ____

3. ___________ Lincoln's 1863 program for a rapid Reconstruction of the South

4. __________ The congressional bill of 1864 requiring 50 percent of a state's voters to take an oath of allegiance before rejoining Union; vetoed by Lincoln

5. __________ The harsh Southern state laws of 1865 that limited black rights and imposed harsh restrictions to ensure a stable black labor supply

6. __________ The constitutional amendment granting civil rights to freed slaves and barring former Confederates from office

7. __________ Law of March 1867 that imposed military rule on the South and disenfranchised former thousands of former Confederates

8. __________ Laudatory term for white southerners who worked to overthrow Reconstruction and establish Home Rule regimes in the southern states

9. __________ The black political organization that promoted self-help and defense of political rights during Reconstruction

10. __________ Supreme Court ruling that military tribunals could not try civilians when the civil courts were open

11. __________ Derogatory term for white Southerners who cooperated with the Republican Reconstruction governments

12. __________ Derogatory term for Northerners who came to the South during Reconstruction and sometimes took part in Republican state governments

13. __________ Constitutional amendment guaranteeing blacks the right to vote

14. __________ White supremacist organization that created a reign of terror against blacks until it was largely suppressed by federal troops

D. Matching People, Places, and Events

Match the person, place, or event in the left column with the proper description in the right column by inserting the correct letter on the blank line.

1. ___ Exodusters
2. ___ Oliver O. Howard
3. ___ Andrew Johnson
4. ___ Abraham Lincoln
5. ___ Andrew Stephens
6. ___ Charles Sumner
7. ___ Thaddeus Stevens
8. ___ Military Reconstruction Act of 1867
9. ___ Hiram Revels
10. ___ Ku Klux Klan
11. ___ Force Acts of 1870 and 1871
12. ___ "swing around the circle"
13. ___ Union League

a. President Andrew Johnson's angry, disastrous political trip attacking Congress in the campaign of 1866

b. Former Confederate vice president whose election to Congress in 1865 infuriated northerners

c. Born a poor white southerner, he became the white South's champion against radical Reconstruction

d. Secretary of state who arranged an initially unpopular but valuable land deal in 1867

e. Laws designed to stamp out Ku Klux Klan terrorism in the South

f. Black Republican senator from Mississippi during Reconstruction

14. ___ Benjamin Wade

15. ___ William Seward

g. Secret organization that intimidated blacks and worked to restore white supremacy

h. Blacks who left the South for Kansas and elsewhere during Reconstruction

i. Congressional law that imposed military rule on the South and demanded harsh conditions for readmission of the seceded states

j. Beaten in the Senate chamber before the Civil War, he became the leader of Senate Republican radicals during Reconstruction

k. Pro-black general who led an agency that tried to assist the freedmen

l. Leading black political organization during Reconstruction

m. Author of the moderate 10 percent Reconstruction plan that ran into congressional opposition

n. The president pro tempore of the Senate who hoped to become president of the United States after Johnson's impeachment conviction

o. Leader of radical Republicans in the House of Representatives

E. Putting Things in Order

Put the following events in correct order by numbering them from 1 to 5.

1. __________ Constitution is amended to guarantee former slaves the right to vote

2. __________ Lincoln announces a plan to rapidly restore southern states to the Union.

3. __________ Northern troops are finally withdrawn from the South, and Southern state governments are reconstituted without federal constraint.

4. __________ An unpopular antiradical president escapes conviction and removal from office by one vote.

5. __________ Johnson's attempt to restore the South to the Union is overturned because of congressional hostility to ex-Confederates and southern passage of the Black Codes.

F. Matching Cause and Effect

Match the historical cause in the left column with the proper effect in the right column by writing the correct letter on the blank line.

Cause

1. ___ The South's military defeat in the Civil War
2. ___ The Freedmen's Bureau
3. ___ The Black Codes of 1865
4. ___ The election of ex-Confederates to Congress in 1865
5. ___ Johnson's "swing around the circle" in the election of 1866
6. ___ Military Reconstruction and the Fourteenth and Fifteenth Amendments
7. ___ The radical Southern state Reconstruction governments
8. ___ The Ku Klux Klan
9. ___ The radical Republicans' hatred of Johnson
10. ___ The whole Reconstruction era

Effect

a. Provoked a politically motivated trial to remove the president from office

b. Intimidated black voters and tried to keep blacks "in their place"

c. Prompted Republicans to refuse to seat Southern delegations in Congress

d. Destroyed the Southern economy but strengthened Southern hatred of yankees

e. Successfully educated former slaves but failed to provide much other assistance to them

f. Forced all the Southern states to establish governments that upheld black voting and other civil rights

g. Embittered white Southerners while doing little to really help blacks

h. Engaged in some corruption but also enacted many valuable social reforms

i. Weakened support for mild Reconstruction policies and helped elect overwhelming Republican majorities to Congress

j. Imposed slavery-like restrictions on blacks and angered the North

G. Developing Historical Skills

Interpreting Photographs and Drawings

Answer the following questions about the photographs and drawings in this chapter.

1. *Educating Young Freedmen and Women, 1870s*

   What appears to be the average age of the students in the photograph? What does the dress of the students suggest about the freedmen's attitudes toward education? From their positioning in the photograph, how might you describe the teachers' relationships with the children?

2. *Sharecroppers Picking Cotton*

What tasks are the sharecroppers engaged in? Is there possibly a gender division of labor among the field workers? How does the white man in the background—likely the landowner—display his social and economic superiority to the black sharecroppers?

3. *Freedmen Voting, Richmond, Virginia, 1871*

What appears to be the economic status of the new black voters portrayed here? How does their condition differ from that of the voting officials, black and white? What does the drawing suggest about the power of the newly enfranchised freedmen?

PART III: APPLYING WHAT YOU HAVE LEARNED

1. What were the major problems facing the South and the nation after the Civil War? How did Reconstruction address them or fail to do so?
2. How did freed blacks react to the end of slavery? How did both Southern and Northern whites react?
3. Why did the white South's treatment of the freed slaves so enrage many northerners in 1865. Was the Republican anger at Johnson motivated primarily by concern that the fruits of emancipation would be lost or by fear that a restored white South would be more powerful than ever?
4. What was the purpose of congressional Reconstruction, and what were its actual effects in the South?
5. What did the attempt at black political empowerment achieve? Why did it finally fail? Could it have succeeded with a stronger Northern political will behind it?
6. How did African Americans take advantage of the political, economic, religious, and social opportunities of Reconstruction, despite their limitations? In what areas were blacks most successful, and in which least?
7. The legend of the Reconstruction state governments is that they were vicious and corrupt failures run by unprepared blacks and greedy northern carpetbaggers. How did the reality of Reconstruction compare with this portrayal?
8. The radical Republicans believed that only a complete economic and social revolution, including redistribution of land and property, could permanently guarantee black rights in the South. Were they right? Why were most northerners of the time, including the moderate Republicans, unwilling to support such a drastic government-sponsored transformation?
9. Why did Reconstruction apparently fail so badly? Was the failure primarily one of immediate political circumstances, or was it more deeply rooted in the history of American sectional and race relations?
10. What was the greatest success of Reconstruction? Would you agree with historians who argue that even though Reconstruction failed at the time, it laid the foundations for the later successes of the civil rights movement?

CHAPTER 23

Political Paralysis in the Gilded Age, 1869–1896

PART I: REVIEWING THE CHAPTER

A. Checklist of Learning Objectives

After mastering this chapter, you should be able to:

1. Describe the political corruption of the Grant administration and the mostly unsuccessful efforts to reform politics in the Gilded Age.
2. Describe the economic crisis of the 1870s, and explain the growing conflict between hard-money and soft-money advocates.
3. Explain the intense political partisanship of the Gilded Age, despite the parties' lack of ideological difference and poor quality of political leadership.
4. Indicate how the disputed Hayes-Tilden election of 1876 led to the Compromise of 1877 and the end of Reconstruction.
5. Describe how the end of Reconstruction led to the loss of black rights and the imposition of the Jim Crow system of segregation in the South.
6. Explain the rise of class conflict between business and labor in the 1870s and the growing hostility to immigrants, especially the Chinese.
7. Explain the economic crisis and depression of the 1890s, and indicate how the Cleveland administration failed to address it.
8. Show how the farm crisis of the depression of the 1890s stirred growing social protests and class conflict, and fueled the rise of the radical Populist Party.

B. Glossary

To build your social science vocabulary, familiarize yourself with the following terms.

1. **coalition** A temporary alliance of political factions or parties for some specific purpose. "The Republicans, now freed from the Union party coalition of war days, enthusiastically nominated Grant. . . ."
2. **corner** To gain exclusive control of a commodity in order to fix its price. "The crafty pair concocted a plot in 1869 to corner the gold market."
3. **censure** An official statement of condemnation passed by a legislative body against one of its members or some other official of government. While severe, a censure itself stops short of penalties or **expulsion**, which is removal from office. "A newspaper exposé and congressional investigation led to formal censure of two congressmen. . . ."
4. **amnesty** A general pardon for offenses or crimes against a government. "The Republican Congress in 1872 passed a general amnesty act. . . ."

5. **civil service** Referring to regular employment by government according to a standardized system of job descriptions, merit qualifications, pay, and promotion, as distinct from **political appointees** who receive positions based on affiliation and party loyalty. "Congress also moved to reduce high Civil War tariffs and to fumigate the Grant administration with mild civil service reform."

6. **unsecured loans** Money loaned without identification of collateral (existing assets) to be forfeited in case the borrower defaults on the loan. "The Freedman's Savings and Trust Company had made unsecured loans to several companies that went under."

7. **contraction** In finance, reducing the available supply of money, thus tending to raise interest rates and lower prices. "Coupled with the reduction of greenbacks, this policy was called 'contraction.' "

8. **deflation (ary)** An increase in the value of money in relation to available goods, causing prices to fall. **Inflation**, a decrease in the value of money in relation to goods, causes prices to rise. "It had a noticeable deflationary effect—the amount of money per capita in circulation actually *decreased*. . . ."

9. **fraternal organization** A society of men drawn together for social purposes and sometimes to pursue other common goals. ". . . the Grand Army of the Republic [was] a politically potent fraternal organization of several hundred thousand Union veterans of the Civil War."

10. **consensus** Common or unanimous opinion. "How can this apparent paradox of political consensus and partisan fervor be explained?"

11. **kickback** The return of a portion of the money received in a sale or contract, often secretly or illegally, in exchange for favors. "The lifeblood of both parties was patronage—disbursing jobs by the bucketful in return for votes, kickbacks, and party service."

12. **lien** A legal claim by a lender or another party on a borrower's property as a guarantee against repayment, and prohibiting any sale of the property. " . . . storekeepers extended credit to small farmers for food and supplies and in return took a lien on their harvest."

13. **assassination** Politically motivated murder of a public figure. " . . . he asked all those who had benefited politically by the assassination to contribute to his defense fund."

14. **laissez-faire** The doctrine of noninterference, especially by the government, in matters of economics or business (literally, "leave alone"). "[The new president was] a staunch apostle of the hands-off creed of laissez-faire. . . ."

15. **pork barrel** In American politics, government appropriations for political purposes, especially projects designed to please a legislator's local constituency. "One [way to reduce the surplus] was to squander it on pensions and 'pork-barrel' bills. . . ."

PART II: CHECKING YOUR PROGRESS

A. True-False

Where the statement is true, circle **T**; where it is false, circle **F**.

1. T F Ulysses Grant's status as a military hero enabled him to become a successful president who stood above partisan politics.

2. T F The scandals of the Grant administration included bribes and corrupt dealings reaching to the cabinet and the vice president of the United States.

3. T F The Liberal Republican movement's political skill enabled it to clean up the corruption of the Grant administration.

4. T F The severe economic downturn of the 1870s caused business failures, labor conflict, and battles over currency.

5. T F The close, fiercely contested elections of the Gilded Age reflected the deep divisions between Republicans and Democrats over national issues.

6. T F The battles between the Stalwart and Half-Breed Republican factions were mainly over who would get patronage and spoils.

7. T F The disputed Hayes-Tilden election was settled by a political deal in which Democrats got the presidency and Republicans got economic and political concessions.

8. T F The Compromise of 1877 purchased political peace between North and South by sacrificing southern blacks and removing federal troops in the South.

9. T F The sharecropping and tenant farming systems forced many Southern blacks into permanent economic debt and dependency.

10. T F Western hostility to Chinese immigrants arose in part because the Chinese provided a source of cheap labor that competed with white workers.

11. T F By reducing politicians' use of patronage, the new civil-service system inadvertently made them more dependent on big campaign contributors.

12. T F The Cleveland-Blaine campaign of 1884 was conducted primarily as a debate about the issues of taxes and the tariff.

13. T F The Republican party, in the post–Civil War era, relied heavily on the political support of veterans' groups, to which it gave substantial pension benefits in return.

14. T F The Populist party's attempt to form a coalition of farmers and workers failed partly because of the racial division between poor whites and blacks in the South.

15. T F President Cleveland's deal to save the gold standard by borrowing $65 million from J.P. Morgan enhanced his popularity among both Democrats and Populists.

B. Multiple Choice

Select the best answer and circle the corresponding letter.

1. Financiers Jim Fisk and Jay Gould involved the Grant administration in a corrupt scheme to
   a. skim funds from the Bureau of Indian Affairs.
   b. sell watered railroad stock at artificially high prices.
   c. corner the gold market.
   d. bribe congressmen in exchange for federal land grants.
   e. provide federal subsidies for bankrupt Wall Street stockbrokers.
2. Boss Tweed's widespread corruption was finally brought to a halt by
   a. federal prosecutors who uncovered the theft.
   b. outraged citizens who rebelled against the waste of public money.
   c. the journalistic exposés of the *New York Times* and cartoonist Thomas Nast.
   d. Tweed's political opponents in New York City.
   e. bank officials who disclosed Tweed's illegal financial maneuvers.

3. The Credit Mobilier scandal involved
   a. the abuse of federal loans intended for urban development.
   b. railroad corporation fraud and the subsequent bribery of congressmen to cover it up.
   c. Secretary of War Belknap's fraudulent sale of contracts to supply Indian reservations.
   d. the attempt of insiders to gain control of New York's gold and stock markets.
   e. illegal gifts and loans to members of President Grant's White House staff.
4. Grant's greatest failing in the scandals that plagued his administration was his
   a. refusal to turn over evidence to congressional investigators.
   b. toleration of corruption and his loyalty to crooked friends.
   c. acceptance of behind-the-scenes payments for performing his duties as president.
   d. use of large amounts of dirty money in his political campaigns.
   e. inability to distinguish innocent members of his staff from the guilty.
5. The depression of the 1870s led to increasing demands for
   a. a new federally controlled Bank of the United States.
   b. federal programs to create jobs for the unemployed.
   c. restoration of sound money by backing all paper currency with gold.
   d. stronger regulation of the banking system.
   e. inflation of the money supply by issuing more paper or silver currency.
6. The political system of the Gilded Age was generally characterized by
   a. split-ticket voting, low voter turnout, and single-issue special-interest groups.
   b. strong party loyalties, low voter turnout, and deep ideological differences.
   c. third-party movements, high voter turnout and strong disagreement on foreign-policy issues.
   d. strong party loyalties, high voter turnout, and few disagreements on national issues.
   e. weak party loyalties, high voter turnout, and focus on personalities rather than parties.
7. The primary goal for which all factions in both political parties contended during the Gilded Age was
   a. racial justice.
   b. a sound financial and banking system.
   c. patronage.
   d. a more assertive American foreign policy.
   e. rapid expansion of the national railway system.
8. The key tradeoff featured in the Compromise of 1877 was that
   a. Republicans got the presidency in exchange for the final removal of federal troops from the South.
   b. Democrats got the presidency in exchange for federal guarantees of black civil rights.
   c. Republicans got the presidency in exchange for Democratic control of the cabinet.
   d. Democrats got the presidency in exchange for increased immigration quotas from Ireland.
   e. Republicans got the presidency in exchange for permitting former Confederate officers to vote.
9. Which of the following was *not* among the changes that affected African Americans in the South after federal troops were withdrawn in the Compromise of 1877?
   a. The forced relocation of black farmers to the Kansas and Oklahoma dust bowl
   b. The imposition of literacy requirements and poll taxes to prevent black voting
   c. The development of the tenant farming and share-cropping systems
   d. The introduction of legal systems of racial segregation
   e. The rise of mob lynching as a means of suppressing blacks who challenged the racial system

10. The Supreme Court's ruling in *Plessy* v. *Ferguson* upholding "separate but equal" public facilities in effect legalized
    a. southern blacks' loss of voting rights.
    b. the right of blacks to establish separate colleges admitting blacks only.
    c. the program of separate black and white economic development endorsed by Booker T. Washington.
    d. the rights to "equal protection of the law" guaranteed by the Fourteenth Amendment.
    e. the system of unequal segregation between the races.
11. The great railroad strike of 1877 revealed the
    a. growing strength of American labor unions.
    b. refusal of the U.S. federal government to intervene in private labor disputes.
    c. ability of American workers to cooperate across ethnic and racial lines.
    d. growing threat of class warfare in response to the economic depression of the mid-1870s.
    e. American economy's capacity to find alternatives to railroad transportation.
12. The final result of the widespread anti-Chinese agitation in the West was
    a. a program to encourage Chinese students to enroll in American colleges and universities.
    b. a congressional law to prohibit any further Chinese immigration.
    c. the stripping of citizenship even from native-born Chinese Americans.
    d. legal segregation of all Chinese into Chinatown districts in San Francisco and elsewhere.
    e. the forced emigration of all but a handful of Chinese back to China.
13. President James Garfield was assassinated by a(n)
    a. fanatically anti-Republican Confederate veteran.
    b. mentally unstable disappointed office seeker.
    c. anticapitalist immigrant anarchist.
    d. corrupt gangster under federal criminal indictment.
    e. bitter supporter of his defeated Democratic opponent, Winfield Scott Hancock.
14. In its first years, the Populist Party advocated, among other things
    a. free silver, a graduated income tax, and government ownership of the railroads, telegraph, and telephone.
    b. higher tariffs and federally sponsored unemployment insurance and pensions.
    c. tighter restriction on black economic, social, and political rights.
    d. a Homestead Act to permit farmers and unemployed workers to obtain free federal land in the West.
    e. greater support for land grant colleges to enhance scientific agriculture.
15. Grover Cleveland stirred a furious storm of protest when, in response to the extreme financial crisis of the 1890s, he
    a. lowered tariffs to permit an influx of cheaper foreign goods into the country.
    b. signed a bill introducing a federal income tax that cut into workers' wages.
    c. pushed the Federal Reserve Board into sharply raising interest rates.
    d. borrowed $65 million dollars from J.P. Morgan and other bankers in order to save the monetary gold standard.
    e. seized federal control of the railroad industry.

C. Identification

Supply the correct identification for each numbered description.

1. __________ The symbol of the Republican political tactic of attacking Democrats with reminders of the Civil War
2. __________ Corrupt construction company whose bribes and payoffs to congressmen and others created a major Grant administration scandal
3. __________ Short-lived third party of 1872 that attempted to curb Grant administration corruption
4. __________ Precious metal that soft-money advocates demanded be coined again to compensate for the Crime of '73
5. __________ Soft-money third party that polled over a million votes and elected fourteen congressmen in 1878 by advocating inflation
6. __________ Mark Twain's sarcastic name for the post–Civil War era, which emphasized its atmosphere of greed and corruption
7. __________ Civil War Union veterans' organization that became a potent political bulwark of the Republican party in the late nineteenth century
8. __________ Republican party faction led by Senator Roscoe Conkling that opposed all attempts at civil-service reform
9. __________ Republican party faction led by Senator James G. Blaine that paid lip service to government reform while still battling for patronage and spoils
10. __________ The complex political agreement between Republicans and Democrats that resolved the bitterly disputed election of 1876
11. __________ Asian immigrant group that experienced discrimination on the West Coast
12. __________ System of choosing federal employees on the basis of merit rather than patronage introduced by the Pendleton Act of 1883
13. __________ Sky-high Republican tariff of 1890 that caused widespread anger among farmers in the Midwest and the South
14. __________ Insurgent political party that gained widespread support among farmers in the 1890s
15. __________ Notorious clause in southern voting laws that exempted from literacy tests and poll taxes anyone whose ancestors had voted in 1860, thereby excluding blacks

D. Matching People, Places, and Events

Match the person, place, or event in the left column with the proper description in the right column by inserting the correct letter on the blank line.

1. ___ Ulysses S. Grant
2. ___ Jim Fisk
3. ___ Boss Tweed
4. ___ Horace Greeley

a. Heavyweight New York political boss whose widespread fraud landed him in jail in 1871

b. Bold and unprincipled financier whose plot to corner the U.S. gold market nearly succeeded in 1869

5. ___ Samuel Tilden
6. ___ Denis Kearney
7. ___ Tom Watson
8. ___ Roscoe Conkling
9. ___ James G. Blaine
10. ___ Rutherford B. Hayes
11. ___ James Garfield
12. ___ Jim Crow
13. ___ Grover Cleveland
14. ___ William Jennings Bryan
15. ___ J. P. Morgan

c. Winner of the contested 1876 election who presided over the end of Reconstruction and a sharp economic downturn

d. Great military leader whose presidency foundered in corruption and political ineptitude

e. Term for the racial segregation laws imposed in the 1890s

f. Eloquent young Congressman from Nebraska who became the most prominent advocate of free silver in the early 1890s

g. President whose assassination after only a few months in office spurred the passage of a civil-service law

h. Irish-born leader of the anti-Chinese movement in California

i. Radical Populist leader whose early success turned sour and who then became a vicious racist

j. New York prosecutor of Boss Tweed who later lost in the disputed presidential election of 1876

k. Imperious New York senator and leader of the Stalwart faction of Republicans

l. First Democratic president since the Civil War; defender of laissez-faire economics and low tariffs

m. Enormously wealthy banker whose secret bailout of the federal government in 1895 aroused fierce public anger

n. Colorful, eccentric newspaper editor who carried the Liberal Republican and Democratic banners against Grant in 1872

o. Charming but corrupt Half-Breed Republican senator and presidential nominee in 1884

E. Putting Things in Order

Put the following events in correct order by numbering them from 1 to 5.

1. __________ A bitterly disputed presidential election is resolved by a complex political deal that ends Reconstruction in the South.

2. __________ Two unscrupulous financiers use corrupt means to manipulate New York gold markets and the U.S. Treasury.

3. __________ A major economic depression causes widespread social unrest and the rise of the Populist party as a vehicle of protest.

4. __________ Grant administration scandals split the Republican party, but Grant overcomes the inept opposition to win reelection.

5. __________ Monetary deflation and the high McKinley Tariff lead to growing agitation for free silver by Congressman William Jennings Bryan and others.

F. Matching Cause and Effect

Match the historical cause in the left column with the proper effect in the right column by writing the correct letter on the blank line.

Cause

1. ___ Favor-seeking businesspeople and corrupt politicians
2. ___ The *New York Times* and cartoonist Thomas Nast
3. ___ Upright Republicans' disgust with Grant administration scandals
4. ___ The economic crash of the mid-1870s
5. ___ Local cultural, moral, and religious differences
6. ___ The Compromise of 1877 that settled the disputed Hayes-Tilden election
7. ___ White workers' resentment of Chinese labor competition
8. ___ Public shock at Garfield's assassination by Guiteau
9. ___ The 1890s depression and the drain of gold from the federal treasury
10. ___ The inability of Populist leaders to overcome divisions between white and black farmers

Effect

a. Created fierce partisan competition and high voter turnouts, even though the parties agreed on most national issues
b. Caused anti-Chinese violence and restrictions against Chinese immigration
c. Led to the formation of the Liberal Republican party in 1872
d. Induced Grover Cleveland to negotiate a secret loan from J. P. Morgan's banking syndicate
e. Forced Boss Tweed out of power and into jail
f. Helped ensure passage of the Pendleton Act
g. Caused numerous scandals during President Grant's administration
h. Led to failure of the third-party revolt in the South and a growing racial backlash
i. Caused unemployment, railroad strikes, and a demand for cheap money
j. Led to the withdrawal of troops from the South and the virtual end of federal efforts to protect black rights there

G. Developing Historical Skills

Historical Fact and Historical Explanation

Historians uncover a great deal of information about the past, but often that information takes on significance only when it is analyzed and interpreted. In this chapter, many facts about the presidents and elections of the Gilded Age are presented: for example, the very close elections in 1876, 1884, 1888, and 1892; the large voter turnouts; and the lack of significant issues in most elections.

These facts take on larger meaning, however, when we examine the reasons for them. Reread the section "Pallid Politics in the Gilded Age" (pp.543–544) and answer each of the following questions in a sentence or two.

1. What fundamental difference between the two parties made partisan politics so fiercely contested in the Glided Age?

2. Why did this underlying difference *not* lead to differences over issues at the national level?

3. Why were so many of the elections extremely close, no matter who the candidates were?

4. Why was winning each election so very important to both parties, even though there was little disagreement on issues?

H. Map Mastery

Map Discrimination

Using the maps and charts in Chapter 23, answer the following questions.

1. *Hayes-Tilden Disputed Election of 1876*: In the controversial Hayes-Tilden election of 1876, how many undisputed electoral votes did Republican Hayes win in the former Confederate states?

2. *Hayes-Tilden Disputed Election of 1876*: Democrat Tilden carried four states in the North—states that did not have slavery before 1865. Which were they?

3. *Growth of Classified Civil Service*: The percentage of offices classified under civil service was approximately how many times greater under President McKinley than under President Arthur: two, three, four, five, or ten?

4. *Presidential Election of 1884*: Which of the following states gained the most electoral votes between 1876 and 1884: New York, Indiana, Missouri, or Texas?

5. *Presidential Election of 1884*: How many states that were carried by Republican Hayes in 1876 were carried by Democrat Cleveland in 1884?

Map Challenge

Using the election map on p. 545 and the account of the Compromise of 1877 in the text (pp. 545–546), discuss the election of 1876 in relation to both Reconstruction and the political balance of the Gilded Age. Include some analysis of the reasons why this was the last time for nearly a century that the states in the Deep South voted Republican.

PART III: APPLYING WHAT YOU HAVE LEARNED

1. What made politics in the Gilded Age so extremely popular—with over 80 percent voter participation—yet so often corrupt and unconcerned with important national issues?
2. What caused the end of the Reconstruction? In particular, why did the majority of Republicans abandon their earlier policy of support for black civil rights and voting in the South?
3. What were the results of the Compromise of 1877 for race relations? How did the suppression of blacks through the sharecropping and crop-lien systems depress the economic condition of the South for whites and blacks alike?
4. What caused the rise of the money issue in American politics? What were the backers of greenback and silver money each trying to achieve?
5. What were the causes and political results of the rise of agrarian protest in the 1880s and 1890s? Why were the Populists' attempts to form a coalition of white and black farmers and industrial workers ultimately unsuccessful?
6. White laborers in the West fiercely resisted Chinese immigration, and white farmers in the South turned toward race-baiting rather than forming a populist alliance with black farmers. How and why did racial animosity trump the apparent economic self-interests of these lower-class whites?
7. In what ways did the political conflicts of the Gilded Age still reflect the aftermath of the Civil War and Reconstruction (see Chapter 22)? To what extent did the political leaders of the time address issues of race and sectional conflict, and to what extent did they merely shove them under the rug?
8. Was the apparent failure of the American political system to address the industrial conflicts and racial tensions of the Gilded Age a result of the two parties' poor leadership and narrow self-interest, or was it simply the natural inability of a previously agrarian, local, democratic nation to face up to a modern, national industrial economy?

CHAPTER 24

Industry Comes of Age, 1865–1900

PART I: REVIEWING THE CHAPTER

A. Checklist of Learning Objectives

After mastering this chapter, you should be able to:

1. Explain how the transcontinental railroad network provided the basis for an integrated national market and the great post–Civil War industrial transformation.
2. Identify the abuses in the railroad industry and discuss how these led to the first efforts at industrial regulation by the federal government.
3. Describe how the economy came to be dominated by giant trusts, such as those headed by Carnegie and Rockefeller in the steel and oil industries, and the growing class conflict it precipitated.
4. Describe how new technological inventions fueled new industries and why American manufacturers increasingly turned toward the mass production of standardized goods.
5. Indicate how industrialists and their intellectual and religious supporters attempted to explain and justify great wealth, and increasing class division through natural law and the Gospel of Wealth.
6. Explain why the South was generally excluded from American industrial development and remained in a Third World economic subservience to the North.
7. Analyze the social changes brought by industrialization, particularly the altered position of working men and women.
8. Explain the failures of the Knights of Labor and the modest success of the American Federation of Labor.

B. Glossary

To build your social science vocabulary, familiarize yourself with the following terms.

1. **pool** In business, an agreement to divide a given market in order to avoid competition. "The earliest form of combination was the 'pool'. . . . "
2. **rebate** A return of a portion of the amount paid for goods or services. "Other rail barons granted secret rebates. . . ."
3. **free enterprise** An economic system that permits unrestricted entrepreneurial business activity; capitalism. "Dedicated to free enterprise . . . , they cherished a traditionally keen pride in progress."
4. **regulatory commission** In American government, any of the agencies established to control a special sphere of business or other activity; members are usually appointed by the president and confirmed by Congress. "It heralded the arrival of a series of independent regulatory commissions in the next century. . . ."

5. **trust** A combination of corporations, usually in the same industry, in which stockholders trade their stock to a central board in exchange for trust certificates. (By extension, the term came to be applied to any large, semi-monopolistic business.) "He perfected a device for controlling bothersome rivals—the 'trust.'"

6. **syndicate** An association of financiers organized to carry out projects requiring very large amounts of capital. "His prescribed remedy was to . . . ensure future harmony by placing officers of his own banking syndicate on their various boards of directors."

7. **patrician** Characterized by noble or high social standing. "An arrogant class of 'new rich' was now elbowing aside the patrician families. . . ."

8. **plutocracy** Government by the wealthy. "Plutocracy . . . took its stand firmly on the Constitution."

9. **Third World** Term developed during the Cold War between the United States and the Soviet Union (1946–1991) for the non-Western (first world) and noncommunist (second world) nations of the world, most of them formerly under colonial rule and still economically poor and dependent. "The net effect was to keep the South in a kind of 'Third World' servitude to the Northeast. . . ."

10. **socialist (socialism)** Political belief in promoting social and economic equality through the ownership and control of the major means of production by the whole community (usually but not necessarily in the form of the state) rather than by individuals or corporations. "Some of it was envious, but much of it rose from the small and increasingly vocal group of socialists. . . ."

11. **radical** One who believes in fundamental change in the political, economic, or social system. " . . .much of [this criticism] rose from . . . socialists and other radicals, many of whom were recent European immigrants."

12. **lockout** The refusal by an employer to allow employees to work unless they agree to his or her terms. "Employers could lock their doors against rebellious workers—a process called the 'lockout'. . . ."

13. **yellow dog contract** A labor contract in which an employee must sign a document pledging not to join a union as a condition of holding the job. "[Employers] could compel them to sign 'ironclad oaths' or 'yellow dog contracts'. . . ."

14. **cooperative** An organization for producing, marketing, or consuming goods in which the members share the benefits. ". . . they campaigned for . . . producers' cooperatives. . . ."

15. **anarchist (anarchism)** Political belief that all organized, coercive government is wrong in principle, and that society should be organized solely on the basis of free cooperation. (Some anarchists practiced violence against the state, while others were nonviolent pacifists.) "Eight anarchists were rounded up, although nobody proved that they had anything to do directly with the bomb."

PART II: CHECKING YOUR PROGRESS

A. True-False

Where the statement is true, circle **T**; where it is false, circle **F**.

1. T F Private railroad companies built the transcontinental rail lines by raising their own capital funds without the assistance of the federal government.

2. T F The rapid expansion of the railroad industry was often accompanied by rapid mergers, bankruptcies, and reorganizations.

3. T F The railroads created an integrated national market, stimulated the growth in cities, and encouraged European immigration.

4. T F The practice of artificially inflating railroads' stock prices (stock watering) often left the companies deeply in debt after promoters absconded with the profits.

5. T F The new Interstate Commerce Commission did end some of the worst railroad abuses, but served more to stabilize the railroad industry than to seriously reform it.

6. T F The Rockefeller oil company technique of horizontal integration involved combining into one organization all the phases of manufacturing from the raw material to the customer.

7. T F Rockefeller, Morgan, and others organized monopolistic trusts and interlocking directorates in order to consolidate business and eliminate cutthroat competition.

8. T F Defenders of unrestrained capitalism like Herbert Spencer and William Graham Sumner primarily used natural law and laissez-faire economics rather than Charles Darwin's theories to justify the "survival of the fittest."

9. T F The pro-industry ideology of the New South enabled that region to make rapid economic gains by 1900.

10. T F Two new inventions that brought large numbers of women into the workplace were the typewriter and the telephone.

11. T F The most successful American manufacturers concentrated on producing high-quality, specialized goods for luxury markets in the United States and Europe.

12. T F The impact of new machines and mass immigration held down wages and gave employers advantages in their dealings with labor.

13. T F The Knights of Labor achieved spectacular growth by enlisting all workers, including skilled and unskilled, male and female, black and white.

14. T F The Haymarket Square bombing severely damaged the Knights of Labor by linking it with anarchist violence, even though the organization had nothing to do with the bombs.

15. T F The American Federation of Labor tried hard but failed to organize unskilled workers, women, and blacks.

B. Multiple Choice

Select the best answer and circle the corresponding letter.

1. The federal government contributed to the building of the national rail network by
   a. importing substantial numbers of Chinese immigrants to build the railroads.
   b. providing free grants of federal land to the railroad companies.
   c. building and operating the first transcontinental rail lines.
   d. transporting the mail and other federal shipments over the rail lines.
   e. establishing clear national standards for railroad routes, track gauge, safety, and fair pricing.
2. A large share of the capital that financed the growth of American industry came from
   a. workers' pension funds and other pooled resources.
   b. the federal government.
   c. European investment in private American corporations.
   d. a system of revolving industrial development loans run by individual states.
   e. immigrants and investors fleeing political instability in Latin America.

3. The railroad most significantly stimulated American industrialization by
   a. opening up the West to settlement.
   b. creating a single national market for raw materials and consumer goods.
   c. eliminating the inefficient canal system.
   d. inspiring greater federal investment in technical research and development.
   e. ending the agricultural domination of the American economy.
4. The railroad barons aroused considerable public opposition by practices such as
   a. forcing Indians off their traditional hunting grounds.
   b. refusing to pay their employees decent wages.
   c. refusing to build railroad lines in less settled areas.
   d. stock watering, rate discrimination, and bribery of public officials.
   e. using federal land grants and other subsidies to finance their construction and operations.
5. The railroads affected even the organization of time in the United States by
   a. introducing regularly scheduled departures and arrivals on railroad timetables.
   b. introducing daylight savings time during the summer.
   c. introducing four standard time zones across the country.
   d. turning travel that had once taken days into a matter of hours.
   e. establishing the practice of a fixed 10-hour work day for all employees.
6. Congress finally stepped in to pass the Interstate Commerce Act to regulate the railroad industry because
   a. labor unions and social reformers demanded a public voice in the railroad industry.
   b. railroad corporations themselves were demanding an end to corruption and cutthroat competition.
   c. President Grover Cleveland gave strong backing for the law.
   d. the Supreme Court had ruled in the *Wabash* case that the states had no power to regulate interstate commerce.
   e. the spectacular failure of several railroads threatened the survival of the industry.
7. Financier J. P. Morgan exercised his tremendous economic power most effectively by
   a. promoting horizontal integration of the oil industry.
   b. lending money to the federal government.
   c. consolidating and controlling rival industries through interlocking directorates.
   d. serving as the middleman between American industrialists and foreign governments.
   e. steering bank loans and investments to the most promising new industries.
8. Two late-nineteenth-century technological inventions that especially drew women out of the home and into the workforce were the
   a. railroad and the telegraph.
   b. electric light and the phonograph.
   c. cash register and the stock ticker.
   d. typewriter and the telephone.
   e. mimeograph and the moving picture.
9. Andrew Carnegie's industrial system of vertical integration involved the
   a. construction of large, vertical steel factories in Pittsburgh and elsewhere.
   b. cooperation between manufacturers like Andrew Carnegie and financiers like J. P. Morgan.
   c. integration of diverse immigrant ethnic groups into the steel industry labor force.
   d. combination of all phases of the steel industry from mining to manufacturing into a single organization.
   e. allying of competitors to monopolize a given market.

10. The large trusts like Standard Oil and Swift and Armour justified their economic domination of their industries by claiming that
    a. they were fundamentally concerned with serving the public interest over private profit.
    b. only large-scale methods of production and distribution could provide superior products at low prices.
    c. competition among many small firms was contrary to the law of economics.
    d. only large American corporations could compete with huge British and German international companies.
    e. price wars were necessary to make a profit.
11. So-called Social Darwinists like Herbert Spencer and William Graham Sumner justified harsh competition and vast disparities in wealth by arguing that
    a. industrialists like Rockefeller and Carnegie foreshadowed the evolution of the human race.
    b. such developments were a natural consequence of the New World environment.
    c. large fortunes could be used to invest in research that would improve the human gene pool.
    d. Charles Darwin had uncovered the scientific basis of economics as well as biology.
    e. the wealthy who came out on top were simply displaying their natural superiority to others.
12. Andrew Carnegie's "Gospel of Wealth" proclaimed his belief that
    a. wealth was God's reward for hard work, while poverty resulted from laziness and immorality.
    b. churches needed to take a stronger stand on the economic issues of the day.
    c. faith in capitalism and progress should take the place once reserved for religion.
    d. those who acquired great wealth were morally responsible to use it for the public good.
    e. Jesus' teachings had revealed the fundamental principles of successful business.
13. The attempt to create an industrialized New South in the late nineteenth century generally failed because
    a. most southerners cherished the aristocratic ideals of leisure and education and looked down on hard work and economic pursuits.
    b. Southerners were too still too bitter at the Union to engage in productive economic pursuits that might benefit the nation.
    c. continued political violence made the South an unattractive place for investment.
    d. there was little demand for southern products like textiles and cigarettes.
    e. the South was discriminated against and kept in constant debt as a supplier of raw materials to northern industry.
14. For American workers, industrialization generally meant
    a. a steady, long-term decline in wages and the standard of living.
    b. an opportunity to create small businesses that would enable them eventually to achieve economic independence.
    c. a long-term rise in the standard of living but a loss of independence and control of work.
    d. a stronger sense of identification with their jobs and employers.
    e. the ability to join unions and achieve solidarity with their fellow workers.
15. In contrast to the Knights of Labor, the American Federation of Labor advocated
    a. uniting both skilled and unskilled workers into a single large union.
    b. concentrating on improving wages and hours and avoiding general social reform.
    c. working for black and female labor interests as well as those of white men.
    d. using secrecy and violence against employers.
    e. using politics and government rather than strikes to achieve labor's goals.

C. Identification

Supply the correct identification for each numbered description.

1. __________ Federally owned acreage granted to the railroad companies in order to encourage the building of rail lines
2. __________ The original transcontinental railroad, commissioned by Congress, which built its rail line west from Omaha
3. __________ The California-based railroad company, headed by Leland Stanford, that employed Chinese laborers in building lines across the mountains
4. __________ The luxurious railroad cars that enabled passengers to travel long distances in comfort and elegance
5. __________ Dishonest device by which railroad promoters artificially inflated the price of their stocks and bonds
6. __________ Supreme Court case of 1886 that prevented states from regulating railroads or other businesses engaging in interstate commerce
7. __________ The region of northern Minnesota that supplied most of the iron ore for tremendously profitable American steel industry
8. __________ Late-nineteenth-century invention that revolutionized communications and created a large new industry that relied heavily on female workers
9. __________ First of the great industrial trusts, organized through the principle of horizontal integration, that ruthlessly incorporated or destroyed competitors in an energy industry.
10. __________ The first billion-dollar American corporation, organized when J. P. Morgan bought out Andrew Carnegie
11. __________ Term that southern promoters used to proclaim their belief in a technologically advanced, industrial South
12. __________ Somewhat misleading term to describe the ideas of theorists like Herbert Spencer and William Graham Sumner, who claimed that vast wealth was the result of the natural superiority of those who achieved it.
13. __________ Secret, ritualistic labor organization that enrolled many skilled and unskilled workers but collapsed suddenly after the Haymarket Square bombing
14. __________ Shorthand term for the image of the independent and athletic new woman created by a popular magazine illustrator of the late nineteenth century.
15. __________ The conservative labor group that successfully organized a minority of American workers but left others out

D. Matching People, Places, and Events

Match the person, place, or event in the left column with the proper description in the right column by inserting the correct letter on the blank line.

1. ___ Leland Stanford
2. ___ Russell Conwell
3. ___ James J. Hill

a. Inventive genius of industrialization who worked on devices such as the electric light, the phonograph, and the motion picture

4. ____ Cornelius Vanderbilt
5. ____ James Buchanan Duke
6. ____ Alexander Graham Bell
7. ____ Thomas Edison
8. ____ Andrew Carnegie
9. ____ John D. Rockefeller
10. ____ J. Pierpont Morgan
11. ____ Henry Grady
12. ____ Terence V. Powderly
13. ____ William Graham Sumner
14. ____ John P. Altgeld
15. ____ Samuel Gompers

b. The only businessperson in America wealthy enough to buy out Andrew Carnegie and organize the United States Steel Corporation

c. Illinois governor who pardoned the Haymarket anarchists

d. Southern newspaper editor who tirelessly promoted industrialization as the salvation of the economically backward South

e. Aggressive energy-industry monopolist who used tough means to build a trust based on horizontal integration

f. Wealthy southern industrialist whose development of mass-produced cigarettes led him to endow a university that later bore his name

g. Aggressive eastern railroad builder and consolidator who scorned the law as an obstacle to his enterprise

h. Pro-business clergyman whose "Acres of Diamonds" speeches criticized the poor

i. Scottish immigrant who organized a vast new industry on the principle of vertical integration

j. Former California governor and organizer of the Central Pacific Railroad

k. Organizer of a conservative craft-union group and advocate of more wages for skilled workers

l. Eloquent leader of a secretive labor organization that made substantial gains in the 1880s before it suddenly collapsed

m. Public-spirited railroad builder who assisted farmers in the northern areas served by his rail lines

n. Intellectual defender of laissez-faire capitalism who argued that the wealthy owed nothing to the poor

o. Former teacher of the deaf whose invention created an entire new industry

E. Putting Things in Order

Put the following events in correct order by numbering them from 1 to 5.

1. ______ J. P. Morgan buys out Andrew Carnegie to form the first billion-dollar U.S. corporation.
2. ______ The first federal law regulating railroads is passed.
3. ______ The killing of policemen during a labor demonstration results in the execution of radical anarchists and the decline of the Knights of Labor.
4. ______ A teacher of the deaf invents a machine that greatly eases communication across distance.
5. ______ A golden spike is driven, fulfilling the dream of linking the nation by rail.

F. Matching Cause and Effect

Match the historical cause in the left column with the proper effect in the right column by writing the correct letter on the blank line.

Cause

1. ___ The vast American national market and the high cost of skilled labor in the United States
2. ___ The building of a transcontinental rail network
3. ___ Corrupt financial dealings and political manipulations by the railroads
4. ___ New developments in steel making, oil refining, and communication
5. ___ The ruthless competitive techniques of Rockefeller and other industrialists
6. ___ The economic investments of European financiers
7. ___ The North's use of discriminatory price practices against the South
8. ___ The growing mechanization and depersonalization of factory work
9. ___ The Haymarket Square bombing
10. ___ The American Federation of Labor's concentration on skilled craft workers

Effect

a. Eliminated competition and created monopolistic trusts in many industries

b. Provided a large share of the capital for the growth of American industry

c. Created a strong but narrowly based union organization

d. Stimulated the growth of a huge unified national market for American manufactured goods

e. Created a public demand for railroad regulation, such as the Interstate Commerce Act

f. Often made laborers feel powerless and vulnerable to their well-off corporate employers

g. Helped destroy the Knights of Labor and increased public fear of labor agitation

h. Laid the technological basis for huge new industries and spectacular economic growth

i. Encouraged industrialists to develop technological innovations that would enable them to produce goods with limited, unskilled labor

j. Kept the South in economic dependency as a poverty-stricken supplier of farm products and raw materials to the Northeast

G. Developing Historical Skills

Interpreting Historical Paintings and Photographs

Historical paintings, lithographs, and photographs not only convey substantive information; they can also tell us how an artist or photographer viewed and understood the society and events of his or her day. Examine the photographs and painting indicated below and answer the following questions about them.

1. Examine the working people in the images on pp. 568, 570, 580, 581, 584, 585, and 587. What is the relationship of the workers in each image to their workplace? What is their relation to one another? What does each of the photos reveal about the nature of industrial labor?

2. Examine the painting of "The Strike" by Robert Koehler on p. 588. Where is the scene taking place? What is the relationship between the place of work and the scene in the painting? What has likely happened to bring the workers to this scene?

3. Analyze the clothing of all the figures in the Koehler painting. What does it tell you about the economic and social condition of the various people?

4. Two main conversations seem to be taking place in the foreground of the painting. What might each be about? What is the artist suggesting by presenting both conversations?

PART III: APPLYING WHAT YOU HAVE LEARNED

1. What was the impact of the transcontinental rail system on the American economy and society in the late nineteenth century?
2. How did the huge industrial trusts develop in industries such as steel and oil, and what was their effect on the economy? Was the growth of enormous, monopolistic corporations simply the natural end result of economic competition, or did it partly result from corrupt practices designed to eliminate competition?
3. What early efforts were made to control the new corporate industrial giants, and how effective were these efforts?
4. What was the effect of the new industrial revolution on American laborers, and how did various labor organizations attempt to respond to the new conditions?
5. Compare the impact of the new industrialization on the North and the South. Why was the New South more a propagandistic slogan than a reality?

6. William Graham Sumner and other so-called Social Darwinists argued that the wealth and luxury enjoyed by millionaires was justifiable as a "good bargain for society" and that natural law should prevent the wealthy classes from aiding the working classes and poor. Why were such views so popular during the Gilded Age? What criticisms of such views might be offered?

7. The text states that "no single group was more profoundly affected by the new industrial age than women." Why was women's role in society so greatly affected by these economic changes?

8. In what ways did industrialization bring a revolution in cultural views of labor, opportunity, and even time?

9. How did the vast scale of the continent-wide American market affect the development of American production, technology, and labor practices?

10. What strains did the new industrialization bring to the American ideals of democracy and equality? Was the growth of huge corporations and great fortunes a successful realization of American principles or a threat to them?

CHAPTER 25

America Moves to the City, 1865–1900

PART I: REVIEWING THE CHAPTER

A. Checklist of Learning Objectives

After mastering this chapter, you should be able to:

1. Describe the rise of the American industrial city, and place it in the context of worldwide trends of urbanization and mass migration (the European diaspora).
2. Describe the New Immigration, and explain how it differed from the Old Immigration and why it aroused opposition from many native-born Americans.
3. Discuss the efforts of social reformers and churches to aid the New Immigrants and alleviate urban problems, and the immigrants' own efforts to sustain their traditions while assimilating to mainstream America.
4. Analyze the changes in American religious life in the late nineteenth century, including the expansion of Catholicism, Orthodoxy, and Judaism, and the growing Protestant division between liberals and fundamentalists over Darwinism and biblical criticism.
5. Explain the changes in American education and intellectual life, including the debate between DuBois and Washington over the goals of African American education.
6. Describe the literary and cultural life of the period, including the widespread trend towards realism in art and literature, and the city beautiful movement led by urban planners.
7. Explain the growing national debates about morality in the late nineteenth century, particularly in relation to the changing roles of women and the family.

B. Glossary

To build your social science vocabulary, familiarize yourself with the following terms.

1. **megalopolis** An extensive, heavily populated area, containing several dense urban centers. ". . . gave way to the immense and impersonal megalopolis. . . ."
2. **tenement** A multidwelling building, often poor or overcrowded. "The cities . . . harbored . . . towering skyscrapers and stinking tenements."
3. **affluence** An abundance of wealth. "These leafy 'bedroom communities' eventually ringed the brick-and-concrete cities with a greenbelt of affluence."
4. **despotism** Government by an absolute or tyrannical ruler. ". . . people had grown accustomed to cringing before despotism."
5. **parochial** Concerning a religious parish or small district. (By extension, the term is used, often negatively, to refer to narrow or local perspectives as distinct from broad or cosmopolitan outlooks.) "Catholics expanded their parochial-school system. . . ."

6. **sweatshop** A factory where employees are forced to work long hours under difficult conditions for meager wages. "The women of Hull House successfully lobbied in 1893 for an Illinois antisweatshop law that protected women workers. . . ."
7. **pauper** A poor person, often one who lives on tax-supported charity. "The first restrictive law . . . banged the gate in the faces of paupers. . . ."
8. **convert** A person who turns from one religion or set of beliefs to another. "A fertile field for converts was found in America's harried, nerve-racked, and urbanized civilization. . . ."
9. **Fundamentalism** A conservative Protestant movement that rejects religious modernism in religion and culture, including biblical higher criticism, and adheres to a strict and literal interpretation of Christian doctrine and Scriptures. "Their rejection of scientific consensus spawned a muscular view of biblical authority that eventually gave rise to fundamentalism...."
10. **philanthropist** A person or organization that works to benefit society through uncompensated gifts, services, or benefits; literally, a "lover of humanity." "Some help came from northern philanthropists. . . . "
11. **behavioral psychology** The branch of psychology that examines human action, often considering it more important than mental or inward states. "His [work] helped to establish the modern discipline of behavioral psychology."
12. **syndicated (syndication)** In journalism, featured writing or drawing that is sold by an organization for publication in several newspapers. "Bare-knuckle editorials were, to an increasing degree, being supplanted by feature articles and non-controversial syndicated material."
13. **tycoon** A wealthy businessperson, especially one who openly displays power and position. "Two new journalistic tycoons emerged."
14. **feminist (feminism)** One who promotes complete political, social, and economic equality of opportunity for women. " . . . in 1898 they heard the voice of a major feminist prophet."
15. **prohibition** Forbidding by law the manufacture, sale, or consumption of liquor. (**Temperance** is the voluntary abstention from liquor consumption.) "Statewide prohibition . . . was sweeping new states into the 'dry' column."

PART II: CHECKING YOUR PROGRESS

A. True-False

Where the statement is true, circle **T**; where it is false, circle **F**.

1. T F Rapid and uncontrolled growth made American cities places of both exciting opportunity and severe social problems.
2. T F The United States was unique in the rapidity and scale of growth in its large cities.
3. T F The largest root cause of the New Immigration was the inability of the European economy to support millions of peasants who were driven off the land.
4. T F Female social workers established settlement houses to aid struggling immigrants and promote social reform, while also advancing women's opportunities.
5. T F American Protestantism was dominated by liberal denominations that adapted religious ideas to modern culture and promoted a social gospel rather than biblical literalism.

6. T F Catholic, Jewish, and Orthodox immigrants often initially clustered in their own neighborhoods, places of worship, and schools.

7. T F Almost all American Protestants eventually accepted Charles Darwin's evolutionary theories as well as nonliteral interpretations of the Bible.

8. T F In the late nineteenth century, secondary (high school) education was increasingly carried on by private schools.

9. T F Booker T. Washington believed that the most talented blacks should be educated for political leadership in academically rigorous black colleges.

10. T F American higher education depended on both public land-grant funding and private donations for its financial support.

11. T F Urban newspapers often promoted a sensational yellow journalism that emphasized sex and scandal rather that politics or social reform.

12. T F Post–Civil War writers like Mark Twain and William Dean Howells turned from social realism toward fantasy and science fiction in their novels.

13. T F There was growing tension in the late nineteenth century between women's traditionally defined sphere of family and home, and the social and cultural changes of the era.

14. T F The new urban environment generally weakened the family but offered new opportunities for women to achieve social and economic independence.

15. T F American urban planners focused on preserving greenbelt suburbs rather than the grand schemes for urban beautification developed in Paris and other European cities.

B. Multiple Choice

Select the best answer and circle the corresponding letter.

1. The new cities' glittering consumer economy was symbolized especially by the rise of
   a. separate districts for retail merchants.
   b. fine restaurants and grocery stories.
   c. large, elegant department stores.
   d. large, carefully constructed urban parks.
   e. large arenas for sports and other forms of urban entertainment.
2. One of the most difficult new problems generated by the rise of cities and the urban American life-style was
   a. dealing with horses and other animals in crowded urban settings.
   b. developing means of communication in densely populated city centers.
   c. disposing of large quantities of consumer-generated waste material.
   d. finding effective methods of high-rise construction for limited urban space.
   e. developing methods for accurately recording urban population growth and movement.
3. Two new technological developments of the late nineteenth century that especially contributed to the spectacular growth of cities in America and elsewhere around the world were the
   a. telegraph and the railroad.
   b. steam drill and the internal combustion engine.
   c. phonograph and the motion picture.
   d. oil furnace and the air conditioner.
   e. electric trolley and the skyscraper.

4. Among the primary countries from which many of the New Immigrants came were
   a. Sweden and Great Britain.
   b. Germany and Ireland.
   c. Poland and Italy.
   d. China and Japan.
   e. Mexico and Cuba.
5. Among the factors driving tens of millions of European peasants from their homeland to America and elsewhere in the late nineteenth century were the
   a. rapid rise of population and cheap American food imports.
   b. rise of European nation-states and the decline of the Catholic Church.
   c. rise of tyrannical communist and fascist regimes.
   d. major international wars among the European great powers.
   e. attempt to impose compulsory state education on tradition-minded parents.
6. Besides providing direct services to immigrants, the reformers of Hull House worked to implement social reforms such as
   a. the secret ballot and direct election of senators.
   b. antisweatshop and child labor laws to protect women and child laborers.
   c. social security and unemployment compensation.
   d. conservation and federal aid to municipal governments.
   e. public ownership of municipal transportation systems.
7. The one immigrant group that was totally banned from America after 1882, as a result of fierce nativist agitation, was the
   a. Irish.
   b. Greeks.
   c. Africans.
   d. Chinese.
   e. Jews.
8. The religious groups that grew most dramatically because of the New Immigration were
   a. Methodists, Baptists, and Disciples of Christ.
   b. Christian Scientists, the Salvation Army, and Buddhists.
   c. Episcopalians, Unitarians, and Congregationalists.
   d. Jews, Roman Catholics, and Orthodox.
   e. Lutherans, Christian Reformed, and Assemblies of God.
9. The phrase "social Gospel" refers to the
   a. evangelical movement that urged people to turn to God as the solution to social problems and class conflict.
   b. theories that Protestant liberals developed to reconcile Darwinian theories with the biblical views of human origins and the special creation of species.
   c. new theories of Biblical interpretation that emphasized the social contexts of ancient religious texts.
   d. conflict between socialists and traditional religious believers.
   e. efforts of Christian reformers like Walter Rauschenbusch to apply their religious beliefs to new social problems.
10. Traditional American Protestant religion received a substantial blow from the
   a. psychological ideas of William James.
   b. theological ideas of the Fundamentalists.
   c. chemical theories of Charles Eliot.
   d. biological ideas of Charles Darwin.
   e. the sermons of Dwight Moody.

11. Unlike Booker T. Washington, W. E. B. Du Bois advocated
    a. economic opportunity for blacks.
    b. turning to wealthy white philanthropist for funds to support black causes.
    c. practical as well as theoretical education for blacks.
    d. that blacks remain in the South rather than move north.
    e. advanced education and complete political and social equality for blacks.
12. In the late nineteenth century, American colleges and universities benefited especially from
    a. federal and state land-grant assistance and the private philanthropy of wealthy donors.
    b. the growing involvement of the churches in higher education.
    c. the fact that a college degree was becoming a prerequisite for employment in industry.
    d. the growth of federal grants and loans to college students.
    e. the growing belief that classical learning and the liberal arts were essential to a well-rounded life.
13. The widely popular American social reformers Henry George and Edward Bellamy advocated
    a. utopian reforms to end poverty and eliminate class conflict.
    b. an end to racial prejudice and segregation.
    c. the resettlement of the urban poor on free western homesteads.
    d. a transformation of the traditional family through communal living arrangements.
    e. detailed urban planning and low-cost housing as keys to ending inequality.
14. Authors like Mark Twain, Stephen Crane, and Jack London turned American literature toward a greater concern with
    a. close observation and contemplation of nature.
    b. postmodernism and deconstruction of traditional narratives.
    c. fantasy and romance.
    d. social realism and contemporary problems.
    e. history and religion.
15. Drawing on European models, American urban planners like Daniel Burnham believed that
    a. public buildings like libraries and museums should be subordinated to planned commercial development.
    b. suburban sprawl should be controlled through strict land use and zoning regulations.
    c. grand urban buildings and public spaces would stimulate progress and inspire civic virtue and loyalty in the city's residents.
    d. a dense concentration of urban skyscrapers and apartments was the best way to inspire civic pride and eliminate slums.
    e. the key to urban planning was a cheap, efficient mass transportation system.

C. Identification

Supply the correct identification for each numbered description.

1. __________ High-rise urban buildings that provided barracks-like housing for urban slum dwellers

2. __________ Term for the post-1880 newcomers who came to America primarily from southern and eastern Europe

3. __________ Term for the passion for migration to the New World that swept across Europe in the late nineteenth century

4. __________ The religious doctrines preached by those who believed that churches should directly address and work to reform economic and social problems

5. __________ Settlement house in the Chicago slums that became a model for women's involvement in urban social reform

6. __________ Profession established by Jane Addams and others that opened new opportunities for women while engaging urban problems

7. __________ Nativist organization that attacked New Immigrants and Roman Catholicism in the 1880s and 1890s

8. __________ Protestant believers who strongly resisted liberal Protestantism's attempts to adapt doctrines to Darwinian evolution and biblical criticism

9. __________ Black educational institution founded by Booker T. Washington to provide training in agriculture and crafts

10. __________ Organization founded by W. E. B. Du Bois and others to advance black social and economic equality

11. __________ Henry George's best-selling book that advocated social reform through the imposition of a single tax on land

12. __________ Federal law promoted by a self-appointed morality crusader and used to prosecute moral and sexual dissidents

13. __________ The American philosophical theory, especially advanced by William James, that the test of the truth of an idea was its practical consequences

14. __________ Urban planning movement, begun in Paris and carried on in Chicago and other American cities, that emphasized harmony, order, and monumental public buildings

15. __________ Women's organization founded by reformer Frances Willard and others to oppose alcohol consumption

D. Matching People, Places, and Events

Match the person, place, or event in the left column with the proper description in the right column by inserting the correct letter on the blank line.

1. ___ Louis Sullivan
2. ___ Walter Rauschenbusch
3. ___ Jane Addams
4. ___ Charles Darwin
5. ___ Horatio Alger
6. ___ Booker T. Washington
7. ___ W. E. B. Du Bois
8. ___ William James
9. ___ Henry George
10. ___ Emily Dickinson
11. ___ Mark Twain
12. ___ Victoria Woodhull

a. Controversial reformer whose book, *Progress and Poverty*, advocated solving problems of economic inequality by a tax on land

b. Midwestern-born writer and lecturer who created a new style of American literature based on social realism and humor

c. Well-connected and socially prominent historian who feared modern trends and sought relief in the beauty and culture of the past

d. Popular novelist whose tales of young people rising from poverty to wealth through hard work and good fortune enhanced Americans' belief in individual opportunity

e. Leading Protestant advocate of the social gospel who tried to make Christianity relevant to urban and industrial problems

13. ___ Daniel Burnham
14. ___ Charlotte Perkins Gilman
15. ___ Henry Adams

f. Former slave who promoted industrial education and economic opportunity but not social equality for blacks

g. Harvard scholar who made original contributions to modern psychology and philosophy

h. Radical feminist propagandist whose eloquent attacks on conventional social morality shocked many Americans in the 1870s

i. Brilliant feminist writer who advocated cooperative cooking and child-care arrangements to promote women's economic independence and equality

j. Leading social reformer who lived with the poor in the slums and pioneered new forms of activism for women

k. American architect and planner who helped bring French Baron Haussman's City Beautiful movement to the United States.

l. Harvard-educated scholar and advocate of full black social and economic equality through the leadership of a talented tenth

m. Chicago-based architect whose high-rise innovation allowed more people to crowd into limited urban space

n. British biologist whose theories of human and animal evolution by means of natural selection created religious and intellectual controversy

o. Gifted but isolated New England poet, the bulk of whose works were not published until after her death

E. Putting Things in Order

Put the following events in correct order by numbering them from 1 to 5.

1. __________ Well-educated young midwesterner moves to Chicago slums and creates a vital center of social reform and activism.

2. __________ Introduction of a new form of high-rise slum housing drastically increases the overcrowding of the urban poor.

3. __________ Nativist organization is formed to limit the New Immigration and attack Roman Catholicism.

4. __________ The formation of a new national organization signals growing strength for the women's suffrage movement.

5. __________ A western territory becomes the first U.S. government to grant full voting rights to women.

F. Matching Cause and Effect

Match the historical cause in the left column with the proper effect in the right column by writing the correct letter on the blank line.

Cause

1. ___ New industrial jobs and urban excitement
2. ___ Uncontrolled rapid growth and the New Immigration from Europe
3. ___ Cheap American grain exports to Europe
4. ___ The cultural strangeness and poverty of southern and eastern European immigrants
5. ___ Social gospel ministers and settlement-house workers
6. ___ Darwinian science and growing urban materialism
7. ___ Government land grants and private philanthropy
8. ___ Popular newspapers and yellow journalism
9. ___ Changes in moral and sexual attitudes
10. ___ The difficulties of family life in the industrial city

Effect

a. Encouraged the mass urban public's taste for scandal and sensation

b. Created intense poverty and other problems in the crowded urban slums

c. Weakened the religious influence in American society and created divisions within the churches

d. Led women and men to delay marriage and have fewer children

e. Helped uproot European peasants from their ancestral lands and sent them seeking new opportunities in America and elsewhere

f. Supported the substantial improvements in American undergraduate and graduate education in the late nineteenth century

g. Lured millions of rural Americans off the farms and into the cities

h. Assisted immigrants and other slum dwellers and pricked middle-class consciences about urban problems

i. Provoked sharp hostility from some native-born Americans and organized labor groups

j. Created sharp divisions about the new morality and issues such as divorce

G. Developing Historical Skills

Interpreting a Line Graph

A line graph is another visual way to convey information. It is often used to present notable historical changes occurring over substantial periods of time. Study the line graph on p.600 and answer the following questions.

1. There are five major peaks of immigration and four major valleys. What factors helped cause each of the periods of heavy immigration? What helped cause each of the sharp declines?

2. About how long did each of the first four periods of major immigration last? About how long did each of the four valleys last? How long has the current (to 2006) phase of rising or steady immigration lasted?

3. During what five-year period was there the sharpest rise in immigration? What five-year period saw the sharpest fall?

4. In about what three years did approximately 800,000 immigrants enter the United States? In about what seven years did approximately 200,000 immigrants enter the United States?

5. Approximately how many fewer immigrants came in 1920 than in 1914? About how many more immigrants came in 1990 than in 1950?

PART III: APPLYING WHAT YOU HAVE LEARNED

1. What new opportunities and social problems did the cities create for Americans?
2. In what ways was American urbanization simply part of a worldwide trend, and in what ways did it reflect particular American circumstances? How did the influx of millions of mostly European immigrants create a special dimension to America's urban problems?
3. How did the New Immigration differ from the Old Immigration, and how did Americans respond to it?
4. How was American religion affected by the urban transformation, the New Immigration, and cultural and intellectual changes?
5. Why was Darwinian evolution such a controversial challenge for American religious thinkers? Why were religious liberals able to dominate Americans' cultural response to evolution? How did a minority resistance to evolution lay the basis for the later rise of fundamentalism?
6. How did American social criticism, fiction writing, and art all reflect and address the urban industrial changes of the late nineteenth century? Which social critics and novelists were most influential, and why?
7. How and why did women assume a larger place in American society at this time? (Compare their status in this period with that of the pre–Civil War period described in Chapter 16.) How were changes in their condition related to changes in both the family and the larger social order?
8. What was the greatest single cultural transformation of the Gilded Age?
9. In what ways did Americans positively and enthusiastically embrace the new possibilities of urban life, and in what ways did their outlooks and actions reflect worries about the threats that cities presented to traditional American democracy and social ideals?

CHAPTER 26

The Great West and the Agricultural Revolution, 1865–1896

PART I: REVIEWING THE CHAPTER

A. Checklist of Learning Objectives

After mastering this chapter, you should be able to:

1. Describe the nature of the cultural conflicts and battles that accompanied the white American migration into the Great Plains and the Far West.
2. Explain the development of federal policy towards Native Americans in the late nineteenth century.
3. Analyze the brief flowering and decline of the cattle and mining frontiers, and the settling of the arid West by small farmers increasingly engaged with a worldwide economy.
4. Summarize Frederick Jackson Turner's thesis regarding the significance of the frontier in American history, describe its strengths and weaknesses, and indicate the ways in which the American West became and remains a distinctive region of the United States.
5. Describe the economic forces that drove farmers into debt, and describe how the Populist Party organized to protest their oppression, attempted to forge an alliance with urban workers, and vigorously attacked the two major parties after the onset of the depression of the 1890s.
6. Describe the Democratic party's revolt against President Cleveland and the rise of the insurgent William Jennings Bryan's free silver campaign.
7. Explain why William McKinley proved able to defeat Bryan's populist campaign and how the Republicans' triumph signaled the rise of urban power and the end of the third party system in American politics.

B. Glossary

To build your social science vocabulary, familiarize yourself with the following terms.

1. **nomadic (nomad)** A way of life characterized by frequent movement from place to place for economic sustenance. ". . . the Sioux transformed themselves from foot-traveling, crop-growing villagers to wide-ranging nomadic traders. . . ."
2. **immunity** Freedom or exemption from some imposition. ". . . [the] militia massacred . . . four hundred Indians who apparently thought they had been promised immunity."
3. **reservation** Public lands designated for use by Indians. "The vanquished Indians were finally ghettoized on reservations. . . ."
4. **ward** Someone considered incompetent to manage his or her own affairs and therefore placed under the legal guardianship of another person or group. ". . . there [they had] to eke out a sullen existence as wards of the government."

5. **probationary** Concerning a period of testing or trial, after which a decision is made based on performance. "The probationary period was later extended. . . ."
6. **folklore** The common traditions and stories of a people. "These bowlegged Knights of the Saddle . . . became part of American folklore."
7. **irrigation** Watering land artificially, through canals, pipes, or other means. ". . . irrigation projects . . . caused the 'Great American Desert' to bloom. . . ."
8. **meridian** In geography, any of the imaginary lines of longitude running north and south on the globe. ". . . settlers . . . rashly pushed . . . beyond the 100th meridian. . . ."
9. **contiguous** Joined together by common borders. "Only Oklahoma, New Mexico, and Arizona remained to be lifted into statehood from contiguous territory on the mainland of North America."
10. **safety valve** Anything, such as the American frontier, that allegedly serves as a necessary outlet for built-up pressure, energy, and so on. "But the 'safety-valve' theory does have some validity."
11. **loan shark** A person who lends money at an exorbitant or illegal rate of interest. "The [farmers] . . . cried out in despair against the loan sharks. . . ."
12. **serfdom** The feudal condition of being permanently bound to land owned by someone else. ". . . the farmers were about to sink into a status suggesting Old World serfdom."
13. **mumbo jumbo** Mysterious and unintelligible words or behavior. "Kelley, a Mason, even found farmers receptive to his mumbo jumbo of passwords and secret rituals. . . ."
14. **prophet** A person believed to speak with divine power or special gifts, sometimes including predicting the future (hence any specially talented or eloquent advocate of a cause). "Numerous fiery prophets leapt forward to trumpet the Populist cause."
15. **citadel** A fortress occupying a commanding height. " . . . join hands with urban workers, and mount a successful attack on the northeastern citadels of power."

PART II: CHECKING YOUR PROGRESS

A. True-False

Where the statement is true, circle **T**; where it is false, circle **F.**

1. T F The acquisition of Spanish horses transformed the Sioux and Cheyenne from crop-growing villagers into nomadic buffalo hunters.
2. T F The Plains Indians were rather quickly and easily defeated by the U.S. Army.
3. T F A crucial factor in defeating the Indians was the destruction of the buffalo, a vital source of food and other supplies.
4. T F Humanitarian reformers respected the Indians' traditional culture and tried to preserve their tribal way of life.
5. T F Individual gold and silver miners proved unable to compete with large mining corporations and trained engineers.
6. T F During the peak years of the Long Drive, the cattlemen's prosperity depended on driving large beef herds great distances to railroad terminal points.
7. T F The fair administration of the Homestead Act enabled many poorer farmers to achieve economic success on the plains of the arid, frontier West.

8. T F Although very few city dwellers ever migrated west to take up farming, the frontier "safety valve" did have some positive effects by luring some immigrants to the West and helping to keep urban wages higher than they otherwise might have been.

9. T F The farmers who settled the Great Plains were usually single-crop producers who became increasingly dependent on competitive and unstable world markets to sell their agricultural products.

10. T F Western and southern farmers were able to organize quickly and effectively to break their cycle of debt, falling prices, and exploitation by the railroads and other "middlemen."

11. T F A fundamental problem of the Farmers' Alliance in the South was their inability to overcome the racial division between poor white and black farmers.

12. T F The economic crisis of the 1890s strengthened the Populists' belief that farmers and industrial workers should form an alliance against economic and political oppression.

13. T F Republican political manager Mark Hanna struggled to raise enough funds to combat William Jennings Bryan's pro-silver campaign.

14. T F Bryan's populist campaign failed partly because he was unable to persuade enough urban workers to join his essentially rural-based cause.

15. T F McKinley's victory in 1896 ushered in an era marked by Republican domination, weakened party organization, and the fading of the money issue in American politics.

B. Multiple Choice

Select the best answer and circle the corresponding letter.

1. The Indians of the western plains offered strong resistance to white expansion through their effective use of
   a. artillery and infantry tactics.
   b. Canada and Mexico as safe havens from which to conduct warfare.
   c. nighttime and winter campaigning.
   d. eastern journalists and artists to publicize their cause.
   e. superb horsemanship and mobility.
2. The federal government's attempt to confine Indians to certain areas through formal treaties was largely ineffective because
   a. the nomadic Plains Indians largely rejected the idea of formal authority and defined territory.
   b. Congress refused to ratify treaties signed with the Indians.
   c. the treaties made no effective provisions for enforcement.
   d. the largest tribe, the Sioux, refused to sign any treaties with the whites.
   e. the Indians repeatedly broke out of the proposed reservations and resumed open warfare.
3. The warfare that led up to the Battle of the Little Big Horn was set off by
   a. white intrusion into the previously reserved Indian territory of Oklahoma.
   b. Indian attacks on the transcontinental railroad construction crews.
   c. the Indians' defeat and killing of Captain William Fetterman's entire military unit in Montana.
   d. a conflict over the interpretation of the second Treaty of Fort Laramie.
   e. white intrusions into the Indians' sacred Black Hills after the discovery of gold there.

4. Which of the following was *not* among the factors that finally led to the defeat of the Plains Indians and their confinement to reservations?
   a. The federal government's willingness to deploy unrelenting military force
   b. The constant political infighting among the Sioux, Cheyenne, Arapaho, and Apache tribes
   c. The destruction of the buffalo upon which the Indian way of life depended
   d. The railroads' intrusive penetration of Indian lands
   e. The Indians' vulnerability to white people's diseases and liquor
5. Many religious reformers, federal boarding schools, and the Dawes Act were all focused on the goal of
   a. enabling Indians to achieve economic opportunity on the reservations.
   b. assisting Indians who chose to migrate from the remote reservations to towns and cities.
   c. helping Indians form an effective pan-Indian alliance beyond their tribal identity.
   d. undermining Indians' traditional culture and assimilating them into white American culture and society.
   e. weakening the Bureau of Indian Affairs' monopoly on Indian policy.
6. Both the mining and cattle frontiers of the late nineteenth-century West saw a/an
   a. increase of ethnic and class conflict.
   b. loss of economic viability after an initial boom.
   c. turn from large-scale investment to the individual entrepreneur.
   d. brief flourishing of individual enterprise eventually followed by large corporate takeovers.
   e. influx of immigrant miners and cowboys from Europe.
7. The problem of sustaining agriculture in the arid West was solved most successfully through
   a. concentrating agriculture in the more fertile mountain valleys.
   b. the use of small-scale family farms rather than large bonanza farms.
   c. the use of irrigation from dammed western rivers.
   d. the turn to desert crops like olives and dates.
   e. revising the Homestead Act to give away free farms of 640 acres instead of the inadequate 160 acres.
8. The safety valve theory of the frontier claims that
   a. Americans were able to divert the most violent elements of the population to the West.
   b. the conflict between farmers and ranchers was relieved by the Homestead Act.
   c. class and labor conflict in America was alleviated because eastern workers could always migrate to the West and become independent farmers.
   d. political movements such as the Populists provided relief for the most serious grievances of western farmers.
   e. the wide-open spaces of the West provided an arena where Americans' attachment to guns and violence could be pursued without threatening the social fabric.
9. Which one of these factors did *not* make the trans-Mississippi West a unique part of the American frontier experience?
   a. The large-scale engagement and struggle between white Anglo and Hispanic cultures.
   b. The problem of applying new technologies in a hostile wilderness
   c. The scale and severity of environmental challenges in an arid environment
   d. The large role of the federal government in economic and social development
   e. The final military defeat of American Indians and their continuing substantial presence in the region.

10. By the 1880s, most western farmers faced hard times because
    a. free land was no longer available under the Homestead Act.
    b. they were unable to increase grain production to keep up with demand.
    c. they were being strangled by excessive federal regulation of agriculture.
    d. they resisted the adoption of technologically improved farming techniques.
    e. they were forced to sell their grain at declining prices in volatile and depressed world markets.
11. Which of the following was *not* among the political goals advocated by the Populist party in the 1890s?
    a. Nationalizing the railroad, telegraph, and telephone
    b. Creation of a national system of unemployment insurance and old-age pensions
    c. A graduated income tax
    d. Free and unlimited coinage of silver money
    e. Federally-owned warehouses where farmers could store their grain until prices rose.
12. The federal government's use of the U.S. Army to crush the Pullman strike in Chicago aroused great anger from both organized labor and the Populists because
    a. it seemed to reflect an alliance of big business and government to destroy the organizing efforts of workers and farmers.
    b. it broke apart the growing alliance between urban workers and farmers.
    c. it undermined efforts to organize federal workers like those in the postal service.
    d. it turned their most effective leader, Eugene V. Debs, into a cautious conservative.
    e. many of the soldiers used to defeat the union were themselves from rural or working class backgrounds.
13. William Jennings Bryan gained the Democratic nomination in 1896 because he strongly advocated
    a. unlimited coinage of silver in order to inflate the currency.
    b. higher tariffs in order to protect the American farmer.
    c. government ownership of the railroads and the telegraph system.
    d. a coalition between white and black farmers in the South and Midwest.
    e. enlisting President Cleveland and other conservative Democrats in the reform cause.
14. McKinley defeated Bryan primarily because he was able to win the support of
    a. white southern farmers.
    b. eastern wage earners and city dwellers.
    c. urban and rural blacks.
    d. former Populists and Greenback Laborites.
    e. western ranchers and miners.
15. Which of the following was *not* a feature of the end of the third party system and its replacement by a fourth party system after the pivotal election of 1896?
    a. The weakening of strong, patronage-driven political party organizations
    b. The end of razor-thin elections and the beginning of an era of Republican domination
    c. The rise of third parties that threatened to replace either the Democrats or Republicans as a major party
    d. The decline of the money issue that had dominated American politics since the Civil War
    e. Gradual decline in voter participation in politics and elections

C. Identification

Supply the correct identification for each numbered description.

1. __________ Major northern Plains Indian nation that fought and eventually lost a bitter war against the U.S. Army, 1876–1877
2. __________ Southwestern Indian tribe led by Geronimo that carried out some of the last fighting against white conquest
3. __________ Generally poor areas where vanquished Indians were eventually confined under federal control
4. __________ Indian religious movement, originating out of the sacred Sun Dance that the federal government attempted to stamp out in 1890
5. __________ Federal law that attempted to dissolve tribal landholding and establish Indians as individual farmers
6. __________ Huge silver and gold deposit that brought wealth and statehood to Nevada
7. __________ General term for the herding of cattle from the grassy plains to the railroad terminals of Kansas, Nebraska, and Wyoming
8. __________ Federal law that offered generous land opportunities to poorer farmers but also provided the unscrupulous with opportunities for hoaxes and fraud
9. __________ Historian Frederick Jackson Turner's argument that the continual westward migration into unsettled territory has been the primary force shaping American character and American society
10. __________ Former Indian Territory where illegal sooners tried to get the jump on boomers when it was opened for settlement in 1889
11. __________ Third political party that emerged in the 1890s to express rural grievances and mount major attacks on the Democrats and Republicans
12. __________ Popular pamphlet written by William Hope Harvey that portrayed pro-silver arguments triumphing over the traditional views of bankers and economics professors
13. __________ Bitter labor conflict in Chicago that brought federal intervention and the jailing of union leader Eugene V. Debs
14. __________ Spectacular convention speech by a young pro-silver advocate that brought him the Democratic presidential nomination in 1896
15. __________ Popular term for those who favored the status quo in metal money and opposed the pro-silver Bryanites in 1896

D. Matching People, Places, and Events

Match the person, place, or event in the left column with the proper description in the right column by inserting the correct letter on the blank line.

1. ___ Sand Creek, Colorado
2. ___ Little Big Horn

a. Ohio industrialist and organizer of McKinley's victory over Bryan in the election of 1896

3. ____ Sitting Bull
4. ____ Chief Joseph
5. ____ Geronimo
6. ____ Helen Hunt Jackson
7. ____ John Wesley Powell
8. ____ Frederick Jackson Turner
9. ____ Jacob S. Coxey
10. ____ William Hope Harvey
11. ____ Eugene V. Debs
12. ____ Oliver H. Kelley
13. ____ James B. Weaver
14. ____ Mary E. Lease
15. ____ Marcus Alonzo Hanna

b. Leader of the Nez Percé tribe who conducted a brilliant but unsuccessful military campaign in 1877

c. Author of the popular pro-silver pamphlet Coin's Financial School

d. Minnesota farm leader whose Grange organization first mobilized American farmers and laid the groundwork for the Populists

e. Former Civil War general and Granger who ran as the Greenback Labor party candidate for president in 1880

f. Leader of the Sioux during wars of 1876–1877

g. Explorer and geologist who warned that traditional agriculture could not succeed west of the 100th meridian

h. Ohio businessman who led his Commonweal Army to Washington, seeking relief and jobs for the unemployed

i. Leader of the Apaches of Arizona in their warfare with the whites

j. Site of Indian massacre by militia forces in 1864

k. Massachusetts writer whose books aroused sympathy for the plight of the Native Americans

l. Site of major U.S. Army defeat in the Sioux War of 1876–1877

m. American historian who argued that the encounter with the ever-receding West had fundamentally shaped America

n. Railway union leader who converted to socialism while serving jail time during the Pullman strike

o. Eloquent Kansas Populist who urged farmers to "raise less corn and more hell"

E. Putting Things in Order

Put the following events in correct order by numbering them from 1 to 5.

1. ______ A sharp economic depression leads to a major railroad strike and the intervention of federal troops in Chicago.
2. ______ The violation of agreements with the Dakota Sioux leads to a major Indian war and a military disaster for the U.S. cavalry.
3. ______ A federal law grants 160 acres of land to farmers at token prices, thus encouraging the rapid settlement of the Great West.
4. ______ The U.S. Census Bureau declares that there is no longer a clear line of frontier settlement, ending a formative chapter of American history.
5. ______ Despite a fervent campaign by their charismatic young champion, pro-silver Democrats lose a pivotal election to Gold Bug Republicans.

F. Matching Cause and Effect

Match the historical cause in the left column with the proper effect in the right column by writing the correct letter on the blank line.

Cause

1. ___ The encroachment of white settlement and the violation of treaties with Indians
2. ___ Railroad building, disease, and the destruction of the buffalo
3. ___ Reformers' attempts to make Native Americans conform to white ways
4. ___ The coming of big-business mining and stock-raising to the West
5. ___ Dry farming, barbed wire, and irrigation
6. ___ The passing of the frontier in 1890
7. ___ The growing economic specialization of western farmers
8. ___ The rise of the Populist party in the early 1890s
9. ___ The economic depression that began in 1893
10. ___ The return of prosperity after 1897 and new gold discoveries in Alaska, South Africa, and elsewhere

Effect

a. Caused widespread protests and strikes like the one against the Pullman Company in Chicago

b. Threatened the two-party domination of American politics by the Republicans and Democrats

c. Created new psychological and economic problems for a nation accustomed to a boundlessly open West

d. Ended the romantic, colorful era of the miners' and the cattlemen's frontier

e. Decimated Indian populations and hastened their defeat at the hands of advancing whites

f. Effectively ended the free-silver agitation and the domination of the money question in American politics

g. Made settlers vulnerable to vast industrial and market forces beyond their control

h. Made it possible to farm the dry, treeless areas of the Great Plains and the West

i. Further undermined Native Americans' traditional tribal culture and morale

j. Led to nearly constant warfare with Plains Indians from 1868 to about 1890

G. Developing Historical Skills

Reading Meteorological/Agricultural Maps

The map on p. 647 is designed to demonstrate the relationship between a key variation in climate and weather, average annual precipitation, and the patterns of agriculture. Study the map to discern these patterns, and then answer the following questions.

1. In 1900, which was the only grain crop regularly grown in areas receiving less than 20 inches of annual rainfall?

2. In 1900, which two grain crops were produced in areas receiving over sixty inches a year of annual precipitation?

3. Which type of livestock evidently thrived *only* in areas receiving moderate rainfall (20–40 inches per year)?

4. Which type of livestock could be raised in low-rainfall country (under 20 inches per year) as well as in moderate rainfall areas?

H. Map Mastery

Map Discrimination

Using the map on p. 663, answer the following questions.

1. In the election of 1896, how many states west of the Mississippi River did William McKinley carry (counting Minnesota as west of the Mississippi)?

2. How many electoral votes did William Jennings Bryan win in the five Border States of Delaware, Maryland, West Virginia, Kentucky, and Missouri?

3. Given the regional division and pattern of the election, which candidate would Oklahoma, New Mexico, and Arizona likely have favored had they been admitted to the Union?

4. How many electoral votes did McKinley win in the eleven southern states of the old Confederacy?

Map Challenge

Using the maps of *American Agriculture in 1900* (p. 647) and *Presidential Election of 1896* (p. 663), discuss the relationship between the Populist and pro-silver movements and the patterns of American agriculture. Include in your analysis some analysis of those Midwestern agricultural states that may have been influenced by Populism but did not vote for Bryan in 1896.

PART III: APPLYING WHAT YOU HAVE LEARNED

1. How did whites finally overcome resistance of the Plains Indians, and what happened to the Indians after their resistance ceased?
2. What social, ethnic, environmental, and economic factors made the trans-Mississippi West a unique region among the successive American frontiers? What makes the West continue to be a region quite distinctive from other regions such as the Northeast, the Midwest, and the South? How does the myth of the frontier West differ from the actual reality, in the late nineteenth century, and after?
3. What were the actual effects of the frontier on American society at different stages of its development? What was valuable in Frederick Jackson Turner's frontier thesis, despite its being discredited by subsequent historians.
4. Why did landowning small American farmers—traditionally considered by Jefferson, Jackson, and others the backbone of American society—suddenly find themselves trapped in a cycle of debt, deflation, and exploitation in the late nineteenth century? Was their plight due primarily to deliberate economic oppression corporate business, as they saw it, or was it simply an inevitable consequence of agriculture's involvement in world markets and economy?
5. Were the Populist and pro-silver movements of the 1880s and 1890s essentially backward-looking protests by a passing rural America, or were they, despite their immediate political failure, genuine prophetic voices raising central critical questions about democracy and economic justice in the new corporate industrial America?
6. What were the major issues in the crucial campaign of 1896? Why did McKinley win, and what were the long-term effects of his victory?
7. Some historians have seen Bryan as the political heir of Jefferson and Jackson, and McKinley as the political heir of Hamilton and the Whigs. Are such connections valid? Why or why not (see Chapters 10, 12, and 13)?
8. The settlement of the Great West and the farmers' revolt occurred at the same time as the rise of industrialism and the growth of American cities. To what extent were the defeat of the Indians, the destruction and exploitation of western resources, and the populist revolt of the farmers in the 1890s caused by the Gilded Age forces of industrialization and urbanization?

CHAPTER 27

Empire and Expansion, 1890–1909

PART I: REVIEWING THE CHAPTER

A. Checklist of Learning Objectives

After mastering this chapter, you should be able to:

1. Explain why the United States suddenly abandoned its isolationism and turned outward at the end of the nineteenth century.
2. Describe the forces pushing for American overseas expansion and the causes of the Spanish-American War.
3. Describe and explain the unintended results of the Spanish-American War, especially the conquest of Puerto Rico and the Philippines.
4. Explain McKinley's decision to keep the Philippines, and list the opposing arguments in the debate about imperialism.
5. Analyze the consequences of the Spanish-American War, including the Filipino rebellion against U.S. rule and the war to suppress it.
6. Explain the growing U.S. involvement in East Asia, and summarize America's Open Door policy toward China.
7. Discuss the significance of the pro-imperialist Republican victory in 1900 and the rise of Theodore Roosevelt as a strong advocate of American power in international affairs.
8. Describe Roosevelt's assertive policies in Panama and elsewhere in Latin America, and explain why his corollary to the Monroe Doctrine aroused such controversy.
9. Discuss Roosevelt's foreign policies and diplomatic achievements, especially regarding Japan.

B. Glossary

To build your social science vocabulary, familiarize yourself with the following terms.

1. **arbitration** An arrangement in which a neutral third party conclusively determines the mandatory outcome of a dispute between two parties. (In **mediation** the third party only serves as a go-between and proposes solutions that the disputing parties may or may not accept.) "A simmering argument between the United States and Canada . . . was resolved by arbitration in 1893."
2. **scorched-earth policy** The policy of burning and destroying all the property in a given area so as to deny it to an enemy. "The desperate insurgents now sought to drive out their Spanish overlords by adopting a scorched-earth policy."
3. **reconcentration** The policy of forcibly removing a population to confined areas in order to deny support to enemy forces. " He undertook to crush the rebellion by herding many civilians into barbed-wire reconcentration camps."

4. **atrocity** A specific act of extreme cruelty. "Where atrocity stories did not exist, they were invented."

5. **proviso** An article or clause in a statute, treaty, or contract establishing a particular stipulation or condition that qualifies or modifies the whole document. "This proviso proclaimed . . . that when the United States had overthrown Spanish misrule, it would give the Cubans their freedom. . . ."

6. **hostage** A person or thing forcibly held in order to obtain certain goals or agreements. "Hereafter these distant islands were to be . . . a kind of indefensible hostage given to Japan."

7. **Americanization** The process of originally non-American people assimilating to American character, manner, institutions, culture, and so on. "The Filipinos, who hated compulsory Americanization, preferred liberty."

8. **sphere of influence** In international affairs, the territory where a powerful state exercises the dominant control over weaker states or territories. ". . . they began to tear away valuable leaseholds and economic spheres of influence from the Manchu government."

9. **partition** In politics, the act of dividing a weaker territory or government among several more powerful states. "Those principles helped to spare China from possible partition in those troubled years. . . .

10. **blue blood** A person of supposedly" pure blood," presumed to be descended directly from nobility or aristocracy. "Born into a wealthy and distinguished New York family, Roosevelt, a red-blooded blue blood. . . ."

11. **bellicose** Disposed to fight or go to war. "Incurably boyish and bellicose, Roosevelt ceaselessly preached the virile virtues. . . ."

12. **preparedness** The accumulation of sufficient armed forces and matériel to go to war. "An ardent champion of military and naval preparedness. . . ."

13. **corollary** A secondary inference or deduction from a main proposition that is assumed to be established or proven. "[Roosevelt] therefore devised a devious policy of 'preventive intervention,' better known as the Roosevelt Corollary of the Monroe Doctrine."

14. **indemnity** A payment assessed to compensate for an injury or illegal action. "Japan was forced to drop its demands for a cash indemnity. . . ."

PART II: CHECKING YOUR PROGRESS

A. True-False

Where the statement is true, circle **T**; where it is false, circle **F**.

1. T F The American people and their government were deeply involved in the key international developments of the 1860s and 1870s.

2. T F The South American boundary dispute over Guyana in 1895–1896 nearly resulted in a U.S. war with Venezuela.

3. T F President Cleveland refused to annex Hawaii because he believed that the white American planters there had unjustly deposed Hawaii's Queen Liliuokalani.

4. T F Americans first became involved in Cuba because they sympathized with the Cubans' revolt against imperialist Spain.

5. T F When war broke out between the United States and Spain, Admiral George Dewey's squadron attacked Spanish forces in the Philippines because of secret orders given by Assistant Navy Secretary Theodore Roosevelt.

6. T F When the United States refused to hand over the Philippines to Filipino rebels, a vicious guerrilla war with racial overtones broke out between the former allies.

7. T F The American military conquest of Cuba was efficient but very costly in battlefield casualties.

8. T F President McKinley declared that religion played a crucial role in his decision to keep the Philippines as an American colony.

9. T F The peace treaty with Spain that made the Philippines an American colony was almost universally popular with the U.S. Senate and the American public.

10. T F The Supreme Court decided in the insular cases that American constitutional law and the Bill of Rights applied to the people under American rule in Puerto Rico and the Philippines.

11. T F American male and female Protestant missionaries helped to foster a strong, sentimental American attachment to China in the early 1900s.

12. T F John Hay's Open Door notes were designed in consultation with the Chinese and welcomed by the European imperialist powers.

13. T F Theodore Roosevelt believed that the United States should exercise caution and restraint in its exercise of power in international affairs.

14. T F President Roosevelt's anger at Colombia's refusal to authorize a canal across Panama led him to unofficially encourage and assist a movement for Panamanian independence.

15. T F The Roosevelt Corollary to the Monroe Doctrine stated that only the United States but no other nation had the right to intervene in Latin American nations' internal affairs.

16. T F In the San Francisco school crisis of 1906, President Roosevelt forced the integration of Japanese children into schools while persuading Japan to stop further immigration to the United States.

B. Multiple Choice

Select the best answer and circle the corresponding letter.

1. The military theorist Captain Alfred Thayer Mahan promoted American overseas expansion by
   a. developing a lurid yellow press that stimulated popular excitement.
   b. arguing that control of the seas through naval power was the key to world domination.
   c. provoking naval incidents with Germany and Britain in the Pacific.
   d. arguing that the Monroe Doctrine required American control of Latin American waters.
   e. pressing the United States to establish naval bases throughout the Pacific Ocean.

2. Which of the following was *not* among the factors propelling America toward overseas expansion in the 1890s?
   a. The desire to expand overseas agricultural and manufacturing exports
   b. The yellow press of Joseph Pulitzer and William Randolph Hearst
   c. Some Protestant leaders' belief that America should spread its religion and culture to backward people
   d. The ideologies of Anglo-Saxon superiority and social Darwinism
   e. The intervention of the German Kaiser in Latin America
3. President Grover Cleveland refused to annex Hawaii in 1893 because
   a. white planters had illegally overthrown Queen Liliuokalani against the wishes of most native Hawaiians.
   b. there was no precedent for the United States to acquire territory except by purchase.
   c. the Germans and the British threatened possible war.
   d. he knew the public disapproved and the Senate would not ratify a treaty of annexation.
   e. he knew that many Americans would object to the incorporation of a non-white territory into the United States.
4. Americans first became actively involved with the situation in Cuba because
   a. it was clear that Spanish control of Cuba violated the Monroe Doctrine.
   b. imperialists and business leaders were looking to acquire colonial territory for the United States.
   c. leading Cuban rebels began advocating that Cuban be incorporated into the United States.
   d. the Battleship *Maine* exploded in Havana harbor.
   e. Americans sympathized with Cuban rebels in their fight for democratic freedom from Spanish imperial rule.
5. Even before the sinking of the *Maine*, the American public's indignation at Spain had been whipped into a frenzy by
   a. Spanish Catholics' persecution of the Protestant minority in Cuba.
   b. Spain's aggressive battleship-building program.
   c. William Randolph Hearst's sensational newspaper accounts of Spanish atrocities in Cuba.
   d. the Spanish government's brutal treatment of American sailors on leave in Havana.
   e. the mistreatment of white American women by Spanish businessmen.
6. Assistant Secretary of the Navy Roosevelt took full advantage of the outbreak of war between the United States and Spain over Cuba by
   a. pushing for the annexation of Hawaii to the United States.
   b. establishing American naval bases at Pearl Harbor, Guam, and Samoa in the Pacific.
   c. secretly ordering Admiral George Dewey to attack the Spanish in the distant Philippines.
   d. organizing an American naval squadron to trap the Spanish fleet in Havana harbor.
   e. ordering the American navy to blockade all shipments in and out of Cuba.
7. Emilio Aguinaldo was the
   a. leader of Cuban insurgents against Spanish rule.
   b. leader of Filipino insurgents against Spanish rule.
   c. commander of the Spanish navy in the Battle of Manila Bay.
   d. first native Hawaiian to become governor of the islands after the American takeover.
   e. scheming Panamanian engineer who helped Panama to declare independence from Colombia.

8. Besides the Philippines, which two other colonial territories did the United States acquire in the Spanish-American War?
   a. Trinidad and Tobago
   b. Puerto Rico and Guam
   c. Cuba and the Dominican Republic
   d. Hawaii and American Samoa
   e. The Virgin Islands and the Panama Canal Zone
9. Which of the following was *not* among the reasons that President McKinley and other pro-imperialists gave for acquiring the Philippines as an American territory?
   a. Other imperial nations like Germany or Japan would seize the Philippines if the United States left.
   b. McKinley believed that handing them back to Spain's cruel misrule would betray American ideals.
   c. Many believed that Manila could open rich trading opportunities in China.
   d. McKinley believed that God had told him to Christianize and civilize the Filipinos.
   e. The Filipinos had been mostly Catholic Christians for centuries and so would welcome American rule.
10. Which of the following was *not* among the arguments that anti-imperialists used to oppose American acquisition of the Philippines?
   a. The Philippines had a large population of a different culture, language, and racial composition.
   b. The Filipinos would never voluntarily convert to Protestantism if they were forced under American rule.
   c. Acquiring colonial territory would violate Americans' historic commitment to self-determination and anti-colonialism.
   d. Ruling over people without their consent was despotism and would undermine American democracy at home.
   e. Ruling the Philippines would be expensive, and the United States could never adequately defend them.
11. The most immediate consequence of American acquisition of the Philippines was
   a. the establishment of Manila as a crucial American defense post in East Asia.
   b. an agreement between Americans and Filipinos to move toward Philippine independence.
   c. an outbreak of vicious guerrilla warfare between the United States and Filipino rebels.
   d. threats by Japan to seize the Philippines from American control.
   e. a successful program to Americanize the Filipinos by bringing them U.S. culture and education.
12. In the Open Door notes, Secretary of State John Hay called on all the imperial powers to
   a. acknowledge American control of the Philippines as the gateway to China.
   b. limit their military forces and control the arms race in China and the Pacific.
   c. respect Chinese rights and uphold China's territorial integrity rather than breaking it up into colonies.
   d. grant the United States an equal share in any possible colonization of China.
   e. treat China fairly despite the attacks on foreigners during the Boxer Rebellion.
13. As president, Theodore Roosevelt gained political strength especially through
   a. his careful use of traditional diplomacy.
   b. his constant threats of military intervention around the world.
   c. his vigorous use of his personal popularity and presidential power to lead Congress and the public.
   d. his ability to quietly mobilize his cabinet to promote his policy objectives.
   e. creating a personal political organization separate from the Republican party.

14. Roosevelt overcame Colombia's refusal to approve a canal treaty by
    a. increasing the amount of money the United States was willing to pay for a canal zone.
    b. encouraging Panamanian rebels to revolt and declare independence from Colombia.
    c. threatening to build the canal on a route through Nicaragua.
    d. seeking mediation of the dispute by other Latin American nations.
    e. sending in U.S. marines to seize control of the canal route.
15. Theodore Roosevelt's slogan that stated his essential foreign policy principle was
    a. "Open covenants openly arrived at."
    b. "Millions for defense but not one cent for tribute."
    c. "Speak softly and carry a big stick."
    d. "Democracy and liberty in a New World Order."
    e. "American does not go abroad in search of monsters to destroy."

C. Identification

Supply the correct identification for each numbered description.

1. __________ Remote Pacific site of a naval clash between the United States and Germany in 1889
2. __________ South American nation that nearly came to blows with the United States in 1892 over an incident involving the deaths of American sailors
3. __________ The principle of American foreign policy invoked by Secretary of State Olney to justify American intervention in the Venezuelan boundary dispute
4. __________ Term for the sensationalistic and jingoistic pro-war journalism practiced by W. R. Hearst and Joseph Pulitzer
5. __________ American battleship sent on a friendly visit to Cuba that ended in disaster and war
6. __________ Site of the dramatic American naval victory that led to U.S. acquisition of rich, Spanish-owned Pacific islands
7. __________ Colorful volunteer regiment of the Spanish-American War led by a militarily inexperienced but politically influential colonel
8. __________ The Caribbean island conquered from Spain in 1898 that became an important American colony
9. __________ Supreme Court cases of 1901 that determined that the U.S. Constitution and Bill of Rights did not apply in colonial territories under the American flag
10. __________ John Hay's clever diplomatic efforts to preserve Chinese territorial integrity and maintain American access to China
11. __________ Antiforeign Chinese revolt of 1900 that brought military intervention by Western troops, including Americans
12. __________ Diplomatic agreement of 1901 that permitted the United States to build and fortify a Central American canal alone, without British involvement
13. __________ Nation whose senate, in 1902, refused to ratify a treaty permitting the United States to build a canal across its territory
14. __________ Questionable extension of a traditional American policy; declared an American right to intervene in Latin American nations under certain circumstances

15. __________ Diplomatic understanding of 1907–1908 that ended a Japanese-American crisis over treatment of Japanese immigrants to the U.S.

D. Matching People, Places, and Events

Match the person, place, or event in the left column with the proper description in the right column by inserting the correct letter on the blank line.

1. ___ Josiah Strong
2. ___ Alfred Thayer Mahan
3. ___ Emilio Aguinaldo
4. ___ Queen Liliuokalani
5. ___ Richard Olney
6. ___ "Butcher" Weyler
7. ___ William Randolph Hearst
8. ___ William McKinley
9. ___ George E. Dewey
10. ___ Theodore Roosevelt
11. ___ John Hay
12. ___ Philippe Bunau-Varilla
13. ___ William James
14. ___ William Jennings Bryan
15. ___ George Washington Goethals

a. Imperialist advocate, aggressive assistant navy secretary, Rough Rider, vice president, and president

b. Harvard philosopher and one of the leading anti-imperialists opposing U.S. acquisition of the Philippines

c. Spanish general whose brutal tactics against Cuban rebels outraged American public opinion

d. Native Hawaiian ruler overthrown in a revolution led by white planters and aided by U.S. troops

e. Scheming engineer who helped stage a revolution in Panama and then became the new country's instant foreign minister

f. American naval officer who wrote influential books emphasizing sea power and advocating a big navy

g. Naval commander whose spectacular May Day victory in 1898 opened the doors to American imperialism in Asia

h. Vigorous promoter of sensationalistic anti-Spanish propaganda and eager advocate of imperialistic war

i. American military engineer who built the Panama Canal

j. American clergyman who preached Anglo-Saxon superiority and called for stronger U.S. missionary effort overseas

k. Filipino leader of a guerrilla war against American rule from 1899 to 1901

l. President who initially opposed war with Spain but eventually supported U.S. acquisition of the Philippines

m. Democratic party nominee who campaigned and lost on a platform opposing imperialism in the presidential election of 1900

n. U.S. secretary of state whose belligerent notes to Britain during the Guiana boundary crisis nearly caused a war

o. American secretary of state who attempted to preserve Chinese independence and protect American interests in China

E. Putting Things in Order

Put the following events in correct order by numbering them from 1 to 5.

1. __________ American rebels in Hawaii seek annexation by the United States, but the American president turns them down.
2. __________ A battleship explosion arouses fury in America and leads the nation into a splendid little war with Spain.
3. __________ A South American boundary dispute leads to aggressive American assertion of the Monroe Doctrine against Britain.
4. __________ Questionable Roosevelt actions in Central America help create a new republic and pave the way for a U.S.-built canal.
5. __________ A San Francisco School Board dispute leads to intervention by President Roosevelt and a Gentleman's Agreement to prohibit further Japanese immigration to the United States.

F. Matching Cause and Effect

Match the historical cause in the left column with the proper effect in the right column by writing the correct letter on the blank line.

Cause

1. ___ Economic expansion, the yellow press, and competition with other powers
2. ___ The Venezuelan boundary dispute
3. ___ The white planter revolt against Queen Liliuokalani
4. ___ The Cuban revolt against Spain
5. ___ The *Maine* explosion

Effect

a. Brought American armed forces onto the Asian mainland for the first time

b. Created an emotional and irresistible public demand for war with Spain

c. Strengthened the Monroe Doctrine and made Britain more willing to accommodate U.S. interests

d. Led to the surprising U.S. victory over Spain at Manila Bay

6. ___ Theodore Roosevelt's secret orders to Commodore Dewey
7. ___ The Boxer Rebellion that attempted to drive all foreigners out of China
8. ___ McKinley's decision to keep the Philippines
9. ___ Colombia's refusal to permit the United States to build a canal across its province of Panama
10. ___ The Spanish-American War

e. Set off the first debate about the wisdom and rightness of American overseas imperialism
f. Turned America away from isolationism and toward international involvements in the 1890s
g. Aroused strong sympathy from most Americans
h. Enhanced American national pride and made the United States an international power in East Asia
i. Set off a bitter debate about imperialism in the Senate and the country
j. Led President Theodore Roosevelt to encourage a revolt for Panamanian independence

G. Map Mastery

Map Discrimination

Using the maps and charts in Chapter 27, answer the following questions.

1. *United States Expansion, 1857–1917*: Of the new American territories acquired in 1898–1899, which three were directly acquired from Spain as a result of conquest in the Spanish-American War (see also text, p. 679)?

2. *United States Expansion, 1857–1917*: Which new American acquisition was located the farthest south in the Pacific Ocean?

3. *Dewey's Route in the Philippines, 1898*: Manila Bay lies off the coast of which island of the Philippine archipelago?

4. *The Cuban Campaign, 1898*: Which of the two battles fought by Rough Riders—San Juan Hill and El Caney—occurred nearer Santiago Harbor?

5. *The Cuban Campaign, 1898*: Which of the two Spanish-owned Caribbean islands conquered by the United States in 1898 was farthest from Florida?

Map Challenge

Using the map of *United States Expansion* on p. 673, discuss the exact geographical relation of each of America's new Pacific colonies—Samoa, Hawaii, the Philippines—to (a) the United States mainland and (b) China and Japan. Which of the colonies was most strategically important to America's position in the Pacific, which least, and which was most vulnerable? Why?

PART III: APPLYING WHAT YOU HAVE LEARNED

1. What were the causes and signs of America's sudden turn toward international involvement at the end of the nineteenth century?
2. How did the United States get into the Spanish-American War over the initial objections of President McKinley?
3. What role did the press and public opinion play in the origin, conduct, and results of the Spanish-American War?
4. What were the key arguments for and against U.S. imperialism?
5. What were some of the short-term and long-term results of American acquisition of the Philippines and Puerto Rico?
6. How was U.S. overseas imperialism in 1898 similar to and different from earlier American expansion across North America or Manifest Destiny (see especially Chapter 13)? Was this new imperialism a fundamental departure from America's traditions or simply a further extension of westward migration?
7. Theodore Roosevelt was an accidental president due to the McKinley's assassination, yet he quickly became one of the most powerful presidents ever. What elements in Roosevelt's personality and political outlook enabled him to dominate American politics as few others have? How did his view of presidential power differ radically from that of most late nineteenth-century American presidents (see Chapter 23)?
8. What were the essential principles of Theodore Roosevelt's foreign policy, and how did he apply them to specific situations?
9. How did Roosevelt's policies in Latin America demonstrate American power in the region, and why did they arouse opposition from many Latin Americans?
10. What were the central issues in America's relations with China and Japan? How did Roosevelt handle tense relations with Japan?
11. What were the strengths and weaknesses of Theodore Roosevelt's aggressive foreign policy? What were the benefits of TR's activism, and what were its drawbacks?
12. The text states that the Roosevelt corollary to the Monroe Doctrine distorted the original policy statement of 1823. How did it do so (see Chapter 10)? Compare the circumstances and purposes of the two policies.

CHAPTER 28

Progressivism and the Republican Roosevelt, 1901–1912

PART I: REVIEWING THE CHAPTER

A. Checklist of Learning Objectives

After mastering this chapter, you should be able to:

1. Discuss the origin, leadership, and goals of progressivism.
2. Describe how the early progressive movement developed at the local and state level and spread to become a national movement.
3. Describe the major role that women played in progressive social reform, and explain why progressivism meshed with many goals of the women's movement.
4. Tell how President Roosevelt began applying progressive principles to the national economy, including his attention to conservation and consumer protection.
5. Explain why Taft's policies offended progressives, including Roosevelt.
6. Describe how Roosevelt led a progressive revolt against Taft that openly divided the Republican party.

B. Glossary

To build your social science vocabulary, familiarize yourself with the following terms.

1. **progressive** In politics, one who believes in continuing social advancement, improvement, or reform. "The new crusaders, who called themselves 'progressives,' waged war on many evils. . ."
2. **conspicuous consumption** The theory, developed by economist Thorstein Veblen, that much spending by the affluent occurs primarily to display wealth and status to others rather than from enjoyment of the goods or services. " . . . a savage attack on 'predatory wealth' and 'conspicuous consumption.' "
3. **direct primary** In politics, the nomination of a party's candidates for office through a special election of that party's voters. "These ardent reformers pushed for direct primary elections. . . ."
4. **initiative** In politics, the procedure whereby voters can, through petition, present proposed legislation directly to the electorate. "They favored the 'initiative' so that voters could directly propose legislation. . . ."
5. **referendum** The submission of a law, proposed or already in effect, to a direct vote of the electorate. "Progressives also agitated for the 'referendum.' "
6. **recall** In politics, a procedure for removing an official from office through popular election or other means. "The 'recall' would enable the voters to remove faithless elected officials. . . ."

7. **city manager** An administrator appointed by the city council or other elected body to manage affairs, supposedly in a nonpartisan or professional way. "Other communities adopted the city-manager system. . . ."

8. **red-light district** A section of a city where prostitution is officially or unofficially tolerated. ". . . wide-open prostitution (vice-at-a-price) . . . flourished in red-light districts. . . ."

9. **franchise** In government, a special privilege or license granted to a company or group to perform a specific function. "Public-spirited city-dwellers also moved to halt the corrupt sale of franchises for streetcars. . . ."

10. **bureaucracy (bureaucrat)** The management of government or business through departments and subdivisions manned by a system of officials (bureaucrats) following defined rules and processes. (The term is often, though not necessarily, disparaging.) "These wedges into the federal bureaucracy, however small, gave female reformers a national stage. . . ."

11. **workers' (workmen's) compensation** Insurance, provided either by government or employers or both, providing benefits to employees suffering work-related injury or disability. " . . . by 1917 thirty states had put workers' compensation laws on the books. . . ."

12. **reclamation** The process of bringing or restoring wasteland to productive use. "Settlers repaid the cost of reclamation. . . ."

13. **collectivism** A political or social system in which individuals are subordinated to mass organization and direction. "He strenuously sought the middle road between unbridled individualism and paternalistic collectivism."

14. **insubordination** Deliberate disobedience or challenge to proper authority. ". . . Taft dismissed Pinchot on the narrow grounds of insubordination. . . ."

PART II: CHECKING YOUR PROGRESS

A. True-False

Where the statement is true, circle **T**; where it is false, circle **F**.

1. T F The progressive movement believed that social and economic problems should be solved at the community level without involvement by the federal government.

2. T F Muckraking journalists, social-gospel ministers, and women reformers all aroused Americans' concern about economic and social problems.

3. T F Early twentieth-century progressivism found its home almost entirely in the Republican party.

4. T F Many female progressives saw the task of improving life in factories and slums as an extension of their traditional roles as wives and mothers.

5. T F President Theodore Roosevelt ended the anthracite coal strike by threatening to use federal troops to break the miners' union.

6. T F Some progressive reforms such as the municipal ownership of utilities were modeled on the admired practices of contemporary German cities.

7. T F Roosevelt believed that all the monopolistic corporate trusts should be broken up so that competition could be restored among smaller businesses.

8. T F Upton Sinclair's novel, *The Jungle*, was intended to arouse consumers' concern about unsanitary practices in the meat industry.

9. T F Conservation of forests, water, and other natural resources was probably Theodore Roosevelt's most popular and enduring presidential achievement.

10. T F Defenders of nature became divided between fervent preservationists who wanted to stop all human intrusions into wilderness areas and more moderate conservationists who thought nature should be available for multiple use.

11. T F Roosevelt effectively used the power of the presidency and the federal government to tame and regulate unbridled capitalism while preserving the basic foundations of the market system and American business.

12. T F William Howard Taft demonstrated his skill as a political campaigner and leader throughout his presidency.

13. T F Progressive Republicans became angry with President Taft because he began to form alliances with Democrats and Socialists.

14. T F The Ballinger-Pinchot conservation controversy pushed Taft further into an alliance with the reactionary Republican Old Guard and against the pro-Roosevelt progressives.

15. T F President Taft used his firm control of the Republican party machinery to deny Theodore Roosevelt the nomination in 1912.

B. Multiple Choice

Select the best answer and circle the corresponding letter.

1. The two primary goals of the progressive movement, as a whole, were to
   a. restore business competition and stimulate entrepreneurship in new areas of the economy.
   b. protect farmers and create a more flexible monetary system.
   c. improve the quality of urban life and help immigrants adjust to American life.
   d. organize workers into class-conscious unions and develop consumer cooperatives.
   e. use the state to curb monopoly power and improve the lives of ordinary people.
2. Prominent among those who aroused the progressive movement by stirring the public's sense of concern were
   a. socialists, social gospelers, women, and muckraking journalists.
   b. union leaders, machine politicians, immigrants, and engineers.
   c. bankers, salesmen, congressmen, and scientists.
   d. athletes, entertainers, filmmakers, and musicians.
   e. farmers, miners, Latinos, and African Americans.
3. Which of the following was *not* among the targets of muckraking journalistic exposés?
   a. Urban politics and government
   b. The oil, insurance, and railroad industries
   c. The U.S. Army and Navy
   d. Child labor and the white slave traffic in women
   e. Makers of patent medicines and other adulterated or dangerous drugs
4. Most progressives were
   a. poor farmers.
   b. urban workers.
   c. immigrants.
   d. wealthy people.
   e. urban middle-class people.

5. Among the political reforms sought by the progressives were
   a. an end to political parties, political conventions, and the Supreme Court's right to judicial review of legislation.
   b. an Equal Rights Amendment, federal financing of election campaigns, and restrictions on negative campaigning.
   c. civil-service reform, racial integration, and free silver.
   d. initiative and referendum, direct election of senators, and women's suffrage.
   e. expanded immigration, literacy tests for voting, and federal loans for higher education.
6. The states where progressivism first gained great influence were
   a. Massachusetts, Maine, and New Hampshire.
   b. Wisconsin, Oregon, and California.
   c. Michigan, Kansas, and Nevada.
   d. New York, Florida, and Texas.
   e. Alabama, Maryland, and Utah.
7. The Supreme Court case of *Muller* v. *Oregon* was seen as a victory for both progressivism and women's rights because it
   a. upheld the right of women to vote in state and local elections.
   b. upheld a law requiring that women receive "equal pay for equal work."
   c. upheld workplace safety regulations to prevent disasters like the Triangle Shirtwaist fire.
   d. opened almost all categories of the new industrial employment to women.
   e. upheld the constitutionality of state laws granting special protections to women in the workplace.
8. President Theodore Roosevelt ended the major Pennsylvania coal strike by
   a. asking Congress to pass a law improving miners' wages and working conditions.
   b. passing federal legislation legalizing unions.
   c. forcing the mine owners and workers to negotiate by threatening to seize the coal mines and operate them with federal troops.
   d. declaring a national state of emergency and ordering the miners back to work.
   e. mobilizing the public to write letters urging the two parties to settle their dispute.
9. The Roosevelt-backed Elkins Act and Hepburn Act were aimed at
   a. better protection for industrial workers.
   b. more effective regulation of the railroad industry.
   c. protection for consumers of beef and fresh produce.
   d. breaking up the Standard Oil and United States Steel monopolies.
   e. prohibiting nonfarm child labor for anyone under age fourteen.
10. The controversy over the Hetch Hetchy Valley in Yosemite National Park revealed
    a. a philosophical disagreement between wilderness preservationists and more moderate multiple-use conservationists.
    b. President Roosevelt's hostility toward creating any more national parks.
    c. a political conflict between the lumber industry and conservationists.
    d. a split between urban California's need for water and environmentalists' concerns to preserve free-flowing streams.
    e. a disagreement over whether or not the National Park system should permit commercial vendors inside the parks.

11. Two issues that President Roosevelt especially promoted as part of his progressive policies were
    a. agricultural exports and housing reform.
    b. stock market regulation and restrictions on false advertising.
    c. freer immigration and racial integration.
    d. consumer protection and conservation of nature.
    e. the advancement of science and federal support for the arts.
12. Roosevelt was blamed by big business for the Panic of 1907 because
    a. his progressive boat-rocking tactics had allegedly unsettled industry and undermined business confidence.
    b. his policies of regulating and protecting industrial workers had caused a depression.
    c. his inability to establish a stable monetary policy led to a Wall Street crash.
    d. the public wanted him to run again for president in 1908.
    e. his administration had run up enormous federal deficits.
13. As a result of his successful presidential campaign in 1908, William Howard Taft was widely expected to
    a. advance the issues of women's suffrage and prohibition of alcohol.
    b. forge a coalition with William Jennings Bryan and the Democrats.
    c. emphasize foreign policy instead of Roosevelt's domestic reforms.
    d. turn away from Theodore Roosevelt and toward the conservative wing of the Republican party.
    e. continue and extend Theodore Roosevelt's progressive policies.
14. Progressive Republicans grew deeply disillusioned with Taft, especially over the issues of
    a. dollar diplomacy and military intervention in the Caribbean and Central America.
    b. labor union protections and women's rights.
    c. trust-busting, tariffs, and conservation.
    d. regulation of the banking and railroad industries.
    e. tax policy and international trade.
15. Roosevelt finally decided to break with the Republicans and form a third party because
    a. he had always regarded the Republican party as too conservative.
    b. he could no longer stand to be in the same party with Taft.
    c. Taft had used his control of the Republican party machine to deny Roosevelt the nomination.
    d. Roosevelt believed that he would have a better chance of winning the presidency as a third-party candidate.
    e. he believed he could win the support of Woodrow Wilson and other mainstream Democrats.

C. Identification

Supply the correct identification for each numbered description.

1. __________ A largely middle-class movement that aimed to use the power of government to correct the economic and social problems of industrialism
2. __________ Popular journalists who used publicity to expose corruption and attack abuses of power in business and government
3. __________ Progressive proposal to allow voters to bypass state legislatures and propose legislation themselves
4. __________ Progressive device that would enable voters to remove corrupt or ineffective officials from office

5. __________ Roosevelt's policy of having the federal government promote the public interest by dealing evenhandedly with both labor and business

6. __________ Effective railroad-regulation law of 1906 that greatly strengthened the Interstate Commerce Commission

7. __________ Disastrous industrial fire of 1911 that spurred workmen's compensation laws and some state regulation of wages and hours in New York

8. __________ Upton Sinclair's novel that inspired pro-consumer federal laws regulating meat, food, and drugs

9. __________ Powerful women's reform organization led by Frances Willard

10. __________ Brief but sharp economic downturn of 1907, blamed by conservatives on the supposedly dangerous president

11. __________ Generally unsuccessful Taft foreign policy in which government attempted to encourage overseas business ventures

12. __________ Powerful corporation broken up by a Taft-initiated antitrust suit in 1911

D. Matching People, Places, and Events

Match the person, place, or event in the left column with the proper description in the right column by inserting the correct letter on the blank line.

1. ___ Thorstein Veblen
2. ___ Lincoln Steffens
3. ___ Ida Tarbell
4. ___ Seventeenth Amendment
5. ___ Robert M. La Follette
6. ___ Hiram Johnson
7. ___ Triangle Shirtwaist Company fire
8. ___ Women's Christian Temperance Union
9. ___ Anthracite coal strike
10. ___ Jane Addams
11. ___ Upton Sinclair
12. ___ *Muller* v. *Oregon*
13. ___ William Howard Taft
14. ___ *Lochner* v. *New York*
15. ___ Gifford Pinchot

a. Politically inept inheritor of the Roosevelt legacy who ended up allied with the reactionary Republican Old Guard

b. Powerful progressive women's organization that sought to "make the world homelike" by outlawing the saloon and the product it sold

c. Case that upheld protective legislation on the grounds of women's supposed physical weakness

d. New York City disaster that underscored urban workers' need for government protection

e. The most influential of the state-level progressive governors and a presidential aspirant in 1912

f. Leading female progressive reformer whose advocacy of pacifism as well as social welfare set her at odds with more muscular and militant progressives

g. Eccentric economist who criticized the wealthy for conspicuous consumption and failure to serve real human needs

h. Leading muckraking journalist whose articles documented the Standard Oil Company's abuse of power

i. Progressive governor of California who broke the stranglehold of the Southern Pacific Railroad on the state's politics

j. Pro-conservation federal official whose dismissal by Taft angered Roosevelt progressives

k. Dangerous labor conflict resolved by Rooseveltian negotiation and threats against business people

l. Early muckraker who exposed the political corruption in many American cities

m. Progressive novelist who sought to aid industrial workers, but found his book, *The Jungle*, instead inspiring middle-class consumer protection.

n. Progressive measure that required U.S. senators to be elected directly by the people rather than by state legislatures

o. Supreme court ruling that overturned a progressive law mandating a ten-hour workday

E. Putting Things in Order

Put the following events in correct order by numbering them from 1 to 5.

1. __________ A former president opposes his handpicked successor for the Republican presidential nomination.

2. __________ Sensational journalistic accounts of corruption and abuse of power in politics and business spur the progressive movement.

3. __________ A progressive forestry official feuds with Taft's secretary of the interior, deepening the division within the Republican party.

4. __________ A novelistic account of Chicago's meat-packing industry sparks new federal laws to protect consumers.

5. __________ A brief but sharp financial crisis leads to conservative criticism of Roosevelt's progressive policies.

F. Matching Cause and Effect

Match the historical cause in the left column with the proper effect in the right column by writing the correct letter on the blank line.

Cause

1. ___ Old-time Populists, muckraking journalists, social-gospel ministers, and European socialist immigrants
2. ___ Progressive concern about political corruption
3. ___ Governors like Robert La Follette
4. ___ Roosevelt's threat to seize the anthracite coal mines
5. ___ Settlement houses and women's clubs
6. ___ Upton Sinclair's *The Jungle*
7. ___ Roosevelt's personal interest in conservation
8. ___ Taft's political mishandling of tariff and conservation policies
9. ___ Russia's and Japan's hostility to an American role in China
10. ___ Roosevelt's feeling that he was cheated out of the Republican nomination by the Taft machine

Effect

a. Ended the era of uncontrolled exploitation of nature and involved the federal government in preserving natural resources

b. Led to reforms like the initiative, referendum, and direct election of senators

c. Forced a compromise settlement of a strike that threatened the national well-being

d. Outraged consumers and led to the Meat Inspection Act and the Pure Food and Drug Act

e. Laid the basis for a third-party crusade in the election of 1912

f. Incensed pro-Roosevelt progressives and increased their attacks on the Republican Old Guard

g. Led the way in using universities and regulatory agencies to pursue progressive goals

h. Made Taft's dollar-diplomacy policy a failure

i. Provided the pioneering forces who laid the foundations for the Progressive movement.

j. Served as the launching pads for widespread female involvement in progressive reforms

G. Developing Historical Skills

Classifying Historical Information

Often a broad historical movement, such as progressivism, can best be understood by breaking it down into various component parts. Among the varieties of progressive reform discussed in this chapter are (A) political progressivism, (B) economic or industrial progressivism, (C) consumer progressivism, and (D) environmental progressivism.

Put each of the following progressive acts, policies, or court cases into one of those categories by writing in the correct letter.

1. ________ The Newlands Act of 1902
2. ________ The ten-hour law for bakers
3. ________ The movement for women's suffrage
4. ________ The anthracite coal strike of 1902
5. ________ Direct election of senators
6. ________ The Meat Inspection Act of 1906
7. ________ The Pure Food and Drug Act
8. ________ Initiative, referendum, and recall
9. ________ *Muller* v. *Oregon*
10. ________ The Hepburn Act of 1906
11. ________ Yosemite and Grand Canyon National Parks
12. ________ Workmen's compensation laws

PART III: APPLYING WHAT YOU HAVE LEARNED

1. The text says that progressivism was less a minority movement than a dominant majority mood. What were the basic social and political conditions that created that reforming mood, and what diverse people and ideas were all sheltered under the broad progressive umbrella?
2. What did the progressive movement accomplish at the local, state, and national levels?
3. What made women such central forces in the progressive crusade? What specific backgrounds and ideologies did they bring to the public arena? What were the strengths and limitations of the progressive emphasis on providing special protection to children and women?
4. The text says that Theodore Roosevelt sought to tame unbridled capitalism, including the largest corporations, without fundamentally altering the American economic system. How do his policies regarding the trusts, labor, and consumer protection reflect this middle way? Why was Roosevelt regarded with hostility by many industrialists and Wall Street financiers, even though he sought to reform rather than attack them?
5. Why were consumer protection and conservation among Theodore Roosevelt's most successful progressive achievements? What does the high visibility of these causes reveal about the character and strength of progressivism, as well as its limits?
6. What caused the Taft-Roosevelt split, and how did it reflect the growing division between Old Guard and progressive Republicans?
7. How was progressivism a response to the development of the new urban and industrial order in America (see Chapters 24 and 25)?
8. It is sometimes argued that progressivism was a uniquely American phenomenon because it addressed the most profound social and economic problems without engaging in the rhetoric of class conflict or economic warfare. Is this true? How did progressives address the problems of the working classes and poor without adopting the ideologies of socialism or communism. How did progressives borrow some ideas from European models, while adapting them to uniquely American conditions?

9. The two key goals of progressivism, according to the text, were to use the government to curb monopolistic corporations and to enhance the ordinary citizen's welfare. How successful was it in attaining these two goals?

CHAPTER 29

Wilsonian Progressivism at Home and Abroad, 1912–1916

PART I: REVIEWING THE CHAPTER

A. Checklist of Learning Objectives

After mastering this chapter, you should be able to:

1. Discuss the key issues of the pivotal 1912 election and the basic principles of Wilsonian progressivism.
2. Describe how Wilson successfully reformed the "triple wall of privilege."
3. State the basic features of Wilson's moralistic foreign policy, and explain how, despite his intentions, it drew him into intervention in Mexico and elsewhere in Latin America.
4. Describe America's initial neutral response to World War I, Wilson's increasingly tough policies on Germany's submarine warfare, and the sharp political divisions over the prospect of American entry into the war.
5. Explain how Wilson's progressive domestic agenda and provisionally successful maintenance of American neutrality enabled him to win a narrow victory in 1916 over still-divided Republicans.

B. Glossary

To build your social science vocabulary, familiarize yourself with the following terms.

1. **entrepreneurship** The process whereby an individual initiates a business at some risk in order to expand it and thereby earn a profit. "Wilson's New Freedom, by contrast, favored small enterprise, entrepreneurship, and the free functioning of . . . markets."
2. **self-determination** In politics, the right of a people to shape its own national identity and form of government, without outside coercion or influence. ". . . [the Confederacy] . . . partly inspired his ideal of self-determination for people of other countries."
3. **piety** Devotion to religious duty and practices. ". . . Wilson was reared in an atmosphere of fervent piety."
4. **graduated income tax** A tax on income in which the taxation rates grow progressively higher for those with higher income. "Congress enacted a graduated income tax. . . ."
5. **levy** A forcible tax or other imposition. ". . . [the] income tax [began] with a modest levy on income over $3,000. . . ."
6. **inelasticity** The inability to expand or contract rapidly. "[The] most serious shortcoming [of the country's financial structure] was the inelasticity of the currency."
7. **commercial paper** Any business document having monetary or exchangeable value. "The . . . paper money [was] backed by commercial paper. . . ."

8. **promissory note** A written pledge to pay a certain person a specified sum of money at a certain time. "The . . . paper money [was] backed by commercial paper, such as promissory notes of business people."

9. **Magna Carta** The "Great Charter" of England, which feudal nobles of England forced King John I to sign in 1215. As the first written guarantee of certain traditional rights, such as trial by a jury of peers, against arbitrary royal power, it served as a model for later assertions of Anglo-Saxon liberties. "Union leader Samuel Gompers hailed the [Clayton] act as the Magna Carta of labor…."

10. **agricultural extension** The system of providing services and advice to farmers through dispersed local agents. "Other laws benefited rural America by providing for . . . the establishment of agricultural extension work in the state colleges."

11. **enclave** A small territory surrounded by foreign or hostile territory. "Though often segregated in Spanish-speaking enclaves, they helped to create a unique borderland culture. . . ."

12. **gringo** Contemptuous Latin American term for North Americans. "Challenging Carranza's authority while also punishing the gringos. . . ."

13. **censor** An official who examines publications, mail, literature, and so forth in order to remove or prohibit the distribution of material deemed dangerous or offensive. "Their censors sheared away war stories harmful to the Allies. . . ."

14. **torpedo** To launch from a submarine or airplane a self-propelled underwater explosive designed to detonate on impact. ". . . the British passenger liner *Lusitania* was torpedoed and sank. . . ."

15. **draft** In politics, to choose an individual to run for office without that person's prior solicitation of the nomination. (A *military* draft, or conscription, legally compels individuals into the armed services.) "Instead, they drafted Supreme Court Justice Charles Evans Hughes, a cold intellectual who had achieved a solid record as governor of New York."

PART II: CHECKING YOUR PROGRESS

A. True-False

Where the statement is true, circle **T**; where it is false, circle **F**.

1. T F Wilson won the election of 1912 largely because the Republican party split in two.

2. T F In the 1912 campaign, Wilson's New Freedom favored a socially activist government and regulating trusts, while Roosevelt's New Nationalist favored strict antitrust laws that would favor small business.

3. T F Wilson was an intellectually gifted leader who tended to look down on ordinary politics and politicians.

4. T F Wilson successfully used his eloquence and popular appeal to push through progressive reforms of the tariff, monetary systems, and trusts.

5. T F Wilson's progressive outlook showed itself clearly in his attempt to improve the conditions and treatment of blacks.

6. T F Wilson initially attempted to overturn the imperialistic big-stick and dollar-diplomacy foreign policies of Roosevelt and Taft in Asia and Latin America.

7. T F Wilson consistently refused to send American troops to intervene in the Caribbean.

8. T F Wilson's initial policy toward the revolutionary Mexican government of General Huerta was to display moral disapproval while trying to avoid American military intervention.

9. T F The mediation of three Latin American nations after the Tampico incident saved Wilson from a full-scale war with Mexico.

10. T F General Pershing's expedition into Mexico was an attempt to bring the pro-American faction of Mexican revolutionaries to power.

11. T F In the early days of World War I, more Americans sympathized with Germany than with Britain.

12. T F The American economy benefited greatly from supplying goods to the Allies.

13. T F After the *Lusitania*'s sinking, the Midwest and West favored war with Germany, while the more isolationist East generally favored attempts at negotiation.

14. T F After the sinking of the *Sussex*, Wilson successfully pressured Germany into stopping submarine attacks against neutral shipping.

15. T F In the 1916 campaign, Wilson ran on the slogan "He Kept Us Out of War," while his opponent Hughes tried to straddle the issue of a possible war with Germany.

B. Multiple Choice

Select the best answer and circle the corresponding letter in the space provided.

1. The basic contrast between the two progressive candidates, Roosevelt and Wilson, was that
   a. Roosevelt wanted genuine political and social reforms, while Wilson wanted only to end obvious corruption.
   b. Roosevelt wanted to promote free enterprise and competition, while Wilson wanted the federal government to regulate the economy and promote social welfare.
   c. Wilson saw advancing women's interests as central to the progressive agenda, while Roosevelt believed women were best served by supporting progressivism outside politics.
   d. Roosevelt wanted to focus on issues of jobs and economic growth, while Wilson pushed for social legislation to protect women, children, and city-dwellers.
   e. Roosevelt wanted the federal government to regulate the corporate economy and expand social welfare, while Wilson wanted to restore economic competition and social equality by breaking up large corporate trusts.
2. Wilson won the election of 1912 primarily because
   a. his policies were more popular with the public.
   b. Taft and Roosevelt split the former Republican vote.
   c. the Socialists took nearly a million votes from Roosevelt.
   d. he was able to win over many of the embittered Roosevelt Republicans to his cause.
   e. his charismatic personal appeal exceeded that of Roosevelt and Taft.
3. Wilson's primary weakness as a politician was his
   a. lack of skill in public speaking.
   b. inability to grasp the complexity of governmental issues.
   c. tendency to be inflexible and refuse to compromise.
   d. lack of overarching political ideals.
   e. background as a professor and college president.

4. The "triple wall of privilege" that Wilson set out to reform consisted of
   a. farmers, shippers, and the military.
   b. the tariffs, the banks, and the trusts.
   c. Ivy League universities, private dining clubs, and segregated urban neighborhoods.
   d. congressional leaders, lobbyists, and lawyers.
   e. labor union officials, big city bosses, and wealthy southern landlords.
5. Under the Wilson administration, Congress exercised the authority granted by the newly enacted Sixteenth Amendment to pass
   a. prohibition of liquor.
   b. women's suffrage.
   c. voting rights for blacks.
   d. rules for the direct election of U.S. Senators.
   e. a progressive federal income tax.
6. The new regulatory agency, created by the Wilson administration in 1914, that attacked unfair business competition, false and misleading advertising, and consumer fraud was the
   a. Federal Trade Commission.
   b. Interstate Commerce Commission.
   c. Federal Reserve System.
   d. Consumer Products Safety Commission.
   e. Antitrust Division of the Justice Department.
7. While outlawing business monopolies, the Clayton Anti-Trust Act created exemptions from antitrust prosecution for
   a. industries essential to national defense.
   b. agricultural and labor organizations.
   c. the oil and steel industries.
   d. professional organizations of doctors and lawyers.
   e. colleges and universities.
8. Wilson effectively reformed the banking and financial system by
   a. requiring that all banks be federally chartered and carry effective deposit insurance.
   b. taking the United States off the gold standard.
   c. establishing a publicly controlled Federal Reserve Board to issue currency and control credit.
   d. transferring authority to regulate banking and currency from the federal government to the states and the private sector.
   e. creating a system of currency exchanges so that people without bank accounts could cash checks and obtain credit.
9. Wilson's general progressive support for the less fortunate in American society was weakened by his actively hostile policies toward
   a. labor unions.
   b. blacks.
   c. farmers.
   d. women.
   e. immigrants.
10. Wilson's initial attitude toward the Mexican revolutionary government was to
   a. refuse recognition of General Huerta's regime but avoid American intervention.
   b. intervene with troops on behalf of threatened American business interests.
   c. provide military and economic assistance to the Huerta regime.
   d. mobilize other Latin American governments to oust Huerta.
   e. follow the lead of publisher William Randolph Hearst.

11. The threatened war between the United States and Mexico in 1914 was avoided by the mediation of the ABC powers, which consisted of
    a. Australia, Britain, and Canada.
    b. Antigua, Brazil, and Cuba.
    c. Angola, Belgium, and China.
    d. the Association of British Commonwealth nations.
    e. Argentina, Brazil, and Chile.
12. General Pershing's expedition into Mexico was sent in direct response to the
    a. refusal of Huerta to abandon power.
    b. threat of German intervention in Mexico.
    c. arrest of American sailors in the Mexican port of Tampico.
    d. killing of American citizens in New Mexico by Pancho Villa.
    e. Mexican revolutionary persecution of the Catholic Church.
13. An early event of World War I that led many Americans to sympathize with the Allies against Germany was
    a. German bribes and payoffs to American journalists.
    b. the Germans' involvement in overseas imperialism.
    c. Germany's invasion of neutral Belgium.
    d. the British refusal to use poison gas in warfare.
    e. Germany's aerial bombing of civilians in France.
14. After the *Lusitania, Arabic,* and *Sussex* sinkings, Wilson successfully pressured the German government to
    a. end the use of the submarine against British warships.
    b. end its attempt to blockade the British Isles.
    c. publish warnings to all Americans considering traveling on unarmed ships.
    d. cease from sinking neutral merchant and passenger ships without warning.
    e. permit Red Cross officials to travel on German submarines to monitor civilian deaths.
15. Wilson's most effective slogan in the campaign of 1916 was
    a. "The full dinner pail."
    b. "Free and unlimited coinage of silver in the ratio of sixteen to one."
    c. "A war to make the world safe for democracy."
    d. "He kept us out of war."
    e. "I will not send your boys to fight in a foreign war."

C. Identification

Supply the correct identification for each numbered description.

1. ___________ Four-footed symbol of Roosevelt's Progressive third party in 1912
2. ___________ A fourth political party, led by a former railroad labor union leader, that garnered nearly a million votes in 1912
3. ___________ Wilson's political philosophy of restoring democracy through trust-busting and economic competition
4. ___________ A twelve-member agency appointed by the president to oversee the banking system under a new federal law of 1913
5. ___________ New presidentially appointed regulatory commission designed to prohibit unfair business competition, unethical advertising, and labeling practices

6. __________ Wilsonian trust-busting law that prohibited interlocking directorates and other monopolistic business practices, while legalizing labor and agricultural organizations

7. __________ Wilson-backed law that promised the Philippines eventual independence from the United States, but only when a stable and secure government was attained

8. __________ Troubled Caribbean island nation where a president's murder led Wilson to send in the marines and assume American control of the police and finances

9. __________ Term for the three Latin American nations whose mediation prevented war between the United States and Mexico in 1914

10. __________ World War I alliance headed by Germany and Austria-Hungary

11. __________ The coalition of powers—led by Britain, France, and Russia—that opposed Germany and its partners in World War I

12. __________ New underwater weapon that threatened neutral shipping and seemed to violate all traditional norms of international law

13. __________ Large British passenger liner whose sinking in 1915 prompted some Americans to call for war against Germany

14. __________ Germany's carefully conditional agreement in 1916 not to sink passenger and merchant vessels without warning

15. __________ Key electoral state where a tiny majority for President Wilson tipped the balance against Republican Charles Evans Hughes in 1916

D. Matching People, Places, and Events

Match the person, place, or event in the left column with the proper description in the right column by inserting the correct letter on the blank line.

1. ___ Thomas Woodrow Wilson
2. ___ Theodore Roosevelt
3. ___ Eugene V. Debs
4. ___ Samuel Gompers
5. ___ Louis D. Brandeis
6. ___ Virgin Islands
7. ___ General Huerta
8. ___ Venustiano Carranza
9. ___ Vera Cruz
10. ___ Pancho Villa
11. ___ John J. Pershing
12. ___ Belgium
13. ___ Serbia
14. ___ Kaiser Wilhelm II
15. ___ Charles Evans Hughes

a. Small European nation in which an Austro-Hungarian heir was killed, leading to the outbreak of World War I

b. Mexican revolutionary whose assaults on American citizens and territory provoked a U.S. expedition into Mexico

c. Port where clashes between Mexicans and American military forces nearly led to war in 1914

d. Socialist party leader who garnered nearly a million votes for president in the election of 1912.

e. Caribbean territory purchased by the United States from Denmark in 1917

f. Narrowly unsuccessful presidential candidate who tried to straddle both sides of the fence regarding American policy toward Germany

g. Small European nation whose neutrality was violated by Germany in the early days of World War I

h. Commander of the American military expedition into Mexico in 1916–1917

i. Southern-born intellectual who pursued strong moral goals in politics and the presidency

j. Leading progressive reformer and the first Jew appointed to the Supreme Court

k. Energetic progressive and vigorous nationalist whose failed third-party effort contributed to Wilson's victory in the election of 1912

l. Labor leader who hailed the Clayton Anti-Trust Act as the "Magna Carta of labor"

m. Second revolutionary Mexican president, who took aid from the United States but strongly resisted American military intervention in his country

n. Autocratic ruler who symbolized ruthlessness and arrogance to many pro-Allied Americans

o. Mexican revolutionary whose bloody regime Wilson refused to recognize and nearly ended up fighting

E. Putting Things in Order

Put the following events in correct order by numbering them from 1 to 5.

1. ___________ Wilson extracts a dangerously conditional German agreement to halt submarine warfare.

2. ___________ Wilson's superb leadership pushes major reforms of the tariff and monetary system through Congress.

3. ___________ The bull moose and the elephant are both electorally defeated by a donkey bearing the banner of "New Freedom."

4. ___________ The heavy loss of American lives to German submarines nearly leads the United States into war with Germany.

5. ___________ Despite efforts to avoid involvement in the Mexican revolution, Wilson's occupation of a Mexican port raises the threat of war.

F. Matching Cause and Effect

Match the historical cause in the left column with the proper effect in the right column by writing the correct letter on the blank line.

1. ___ The split between Taft and Roosevelt
2. ___ Wilson's presidential appeals to the public over the heads of Congress
3. ___ The Federal Reserve Act
4. ___ Conservative justices of the Supreme Court
5. ___ Political turmoil in Haiti and Santo Domingo (Dominican Republic)
6. ___ The Mexican revolution
7. ___ Pancho Villa's raid on Columbus, New Mexico
8. ___ America's close cultural and economic ties with Britain
9. ___ Germany's sinking of the *Lusitania, Arabic,* and *Sussex*
10. ___ Wilson's apparent success in keeping America at peace through diplomacy

a. Caused most Americans to sympathize with the Allies rather than the Central Powers

b. Helped push through sweeping reforms of the tariff and the banking system in 1913

c. Enabled the Democrats to win a narrow presidential victory in the election of 1916

d. Allowed Wilson to win a minority victory in the election of 1912

e. Declared unconstitutional progressive Wilsonian measures dealing with labor unions and child labor

f. Caused President Wilson and other outraged Americans to demand an end to unrestricted submarine warfare

g. Created constant political instability south of the border and undermined Wilson's hopes for better U.S. relations with Latin America

h. Was the immediate provocation for General Pershing's punitive expedition into Mexico

i. Finally established an effective national banking system and a flexible money supply

j. Caused Wilson to send in U.S. marines to restore order and supervise finances

G. Developing Historical Skills

Understanding Documents in Context

Historical documents cannot usually be understood in isolation. Awareness of the circumstances and conditions under which they were written is essential to comprehending their importance. The text reproduces on p. 741 the advertisement with notice from the German government that appeared in the New York *Herald* on May 1, 1915, six days before the *Lusitania* was sunk. Read the ad carefully, and reread text pp. 739–742 to understand and evaluate the context in which the warning appeared. Then answer the following questions.

1. What was the policy of the German government regarding submarine use at the time the ad was taken out?

2. Why might the German government be particularly concerned about warning American passengers thinking of traveling on a British liner? How would the notice be useful even if some Americans did travel on the ship?

3. What fact about the *Lusitania*'s cargo did the German government know that it did not put into the warning?

4. Why were many Americans outraged about the *Lusitania* sinking despite the warning?

PART III: APPLYING WHAT YOU HAVE LEARNED

1. What were the essential qualities of Wilson's presidential leadership, and how did he display them in 1913–1914?
2. What were the results of Wilson's great reform assault on the "triple wall of privilege"—the tariff, the banks, and the trusts?
3. In what ways was Wilson the most pro-labor president up to that point in American history? Which specific laws, policies, and appointments reflect his support for ordinary workers?
4. How was Wilson's foreign policy an attempt to expand idealistic progressive principles from the domestic to the international arena? Why did Wilson's progressive democratic idealism lead to the very kind of U.S. interventions in other countries that he professed to dislike?
5. What were the causes and consequences of U.S. entanglement with Mexico in the wake of the Mexican Revolution? Could the United States have avoided involvement in Mexican affairs?
6. Why was it so difficult for Wilson to maintain America's neutrality from 1914 to 1916?
7. How did Wilson's prejudicial attitudes toward non-whites, in the United States and elsewhere, affect his domestic and foreign policies? Should these policies be seen as a major blot on his overall progressive reputation or as simply a reflection of the general racial prejudice of the time?
8. How did Wilson's foreign policy differ from that of the other great progressive president, Theodore Roosevelt (see Chapter 27)? Which president was more effective in foreign policy and why?
9. Wilsonianism is defined as an approach to American foreign policy that seeks to spread democracy and freedom throughout the whole world. In what ways does Wilson's foreign policy from 1913 to 1916 fit this definition? In what ways was his administration's policy during this period *not* Wilsonian?
10. Why was America so determined to stay out of World War I during the early years of the conflict? What were the factors that gradually turned the government and the majority of Americans against Germany?

CHAPTER 30

The War to End War, 1917–1918

PART I: REVIEWING THE CHAPTER

A. Checklist of Learning Objectives

After mastering this chapter, you should be able to:

1. Explain what caused America to enter World War I.
2. Describe how Wilsonian idealism turned the war into an ideological crusade for democracy that inspired public fervor and suppressed dissent.
3. Discuss America's mobilization for war and its reliance primarily on voluntary methods rather than government force.
4. Explain the consequences of World War I for labor, women, and African Americans.
5. Describe America's participation in the War, and explain why its economic and political importance exceeded its military contribution to the Allied victory and German defeat.
6. Analyze Wilson's attempt to forge a peace based on his idealistic Fourteen Points, the political mistakes that weakened his hand, and the compromises he was forced to make by the other Allied statesmen at Versailles.
7. Discuss how Lodge and others resisted Wilson's League of Nations, how Wilson's total refusal to compromise doomed the Treaty of Versailles, and why Harding's victory in the election of 1920 became the final death sentence for the League.

B. Glossary

To build your social science vocabulary, familiarize yourself with the following terms.

1. **isolationism** In American diplomacy, the traditional belief that the United States should refrain from involvement in overseas politics, alliances, or wars, and confine its national security interest to its own borders (sometimes along with the Caribbean and Central America). **Internationalism** or **Wilsonianism** is the contrasting belief that America's national security requires involvement and sometimes diplomatic or military alliances overseas. "But their obstruction was a powerful reminder of the continuing strength of American isolationism."
2. **collective security** In international affairs, reliance on a group of nations or an international organization as protection against aggressors, rather than on national self-defense alone. " . . . an international organization that Wilson dreamed would provide a system of collective security."
3. **mobilization** The organization of a nation and its armed forces for war. "Creel typified American war mobilization. . . ."
4. **pardon** The official release of a person from punishment for a crime. ". . . presidential pardons were rather freely granted. . . ."
5. **ration** A fixed allowance of food or other scarce commodity. "He deliberately rejected issuing ration cards. . . ."

6. **conscientious objector** A person who refuses to participate in war on grounds of conscience or belief. ". . . about 4,000 conscientious objectors were excused."

7. **Bolshevik** The radical majority faction of the Russian Socialist party that seized power in the October 1917 revolution; they later took the name *Communist*. (Bolshevik is the Russian word for "majority"; their rivals for power were **Mensheviks**, or minority.) "The Bolsheviks long resented these 'capitalistic' interventions. . . ."

8. **salient** A portion of a battle line that extends forward into enemy territory. ". . . nine American divisions . . . joined four French divisions to push the Germans from the St. Mihiel salient. . . ."

9. **parliamentary** Concerning political systems in which the government is constituted from the controlling party's members in the legislative assembly. "Unlike all the parliamentary statesmen at the table, [Wilson] did not command a legislative majority at home."

10. **protectorate** In international affairs, a weaker or smaller country held to be under the guidance or protection of a major power; the arrangement is a weaker form of imperialism or colonialism. (A **colony** is a territory owned outright by a more powerful nation.) ". . . preventing any vengeful parceling out of the former colonies and protectorates of the vanquished powers."

11. **trustee** A nation that holds the territory of a former colony as the conditional agent of an international body under defined terms. "The victors would . . . receive the conquered territory . . . only as trustees of the League of Nations."

12. **mandate** Under the League of Nations (1919–1939), a specific commission that authorized a trustee to administer a former colonial territory. "Japan was conceded the strategic Pacific islands under a League of Nations mandate. . . ."

13. **self-determination** The Wilsonian doctrine that each people should have the right to freely choose its own political affiliation and national future, e.g., independence or incorporation into another nation. "Faced with fierce Wilsonian opposition to this violation of self-determination...."

14. **reservation** A portion of a deed, contract, or treaty that places conditions or restrictions on the general obligations. ". . . he finally came up with fourteen formal reservations. . . ."

15. **demagogue** A politician who arouses fervor by appealing to the lowest emotions of a mass audience, such as fear, hatred, and greed. " . . . a debacle that played into the hands of the German demagogue Adolf Hitler."

PART II: CHECKING YOUR PROGRESS

A. True-False

Where the statement is true, circle **T**; where it is false, circle **F**.

1. T F Germany responded to Wilson's call for "peace without victory" with a proposal for a negotiated settlement of the war.

2. T F Wilson's proclamation of the war as a crusade to end all war and spread democracy around the world inspired intense ideological enthusiasm among Americans.

3. T F Among Wilson's Fourteen Points were freedom of the seas, national self-determination for oppressed smaller nations, and an international organization to secure peace.

4. T F The Committee on Public Information used varied forms of propaganda to stir fervent American patriotism and support for the war.

5. T F The primary targets of prosecution under the Espionage and Sedition Acts were German and Austrian agents in the United States.

6. T F Even during the war mobilization, Americans were extremely reluctant to grant the federal government extensive powers over the civilian economy.

7. T F Despite bitter and sometimes violent strikes, American labor made economic and organizational gains as a result of World War I.

8. T F War-inspired black migration into northern cities led to major racial riots in 1917–1919.

9. T F America's granting of women's right to vote under the Nineteenth Amendment represented the first breakthrough for women's suffrage in the world.

10. T F One of the few major instances of using coercive power during the war was the federal government's seizure and operation of the nation's railroads.

11. T F The arrival of the main force American troops in May 1918 came just in time to block the last German offensive and turn the tide toward Allied victory.

12. T F When Woodrow Wilson first arrived in Europe, the European public hailed him as a hero and a peacemaking savior.

13. T F Wilson successfully thwarted other Allied nations' attempts to make imperialistic gains from the war.

14. T F Wilson's unwillingness to compromise or accept any Republican reservations to the Treaty of Versailles guaranteed that the whole treaty would go down to defeat.

15. T F In the election of 1920, Republican Harding supported the League of Nations, while Democrat Cox tried to straddle both sides of the issue.

B. Multiple Choice

Select the best answer and circle the corresponding letter.

1. The immediate cause of American entry into World War I was
   a. German support for a possible Mexican invasion of the southwestern United States.
   b. Germany's resumption of unrestricted submarine warfare.
   c. the imminent danger of a French surrender to Germany.
   d. desire of the American munitions makers to gain larger profits.
   e. Wilson's recognition that German militarism threatened the ideals of American democracy.
2. Wilson and his administration aroused the still-divided American people to fervent support of the war by
   a. seizing control of the means of communication and demanding national unity.
   b. declaring the German people to be immoral Huns and barbarians.
   c. proclaiming the conflict an ideological war to end all war and make the world safe for democracy.
   d. proclaiming the war a religious crusade to save Western, Christian civilization
   e. asserting that a victorious Germany might well attack or invade the United States.

3. The capstone Fourteenth Point of Wilson's declaration of war aims called for
   a. the establishment of parliamentary democracies throughout Europe.
   b. guarantees of basic human rights for all people in the world.
   c. an international organization to guarantee collective security.
   d. freedom of travel without restrictions.
   e. a severe limitation on all nations' military forces and armaments as soon as the war ended.
4. George Creel's Committee on Public Information typified the entire American war effort because it
   a. maintained respect for American ideals of free speech and dissent even as it promoted the war.
   b. effectively used statistics and scientific information to enable the government to mobilize for war.
   c. relied more on whipped-up patriotism and voluntary compliance than on formal laws or government coercion.
   d. brought all the resources of private business into support of the war effort.
   e. used the constant threat of government takeover to force business and labor to support the war.
5. The two key laws aimed at enforcing loyalty and suppressing antiwar dissent were the
   a. War Mobilization Act and the National Defense Act.
   b. Selective Service Act and the Public Information Act.
   c. Eighteenth Amendment and the Anti-German Language Act.
   d. Espionage Act and the Sedition Act.
   e. War Industries Act and the Council of National Defense authorization law.
6. Two groups that experienced the most direct attacks and suppression during the war were
   a. German Americans and socialists.
   b. communists and labor leaders.
   c. Mexican Americans and immigrants.
   d. African Americans and feminists.
   e. conscientious objectors and draft dodgers.
7. The immediate postwar passage of the Nineteenth Amendment, granting American women the right to vote
   a. was the breakthrough that opened the door to worldwide women's suffrage.
   b. enabled women to consolidate the permanent economic gains they had made during the war.
   c. came in the face of continued opposition by President Wilson.
   d. reflected the general American belief that the war should really lead to an expansion of democracy.
   e. followed similar adoption of suffrage in many Western nations.
8. Particularly violent strikes erupted during and after World War I in
   a. the shipping and railroad industries.
   b. the steel industry.
   c. the textile and clothing manufacturing industries.
   d. factories employing women war workers.
   e. Chicago and East St. Louis.
9. The major result of the substantial wartime migration of blacks to northern cities was
   a. a growing acceptance of the idea of a strong black presence in the military.
   b. federal government efforts to block further black migration from southern farms.
   c. a growing agitation by blacks and northern liberals for racial integration.
   d. the incorporation of blacks into the major industrial unions.
   e. a series of vicious race riots in northern cities.

10. A major difference between the World War I Selective Service Act and the Civil War draft was that in World War I
    a. women as well as men were drafted.
    b. there was no provision for conscientious objection as there had been during the Civil War.
    c. draftees were sent immediately into front line combat.
    d. draftees received the same training as professional soldiers.
    e. it was not possible to purchase an exemption or to hire a substitute as during the Civil War.
11. American soldiers were especially needed in France in the spring of 1918 because
    a. the Allied invasion of Germany was stalling and in danger of failing.
    b. the Italian front was about to collapse and permit the Austro-Hungarians to join German forces in France.
    c. the British were in danger of starving due to German submarine warfare.
    d. the Russians had left the Allied war effort and were threatening to switch to the German side.
    e. a renewed German offensive was threatening to break through to Paris and force France to surrender.
12. The major American military contribution to Germany's decision to give up fighting was
    a. American armies' victories in a dozen critical battles during 1918.
    b. the U.S. Navy's successful destruction of most German submarines.
    c. the prospect of endless supplies of future, fresh American troops to fight the war.
    d. General Pershing's brilliant strategy that final broke the stalemate of trench warfare.
    e. the effective use of new American military weapons like the tank and the airplane.
13. Wilson blundered badly when leading the American peace delegation to Paris by
    a. failing to develop any set of clear diplomatic goals for the peace treaty.
    b. refusing to include any Republican senators in the American delegation.
    c. not consulting with his key allies, Britain and France, about their war aims.
    d. suggesting that he would abandon his idealistic Fourteen Points in order to appease the Allies.
    e. believing Senator Henry Cabot Lodge when he said he supported Wilson one hundred percent.
14. The European Allied powers and Japan were able to undermine Wilson's goal of a nonimperialistic peace treaty partly because
    a. they regarded his proposed League of Nations as largely a useless symbol.
    b. American ethnic groups were working for imperialistic goals of their own.
    c. they knew he could not promise continuing American aid and involvement in European affairs.
    d. Germany's constant threat to resume fighting made them insistent on harshly punishing the war's loser.
    e. Republicans were forcing Wilson to change the League of Nations covenant to guarantee the Monroe Doctrine and other American interests.
15. Wilson bore considerable responsibility for the failure of the United States to join the League of Nations because he
    a. linked the League too closely to European politics.
    b. ordered Democratic senators to defeat the pro-League treaty with the Lodge reservations.
    c. failed to take the case for the League to the American public.
    d. had agreed that America would pay most of the cost of the League.
    e. failed to effectively campaign for pro-League Governor James Cox in the 1920 election.

C. Identification

Supply the correct identification for each numbered description.

1. ___________ Message sent to Mexico from the German foreign minister proposing a secret German-Mexican alliance and possible support for Mexico's recovery of Texas, New Mexico, and Arizona
2. ___________ Wilson's idealistic statement of American war aims in January 1918 that inspired the Allies and demoralized the Germans
3. ___________ American government propaganda agency that aroused zeal for Wilson's ideals and whipped up hatred for the Kaiser
4. ___________ Radical antiwar labor union whose members were prosecuted under the Espionage and Sedition Act
5. ___________ Originally weak wartime agency that gradually expanded the federal government's power over the economy by setting production quotas and allocating natural resources.
6. ___________ Constitutional revision endorsed by Wilson as a war measure whose ratification finally achieved a goal long sought by American women
7. ___________ Treasury Department bond-selling drives that raised about $21 billion to provide most of the funds to finance the American war effort
8. ___________ Popular term for American soldiers during World War I
9. ___________ Collective term for the major powers that dominated the Paris Peace Conference—Britain, France, Italy, and the United States
10. ___________ Wilson's proposed international body that constituted the key provision of the Versailles treaty
11. ___________ Controversial peace agreement that compromised many of Wilson's idealistic Fourteen Points but retained his cherished League of Nations among its provisions
12. ___________ Senatorial committee whose chairman used delaying tactics and hostile testimony to develop opposition to Wilson's treaty and League of Nations
13. ___________ A hard core of isolationist senators who bitterly opposed any sort of league; also called the "Battalion of Death"
14. ___________ Amendments to the proposed Treaty of Versailles, sponsored by Wilson's hated senatorial opponent, that attempted to guarantee America's sovereign rights in relation to the League of Nations
15. ___________ Wilson's belief that the presidential election of 1920 should constitute a direct popular vote on the League of Nations

D. Matching People, Places, and Events

Match the person, place, or event in the left column with the proper description in the right column by inserting the correct letter on the blank line.

1. ___ George Creel
2. ___ Eugene V. Debs

a. Inspirational leader of the Western world in wartime who later stumbled as a peacemaker

3. ___ Bernard Baruch
4. ___ Herbert Hoover
5. ___ John J. Pershing
6. ___ Alice Paul
7. ___ Franklin D. Roosevelt
8. ___ Kaiser Wilhelm II
9. ___ Woodrow Wilson
10. ___ Henry Cabot Lodge
11. ___ Georges Clemenceau
12. ___ William Borah
13. ___ James Cox
14. ___ Calvin Coolidge
15. ___ Warren G. Harding

b. Senatorial leader of the isolationist irreconcilables who absolutely opposed all American involvement in Europe

c. Exciting vice-presidential candidate from New York in the losing Democratic campaign of 1920.

d. The "tiger" of France, whose drive for security forced Wilson to compromise at Versailles

e. Head of the American propaganda agency that mobilized public opinion for World War I

f. Folksy Ohio senator whose 1920 presidential victory ended the last hopes for U.S. participation in the League of Nations

g. Hated leader of America's enemy in World War I

h. Head of the Food Administration who pioneered successful voluntary mobilization methods

i. Leader of the pacifist National Women's Party who opposed U.S. involvement in World War I

j. Defeated Democratic presidential candidate in the election of 1920

k. Commander of the overseas American Expeditionary Force in World War I

l. Massachusetts governor and Warren G. Harding's vice presidential running mate in the election of 1920

m. Wilson's great senatorial antagonist who fought to keep America out of the League of Nations

n. Head of the War Industries Board, which attempted to impose some order on U.S. war production

o. Socialist leader who won nearly a million votes as a presidential candidate while in federal prison for antiwar activities

E. Putting Things in Order

Put the following events in correct order by numbering them from 1 to 5.

1. __________ Germany's resumption of submarine warfare forces the United States into a declaration of war.

2. __________ The Senate's final defeat of the Versailles treaty and a Republican election victory end Wilson's last hopes for American entry into the League of Nations.

3. __________ The United States takes the first hesitant steps toward preparedness in the event of war.

4. __________ The effectiveness of American combat troops in crucial battles helps bring about an Allied victory in World War I.

5. __________ Wilson struggles with other Allied leaders in Paris to hammer out a peace treaty and organize the postwar world.

F. Matching Cause and Effect

Match the historical cause in the left column with the proper effect in the right column by writing the correct letter on the blank line.

Cause

1. ___ Germany's resumption of unrestricted submarine warfare
2. ___ Wilson's Fourteen Points
3. ___ The wartime atmosphere of emotional patriotism and fear
4. ___ Women's labor in wartime factories
5. ___ The migration of African Americans to northern cities
6. ___ American troops' entry into combat in the spring and summer of 1918
7. ___ Wilson's political blunders in the fall of 1918
8. ___ The strong diplomatic demands of France, Italy, and Japan
9. ___ Senator Lodge's tactics of delaying and proposing reservations in the Versailles treaty
10. ___ Wilson's refusal to accept any reservations supported by Lodge.

Effect

a. Led to major racial violence in Chicago and East St. Louis, Illinois

b. Forced Democrats to vote against a modified treaty and killed American participation in the League of Nations

c. Stopped the final German offensive and turned the tide toward Allied victory

d. Allowed domestic disillusionment and opposition to the treaty and League to build strength

e. Finally pushed the United States into World War I

f. Weakened the president's position during the peacemaking process

g. Caused harsh attacks on German Americans and other Americans who opposed the war

h. Lifted Allied and American spirits and demoralized Germany and its allies

i. Forced Wilson to compromise his Fourteen Points in order to keep the League as part of the peace treaty

j. Helped pass the Nineteenth Amendment but did not really change society's emphasis on the maternal role

G. Developing Historical Skills

Analyzing Visual Propaganda

This exercise involves analyzing visual propaganda designed to make emotional appeals on behalf of a cause. In this case, the propaganda was designed to enlist the American public's support for the war effort against Germany. The kinds of propaganda used on behalf of a cause can tell the historian a great deal about what issues were perceived to be at stake and what public values were being appealed to.

Answer the following questions about the cartoons and drawings in this chapter.

1. *Anti-German Propaganda* (p.749): How do the words and image of this poster work together to persuade an American audience to buy liberty loans? Besides the specific message, what general portrait of Germany, the war, and America's reasons for fighting are conveyed?

2. *Patriotic Persuasion* (p. 749): How does this army recruitment poster convey the idea that both patriotism and social solidarity can be served by joining the military? At what social class of young man is the poster evidently aimed?

3. *Food for Thought* (p. 755): How does this poster visually make the connection between the patriotic war effort and gardens? What specific words or phrases create the link between women's food-growing effort and military service on fields of combat? What specific appeal is this image making to women?

PART III: APPLYING WHAT YOU HAVE LEARNED

1. What caused American entry into World War I, and how did Wilson turn the war into an ideological crusade?
2. What did American women gain from their participation in the war effort? What did they fail to obtain?
3. What was America's military and ideological contribution to the Allied victory?
4. How were the goals of the war presented to the American public? Did these lofty and idealistic goals eventually contribute to the deep American disillusionment at the conclusion of the war? Why or why not?
5. How was Wilson forced to compromise during the peace negotiations, and why did America, in the end, refuse to ratify the treaty and join the League of Nations?
6. Do you agree that despite Wilson's failure to obtain all his goals, he made the Versailles Peace Treaty much better than it would have been had he not been in Paris? Why or why not?
7. Apart from such immediate factors as the Lodge-Wilson antagonism, what general features of earlier American history worked against American involvement in European affairs and participation in the League of Nations?

8. Do you agree that the final responsibility for the failure of America to join the League of Nations lies with Woodrow Wilson rather than with his opponents like Henry Cabot Lodge? Why or why not?
9. What really caused the overwhelming Republican victory in the election of 1920?
10. Ever since World War I and its aftermath, many of the fundamental debates about American foreign policy have been defined by whether the United States should pursue Wilsonianism or not. Using the account of Wilson's policies in the text and "Varying Viewpoints," outline the essential principles of Wilsonianism and explain why they have been so powerful and yet so controversial in American history.

CHAPTER 31

American Life in the "Roaring Twenties," 1919–1929

PART I: REVIEWING THE CHAPTER

A. Checklist of Learning Objectives

After mastering this chapter, you should be able to:

1. Explain and analyze America's turn toward social conservatism and normalcy following World War I.
2. Describe the cultural conflicts of the 1920s over such issues as immigration, cultural pluralism, and prohibition; and describe the rise of organized crime during the decade.
3. Describe the rise of Protestant Fundamentalism and its apparent defeat in the landmark Scopes Trial.
4. Discuss the rise of the mass-consumption economy, led by the automobile industry.
5. Describe the cultural revolution brought about by radio, films, and changing sexual standards, and the resulting anxiety it produced.
6. Explain how new ideas and values were reflected and promoted in the innovative American literature and music of the 1920s, including the African American Harlem Renaissance.
7. Explain how the era's cultural changes affected women and African Americans.

B. Glossary

To build your social science vocabulary, familiarize yourself with the following terms.

1. **syndicalism** A theory or movement that advocates bringing all economic and political power into the hands of labor unions by means of strikes. ". . . a number of legislatures . . . passed criminal syndicalism laws."
2. **Bible Belt** The region of the American South, extending roughly from North Carolina west to Oklahoma and Texas, where Protestant Fundamentalism and belief in literal interpretation of the Bible have traditionally been strongest. ". . . the Klan spread with astonishing rapidity, especially in the Midwest and the 'Bible Belt' South."
3. **provincial** Narrow and limited; isolated from cosmopolitan influences. "Isolationist America of the 1920s, ingrown and provincial, had little use for the immigrants. . . ."
4. **racketeer** A person who obtains money illegally by fraud, bootlegging, gambling, or threats of violence. "Racketeers even invaded the ranks of local labor unions. . . ."
5. **underworld** Those who live outside society's laws, by vice or crime. ". . . the annual 'take' of the underworld was estimated to be from $12 billion to $18 billion. . . ."

6. **credit** In business, the arrangement of purchasing goods or services immediately but making the payment at a later date. "Buying on credit was another innovative feature of the postwar economy."
7. **installment plan** A credit system by which goods already acquired are paid for in a series of payments at specified intervals. ". . . encouraged by tempting installment-plan buying, countless Americans with shallow purses acquired the habit of riding as they paid."
8. **magnate** An influential person in a large-scale enterprise. ". . . an outraged public forced the screen magnates to set up their own rigorous code of censorship."
9. **repression** In psychology, the forcing of instincts or ideas painful to the conscious mind into the unconscious, where they continue to exercise influence. "The Viennese physician appeared to argue that sexual repression was responsible for a variety of nervous and emotional ills."
10. **charismatic** Concerning the personal magnetism or appeal of a leader for his or her followers; literally, "gift of grace." "Harlem in the 1920s also spawned a charismatic political leader, Marcus Garvey."
11. **functionalism** The theory that a plan or design should be derived from practical purpose. "Architecture also married itself to the new materialism and functionalism."
12. **surtax** A special tax, usually involving a raised percentage increase on an already existing tax. ". . . Congress . . . abolish[ed] the surtax, the income tax, and estate taxes."

PART II: CHECKING YOUR PROGRESS

A. True-False

Where the statement is true, circle **T**; where it is false, circle **F**.

1. T F The red scare of 1919–1920 brought the United States to the brink of war with the revolutionary Communist government in Russia.
2. T F The Sacco-Vanzetti case aroused worldwide protest because of alleged prejudice by the judge and jury against the atheistic immigrant defendants.
3. T F The revived Ku Klux Klan remained a powerful force in American politics until the onset of the Great Depression.
4. T F The Immigration Act of 1924, for the first time, severely limited the numbers of immigrants and discriminated against those from eastern and southern Europe.
5. T F Some intellectuals, like Horace Kallen and Randolph Bourne, believed that immigrants should be able to retain elements of their own cultures and thus contribute to a more diverse and cosmopolitan America.
6. T F One major consequence of prohibition was the rise of organized crime that controlled liquor distribution as well as drugs, gambling, and prostitution.
7. T F The Scopes trial verdict acquitted biology teacher John Thomas Scopes and overturned the Tennessee law prohibiting the teaching of evolution in the schools.
8. T F Two major innovations of the new consumer economy were mass advertising and the ability to purchase goods on credit without paying the full price immediately.
9. T F The automobile had major social and cultural effects in weakening family life and offering new freedom to women and youth.

10. T F D.W. Griffiths' film, *The Birth of a Nation*, was the first major Hollywood production to present African Americans in a positive light.

11. T F The 1920s saw attempts to restore stricter standards of sexual behavior, especially for women.

12. T F The Harlem Renaissance and the rise of jazz both reflected a new racial pride among African Americans.

13. T F The most prominent writers of the 1920s upheld the moral virtues of small-town American life against the critical attitudes and moral questioning of the big cities.

14. T F Many American writers and artists of the 1920s sought escape from what they saw as the narrow culture of the United States by moving abroad to Mexico.

15. T F The real estate and stock market booms of the 1920s were fueled by large amounts of risky speculation and excessive credit.

B. Multiple Choice

Select the best answer and circle the corresponding letter.

1. The red scare of the early 1920s was initially set off by
   a. the Sacco-Vanzetti case.
   b. the rise of the radical Industrial Workers of the World.
   c. the Bolshevik revolution in Russia.
   d. an influx of radical immigrants.
   e. the revelation of American Communist infiltration of the federal government.
2. Besides attacking minorities like Catholics, blacks, and Jews, the Ku Klux Klan of the 1920s opposed contemporary cultural changes, such as
   a. evolution and birth control.
   b. prohibition and higher education.
   c. automobiles and airplanes.
   d. patriotism and immigration restriction.
   e. novels and modern architecture.
3. The quota system established for immigration in the 1920s was based partly on the idea that
   a. many of the political refugees from war-torn Europe were likely radicals or communists.
   b. immigrants from northern and western Europe were superior to those from southern and eastern Europe.
   c. the era of European immigration would be replaced by immigration from Latin America.
   d. immigration should be based on family connections, education, and job skills, not ethnic group.
   e. the United States was becoming increasingly overpopulated.
4. Progressive intellectuals, like Horace Kallen and Randolph Bourne, differed from most Americans of the 1920s in believing that
   a. the continuing divisions of language and religion among the working class enabled employers to exploit workers and crush unions.
   b. southern and eastern European cultures were as sophisticated as those from northern and western Europe.
   c. racial and economic justice was more important that cultural issues.
   d. immigrants should be able to preserve elements of their culture and not be forced to conform to a single American model.
   e. the U.S. government should recognize more than one official language.

5. One major impact of prohibition was
   a. a rise in criminal organizations that supplied illegal liquor.
   b. an improvement in family relations and the general moral tone of society.
   c. a turn from alcohol to other forms of substance abuse.
   d. the rise of voluntary self-help organizations like Alcoholics Anonymous.
   e. a heightened respect for law enforcement at the local, state, and federal levels.
6. The essential issue in the Scopes trial was whether
   a. scientists ought to be allowed to investigate the biological origins of humanity.
   b. the teachings of Darwin could be reconciled with those of religion.
   c. Darwinian evolutionary science could be taught in the public schools.
   d. Fundamentalist Protestants could use public school facilities for their meetings.
   e. the teaching of Darwinism would inevitably lead to sex education in the schools.
7. The term *Fordism* was widely used to describe businessman Henry Ford's innovation of
   a. Ford's anti-Semitism and hostility to education.
   b. applying the internal combustion engine to a vehicle that the ordinary person could own.
   c. a system of time and motion studies designed to improve efficiency in manufacturing.
   d. assembly-line mass production of identical, relatively cheap manufactured goods.
   e. permitting customers to purchase automobiles on credit with little money down.
8. One of the primary social effects of the new automobile age was a
   a. growing migration from cities to smaller towns and rural areas.
   b. strengthening of intergenerational ties among parents, children, and grandchildren.
   c. tightening of restrictions on women.
   d. closing of the gap between the working class and the wealthy.
   e. weakening of traditional family ties between parents and youth.
9. Radio and the movies both had the cultural effect of
   a. increasing Americans' interest in history and literature.
   b. enabling the sophisticated culture of the wealthy elite to spread to the masses.
   c. encouraging producers of culture to adapt their products to a wide a variety of individual tastes.
   d. encouraging local creativity and ending cultural dependence on a few big cities.
   e. increasing standardized mass culture and weakening traditional forms of family and neighborhood culture.
10. Among the major changes vigorously pursued by many American women in the 1920s were
    a. expanded voting rights and political equality.
    b. economic equality and equal pay for equal work.
    c. social reform and family welfare.
    d. leadership in national business and politics.
    e. opportunities for adventure and sexual liberation.
11. The primary achievement of Marcus Garvey's Universal Negro Improvement Association was its
    a. promotion of black jazz and blues.
    b. positive impact on black racial pride.
    c. economic program of economic development in Harlem.
    d. successful transportation of numerous America blacks to Africa.
    e. formation of an organization designed to promote racial integration and equality.

12. H.L. Mencken's magazine, *American Mercury*, appealed to many young literary rebels by
    a. encouraging American writers to migrate abroad to Paris.
    b. promoting a program of progressive economic and social reform.
    c. its regular publication of sexually explicit writing and images.
    d. attacking the American middle class, patriotism, and Puritan do-gooders.
    e. its popular appeal to a great variety of Americans.
13. Many of the prominent new writers of the 1920s were
    a. fascinated by their historical roots in old New England.
    b. disgusted with European domination of American culture.
    c. interested especially in nature and social reform.
    d. rooted in the traditions and values of the South.
    e. highly critical of traditional American Puritanism and small-town life.
14. The center of the African-American literary and cultural revival of the 1920s was
    a. Atlanta.
    b. New Orleans.
    c. Chicago.
    d. Harlem, in New York City.
    e. Paris.
15. During the 1920s, Treasury Secretary Andrew Mellon and the Republican Congress pursued the economic policy of
    a. encouraging stock and real estate speculation.
    b. permitting the federal debt to grow substantially in order to stimulate the economy.
    c. cutting taxes for the wealthy and shifting the tax burden to the middle class.
    d. promoting higher wages so that the lower income groups could purchase goods and keep the economy growing.
    e. favoring old industries, like textiles and steel, over new industries, like consumer appliance manufacturing.

C. Identification

Supply the correct identification for each numbered description.

1. __________ The public panic of 1919–1920, spawned by fear of Bolshevik revolution, that resulted in the arrest and deportation of many political radicals

2. __________ Hooded defenders of Anglo-Saxon and Protestant values against immigrants, Catholics, and Jews

3. __________ Restrictive legislation of 1924 that reduced the number of newcomers to the United States and discriminated against immigrants from southern and eastern Europe

4. __________ Theory advocated by Bourne, Kallen, and others that immigrants should be able to retain elements of their traditions within a diverse America, rather than being forced to melt all differences

5. __________ National policy created by the passage of the Eighteenth Amendment, which led to widespread lawbreaking and the rise of organized crime

6. __________ Legal battle over teaching evolution that pitted modern science against Fundamentalist religion

7. __________ Henry Ford's cheap, rugged, mass-produced automobile

8. ______ D. W. Griffiths' epic film of 1915 about the Reconstruction era that prompted protests and boycotts by African Americans

9. ______ One of the few new consumer products of the 1920s that encouraged people to stay at home rather than pulling them away from home and family

10. ______ Movement led by feminist Margaret Sanger that contributed to changing sexual behaviors, especially for women

11. ______ Syncopated style of music created by blacks that first attained widespread national popularity in the 1920s

12. ______ Marcus Garvey's self-help organization that proposed to the resettlement of blacks in Africa

13. ______ H. L. Mencken's monthly magazine that led the literary attack on traditional moral values, the middle class, and Puritanism

14. ______ F. Scott Fitzgerald's influential first novel of 1920 that celebrated youth and helped set the tone for the emerging jazz age of the decade

15. ______ The explosion of creative expression in a district of New York City that encouraged African American artists, writers, and musicians to celebrate their racial pride

D. Matching People, Places, and Events

Match the person, place, or event in the left column with the proper description in the right column by inserting the correct letter on the blank line.

1. ___ A. Mitchell Palmer
2. ___ Nicola Sacco and Bartolomeo Vanzetti
3. ___ Al Capone
4. ___ John Dewey
5. ___ William Jennings Bryan
6. ___ Henry Ford
7. ___ Bruce Barton
8. ___ Langston Hughes
9. ___ Charles A. Lindbergh
10. ___ Marcus Garvey
11. ___ Randolph Bourne
12. ___ H. L. Mencken
13. ___ F. Scott Fitzgerald
14. ___ Ernest Hemingway
15. ___ Gertrude Stein

a. The Poet Laureate of Harlem and author of *The Weary Blues*

b. Innovative writer whose novels reflected the disillusionment of many Americans with propaganda and patriotic idealism

c. Italian American anarchists whose trial and execution aroused widespread protest

d. Mechanical genius and organizer of the mass-produced automobile industry

e. U.S. attorney general who rounded up thousands of alleged Bolsheviks in the red scare of 1919–1920

f. Baltimore writer who criticized the supposedly narrow and hypocritical values of American society

g. Top gangster of the 1920s, eventually convicted of income-tax evasion

h. Former presidential candidate who led the fight against evolution at the 1925 Scopes trial

i. Experimental writer whose Paris salon became a gathering place for American writers and artists in the 1920s

j. A leader of the new advertising industry, author of a pro-business interpretation of Jesus in *The Man Nobody Knows*

k. Cosmopolitan intellectual who advocated cultural pluralism and said America should be "not a nationality but a trans-nationality"

l. Leading American philosopher and proponent of progressive education

m. Wholesome, shy aviation pioneer who became a cultural hero of the 1920s for his pathbreaking flight

n. Minnesota-born writer whose novels were especially popular with young people in the 1920s

o. Jamaican-born leader who enhanced African American pride despite his failed migration plans

E. Putting Things in Order

Put the following events in correct order by numbering them from 1 to 5.

1. __________ The trial of a Tennessee high-school biology teacher symbolizes a national conflict over values of religion and science.
2. __________ Fear of the Bolshevik revolution sparks a crusade against radicals and Communists in America.
3. __________ A modest young man becomes a national hero by accomplishing a bold feat of aviation.
4. __________ Two Italian immigrants are convicted of murder and robbery, provoking charges of prejudice against the judge and jury.
5. __________ A new immigration law tightens up earlier emergency restrictions and imposes discriminatory quotas against the New Immigrants.

F. Matching Cause and Effect

Match the historical cause in the left column with the proper effect in the right column by writing the correct letter on the blank line.

		Cause		Effect
1.	___	American fear of Bolshevism	a.	Caused the rise of the Ku Klux Klan and the imposition of immigration restrictions
2.	___	Nativist American fear of immigrants and Catholics		

3. ____ Prohibition
4. ____ The automobile industry
5. ____ The radio
6. ____ Rising prosperity, new technologies, and the ideas of Sigmund Freud
7. ____ Resentment against conventional small-town morality
8. ____ The economic boom of the 1920s
9. ____ The ability to buy stocks with only a small down payment
10. ____ Andrew Mellon's tax policies

b. Caused many influential writers of the 1920s to criticize traditional values and search for new moral standards
c. Caused the red scare and the deportation of foreign radicals
d. Enabled many ordinary citizens to join in a speculative Wall Street boom
e. Stimulated highway construction, petroleum production, and other related industries
f. Helped stimulate mass attention to sports and entertainment while spreading the reach of advertising
g. Reduced the tax burden on the wealthy and contributed to the stock-market boom
h. Greatly raised the incomes and living standards of many Americans
i. Created a new atmosphere of sexual frankness and liberation, especially among the young
j. Helped spawn bootlegging and large-scale organized crime

G. Developing Historical Skills

Understanding Cultural Developments in Historical Context

The first part of this chapter describes the major social and economic changes of the 1920s. The second part describes the cultural developments that also occurred in the 1920s. Since the artists, writers, and others who produced the culture and ideas of the period were living amidst these very same social changes, your knowledge of the historical context can help you understand why they created the kind of works they did.

Answer the following questions:

1. In what ways were the movies, for all their glamour, similar to the automobile industry as developed by Henry Ford?

2. How did new technological and economic innovations like the automobile (pp. 781–785) and social changes like urbanization help bring about the cultural liberation of women?

3. In what ways did the novels of F. Scott Fitzgerald (pp.792–793) or musical developments like jazz (pp. 790–791) especially appeal to people living amid the social and economic changes of the 1920s? Did these cultural developments simply mirror existing politics and society, or were they in some ways a challenge to them?

4. Why were writers like H. L. Mencken, Sinclair Lewis, Sherwood Anderson, and others (pp.792–793) so harshly critical of American middle-class and small-town life in their work? Why did such writers strike a popular chord in the 1920s?

PART III: APPLYING WHAT YOU HAVE LEARNED

1. How and why did America turn toward domestic isolation and social conservatism in the 1920s?
2. How was the character of American culture affected by the social and political changes of the 1920s? (Include both white ethnic groups and blacks in your discussion.)
3. Why was immigration, which had been part of American experience for many generations, seen as such a great threat to American identity and culture in the prosperous 1920s? How did the severe and discriminatory immigration restriction laws passed in the 1920s affect the country?
4. Why did critics, like Horace Kallen and Randolph Bourne, dislike the pressure on immigrants to Americanize and join the melting pot? What kind of future America did their ideals of cultural pluralism promote. Why was this view not widely accepted in the 1920s?
5. How did the Eighteenth Amendment outlawing alcohol both reflect and deepen the cultural divisions in the United States, including urban-rural conflicts?
6. How did some of the major public events of the 1920s reflect national disagreements over fundamental social, cultural, and religious values?
7. How did the automobile and other new products create a mass-consumption economy in the 1920s?
8. How did the new films, literature, and music of the 1920s affect American values in areas of religion, sexuality, and family life?
9. How and why did African Americans in the Harlem Renaissance and elsewhere begin celebrating racial pride and the New Negro in the 1920s? Was Marcus Garvey's movement to encourage black migration to Africa an expression of that same spirit or a reflection of the still-harsh oppression that most blacks experienced?
10. In what ways were the twenties a vigorous social and cultural reaction against the progressive movement in the decades leading up to World War I (see Chapters 29, 30, and 31)? Was this hostility to progressivism primarily a result of disillusionment with the outcome of the war or a reflection of the limits of progressive reform itself?

CHAPTER 32

The Politics of Boom and Bust, 1920–1932

PART I: REVIEWING THE CHAPTER

A. Checklist of Learning Objectives

After mastering this chapter, you should be able to:

1. Analyze the domestic political conservatism and economic prosperity of the 1920s.
2. Explain the Republican administrations' policies of isolationism, disarmament, and high-tariff protectionism.
3. Compare the easygoing corruption of the Harding administration with the straight-laced uprightness of his successor Coolidge.
4. Describe the international economic tangle of loans, war debts, and reparations, and indicate how the United States tried to address it.
5. Discuss how Hoover went from being a symbol of twenties business success to a symbol of depression failure.
6. Describe the stock market crash of 1929, and explain the deeper causes of the Great Depression.
7. Indicate how Hoover's response to the depression reflected a combination of old-time rugged individualism and the new view that the federal government had some responsibility for the economy.

B. Glossary

To build your social science vocabulary, familiarize yourself with the following terms.

1. **nationalization** Ownership of the major means of production by the national or federal government. ". . . wartime government operation of the lines might lead to nationalization."
2. **dreadnought** A heavily armored battleship with large batteries of twelve-inch guns. ". . . Secretary Hughes startled the delegates . . . with a comprehensive, concrete plan for . . . scrapping some of the huge dreadnoughts. . . ."
3. **accomplice** An associate or partner of a criminal who shares some degree of guilt. ". . . he and his accomplices looted the government to the tune of about $200 million. . . ."
4. **reparations** Compensation by a defeated nation for damage done to civilians and their property during a war. "Overshadowing all other foreign-policy problems . . . was . . . a complicated tangle of private loans, Allied war debt, and German reparations payments."
5. **pump priming** In economics, the spending or lending of a small amount of funds in order to stimulate a larger flow of economic activity. "'Pump-priming' loans by the RFC were no doubt of widespread benefit. . . ."

PART II: CHECKING YOUR PROGRESS

A. True-False

Where the statement is true, circle **T**; where it is false, circle **F**.

1. T F The most corrupt members of Harding's cabinet were the secretaries of state and the treasury.
2. T F The Republican administrations of the 1920s believed in strict enforcement of antitrust laws to maintain strong business competition.
3. T F The Republican administrations of the 1920s pursued an isolationist policy toward national security by engaging in a large military buildup.
4. T F The high tariff policies of the 1920s enhanced American prosperity but crippled international trade and Europe's economic recovery from World War I.
5. T F Calvin Coolidge's image of honesty and thrift helped restore public confidence in the government after the Harding administration scandals.
6. T F One sector of the American economy that did not share the prosperity of the 1920s was agriculture.
7. T F The major sources of support for liberal third-party presidential candidate Robert La Follette in the election of 1924 were among the urban working class and in the South
8. T F The main exception to America's isolationist foreign policy in the 1920s was continuing U.S. armed intervention in the Caribbean and Central America.
9. T F Britain, France, and America's other Allies vigorously protested U.S. demands for repayment of loans made during World War I.
10. T F In the election of 1928, Democratic nominee Al Smith's urban, Catholic, and wet background cost him support from many traditionally Democratic southern voters.
11. T F The Hawley-Smoot Tariff strengthened the trend toward expanded international trade and economic cooperation.
12. T F The American economic collapse during the Great Depression was the most severe suffered by any major industrial nation in the 1930s.
13. T F The Great Depression was caused partly by overexpansion of credit and excessive consumer debt.
14. T F Throughout his term, Hoover consistently adhered to his firm belief that the federal government should play no role in providing economic relief and assisting the recovery from the Depression.
15. T F Hoover's harsh use of the U.S. Army to disperse the veterans' Bonus Army from Washington brought him widespread condemnation.

B. Multiple Choice

Select the best answer and circle the corresponding letter.

1. As president, Warren G. Harding proved to be
   a. thoughtful and ambitious but impractical.
   b. an able administrator and diplomat but a poor politician.
   c. politically competent and concerned for the welfare of ordinary people.
   d. weak-willed and tolerant of corruption among his friends and his cabinet.
   e. better at managing domestic policy than foreign policy.
2. The relationship between government and big business advocated by the Republican presidents of the 1920s was that
   a. regulation of business should be weakened and the government should actively promote business profits.
   b. federal regulation should take precedence over state and local government.
   c. antitrust laws should be vigorously enforced to prevent monopolies.
   d. the government should retain a role in operating key businesses like the railroads and utilities.
   e. the government should keep hands off business and actively promote laissez-faire.
3. Two groups that suffered severe political setbacks in the immediate post–World War I environment were
   a. Protestants and Jews.
   b. organized labor and blacks.
   c. small businesses and farmers.
   d. women and city dwellers.
   e. southerners and Midwesterners.
4. Which two terms best describe the Harding and Coolidge administrations' approach to foreign policy?
   a. Internationalism and moralism
   b. Interventionism and militarism
   c. Isolationism and disarmament
   d. Balance of power and alliance-seeking
   e. Imperialism and racism
5. The proposed ratio of 5:5:3 in the Washington Disarmament Conference of 1921–1922 referred to the
   a. ratio of American, British, and Japanese troops to be maintained in China.
   b. respective number of votes Britain, France, and the United States would have in the League of Nations.
   c. allowable ratio of battleships and carriers among the United States, Britain, and Japan.
   d. number of nations from Europe, the Americas, and Asia, respectively, that would have to ratify the disarmament treaties before they went into effect.
   e. number of negotiators that the United States, Britain, and Japan sent to the conference.
6. The very high tariff rates of the 1920s had the primary economic effect of
   a. stimulating the formation of common markets among the major industrial nations.
   b. causing severe deflation in the United States and Europe.
   c. turning American trade away from Europe and toward Asia.
   d. stimulating American technological developments and raising wages.
   e. causing the Europeans to erect their own tariff barriers and thus severely reduce international trade

7. The central scandal of Teapot Dome involved members of Harding's cabinet who
   a. sold spoiled foodstuffs to the army and navy.
   b. took bribes for leasing federal oil lands.
   c. violated prohibition by tolerating gangster liquor deals.
   d. stuffed ballot boxes and played dirty tricks on campaign opponents.
   e. took expensive trips at taxpayer expense.
8. The farm bloc's favorite solution to the severe drop in prices that caused farmers' economic suffering in the 1920s was
   a. direct federal assistance to encourage farmers not to grow grain or cotton.
   b. for the federal government to buy up agricultural surpluses at higher prices and sell them abroad.
   c. for the United States to impose high tariffs on agricultural imports from foreign countries.
   d. for farmers to form producers' unions to obtain higher prices from consumers.
   e. for farmers to switch from corn, cotton, and wheat to more profitable crops.
9. Besides deep divisions within the Democratic party, the elections of 1924 revealed
   a. Coolidge's inability to attain Harding's level of personal popularity.
   b. the close political division between Republicans and Democrats.
   c. the turn of the solid South from the Democrats to the Republicans.
   d. the rise of liberalism within the Democratic party.
   e. that the progressive movement was much weaker than it had been before World War I.
10. The international economic crisis caused by unpaid war reparations and loans was partially resolved by
   a. private American bank loans to Germany that enabled Germany to pay war reparations.
   b. forgiving the Allied loans and German reparations.
   c. the creation of a new international economic system by the League of Nations.
   d. the rise of Mussolini and Hitler.
   e. forcing Germany to pay off the Allied loans to the United States.
11. Al Smith's Roman Catholicism and opposition to prohibition hurt him especially
   a. among northeasterners
   b. among ethnic voters.
   c. among African Americans.
   d. among women voters.
   e. in the South.
12. In the political campaign of 1928, Herbert Hoover revealed himself to be
   a. a charismatic and eloquent campaigner.
   b. a combination of nineteenth-century small-town virtues with big business efficiency.
   c. willing to engage in anti-Catholic rhetoric to defeat Al Smith.
   d. hostile to new forms of technology and progress.
   e. interested primarily in foreign policy.
13. One important cause of the great stock market crash of 1929 was
   a. overexpansion of production and credit beyond people's ability to pay for goods.
   b. a tight money policy that made it difficult to obtain loans.
   c. the lack of tariff protection for American markets from foreign competitors.
   d. excessive government regulation of business.
   e. the agricultural depression that had weakened the American farm economy.

14. The sky-high Hawley-Smoot Tariff of 1930 had the economic effect of
    a. providing valuable protection for hard-pressed American manufacturers.
    b. lowering the value of American currency in international money markets.
    c. crippling international trade and deepening the depression.
    d. forcing foreign governments to negotiate fairer trade agreements.
    e. raising so much revenue that the federal government was running surpluses..
15. The federal agency that Hoover established in order to provide pump-priming loans to business was the
    a. Tennessee Valley Authority.
    b. Bonus Expeditionary Force.
    c. Grain Stabilization Corporation.
    d. American Legion.
    e. Reconstruction Finance Corporation.

C. Identification

Supply the correct identification for each numbered description.

1. __________ Poker-playing cronies from Harding's native state who contributed to the morally loose and corrupt atmosphere in his administration
2. __________ Supreme Court ruling that removed women's workplace protection, invalidated a minimum wage for women, and undermined the earlier Court decision in *Muller* v. *Oregon*
3. __________ World War I veterans' group that vigorously promoted militant patriotism, political conservatism, and economic benefits for former servicemen
4. __________ Agreement emerging from the Washington Disarmament Conference that reduced naval strength and established a 5:5:3 ratio of warships among the major naval powers
5. __________ Toothless international agreement of 1928 that pledged nations to outlaw war
6. __________ Naval oil reserve in Wyoming that gave its name to one of the major Harding administration scandals
7. __________ Farm proposal of the 1920s, passed by Congress but vetoed by the president, that provided for the federal government to buy farm surpluses and sell them abroad
8. __________ American-sponsored arrangement for rescheduling German reparations payments that opened the way to private American bank loans to Germany.
9. __________ Southern Democrats who turned against their party's wet, Catholic nominee and voted for the Republicans in 1928
10. __________ Sky-high tariff bill of 1930 that deepened the depression and caused international financial chaos
11. __________ The climactic day of the October 1929 Wall Street stock-market crash
12. __________ Depression shantytowns, named after the president whom many blamed for their financial distress
13. __________ Hoover-sponsored federal agency that provided loans to hard-pressed banks and businesses after 1932

14. __________ Encampment of unemployed veterans who were driven out of Washington by General Douglas MacArthur's forces in 1932

15. __________ The Chinese province invaded and overrun by the Japanese army in 1932

D. Matching People, Places, and Events

Match the person, place, or event in the left column with the proper description in the right column by inserting the correct letter on the blank line.

1. ___ Warren G. Harding
2. ___ Charles Evans Hughes
3. ___ Andrew Mellon
4. ___ Henry Sinclair
5. ___ John Davis
6. ___ Albert B. Fall
7. ___ Harry Daugherty
8. ___ Calvin Coolidge
9. ___ Robert La Follette
10. ___ Herbert Hoover
11. ___ Al Smith
12. ___ Black Tuesday
13. ___ Charles Dawes
14. ___ Douglas MacArthur
15. ___ Henry Stimson

a. The worst single event of the great stock market crash of 1929

b. Negotiator of a plan to reschedule German reparations payments and Calvin Coolidge's vice president after 1925

c. The "Happy Warrior" who attracted votes in the cities but lost them in the South

d. Harding's interior secretary, convicted of taking bribes for leases on federal oil reserves

e. Weak, compromise Democratic candidate in 1924

f. U.S. attorney general and a member of Harding's corrupt Ohio Gang who was forced to resign in administration scandals

g. Strong-minded leader of Harding's cabinet and initiator of major naval agreements

h. Wealthy industrialist and conservative secretary of the treasury in the 1920s

i. Weak-willed president whose easygoing ways opened the door to widespread corruption in his administration

j. Hoover's secretary of state, who sought sanctions against Japan for its aggression in Manchuria

k. Secretary of commerce, through much of the 1920s, whose reputation for economic genius became a casualty of the Great Depression

l. Leader of a liberal third-party insurgency who attracted little support outside the farm belt

m. Wealthy oilman who bribed cabinet officials in the Teapot Dome scandal

n. Commander of the troops who forcefully ousted the army of unemployed veterans from Washington in 1932

o. Tight-lipped Vermonter who promoted frugality and pro-business policies during his presidency

E. Putting Things in Order

Put the following events in correct order by numbering them from 1 to 5.

1. __________ Amid economic collapse, Congress raises tariff barriers to new heights and thereby deepens the depression.
2. __________ An American-sponsored plan to ease German reparations payments provides a temporarily successful approach to the international war-debt tangle.
3. __________ An American-sponsored international conference surprisingly reduces naval armaments and stabilizes Far Eastern power relations.
4. __________ The prosperous economic bubble of the 1920s suddenly bursts, setting off a sustained period of hardship.
5. __________ A large number of corrupt dealings and scandals become public knowledge just as the president who presided over them is replaced by his impeccably honest successor.

F. Matching Cause and Effect

Match the historical cause in the left column with the proper effect in the right column by writing the correct letter on the blank line.

Cause

1. ___ Republican pro-business policies
2. ___ American concern about the arms race and the danger of war
3. ___ The high-tariff Fordney-McCumber Law of 1922
4. ___ The loose moral atmosphere of Harding's Washington
5. ___ The improved farm efficiency and production of the 1920s
6. ___ America's demand for complete repayment of the Allies' war debt
7. ___ Hoover's media campaign and Smith's political liabilities

Effect

a. Led to a Republican landslide in the election of 1928

b. Weakened labor unions and prevented the enforcement of progressive antitrust legislation

c. Plunged the United States into the worst economic depression in its history

d. Drove crop prices down and created a rural economic depression

e. Led to the successful Washington Disarmament Conference and the Five Power Naval Agreement of 1922

8. ___ The stock-market crash
9. ___ Domestic overexpansion of production and dried-up international trade
10. ___ Hoover's limited efforts at federally sponsored relief and recovery

f. Encouraged numerous federal officials to engage in corrupt dealings
g. Helped cause the stock-market crash and deepen the Great Depression
h. Failed to end the depression but did prevent more serious economic suffering
i. Sustained American prosperity, but pushed Europe into economic protectionism and turmoil
j. Aroused British and French anger and toughened their demands for German war reparations

G. Developing Historical Skills

Reading Diagrams

Sometimes a schematic drawing or diagram can help explain a complicated historical process in a simpler way than words. The international financial tangle of the 1920s is an exceptionally complicated affair, but examining the diagram on p. 808 makes it much easier to understand.

Answer the following questions.

1. What two roles did Americans play in the process?

2. What economic relationship did Great Britain and France have with Germany?

3. To whom did Britain owe war debts? To whom did France owe war debts?

4. Why was credit from American bankers so essential to all the European powers? Can you explain what happened when that credit was suddenly cut off after the stock-market crash of 1929?

PART III: APPLYING WHAT YOU HAVE LEARNED

1. What basic economic and political policies were pursued by the three conservative Republican administrations of the 1920s?
2. What were the causes and effects of America's international economic and political isolationism in the 1920s?
3. What weakness existed beneath the surface of the general 1920s prosperity? How did these weaknesses help cause the Great Depression?

4. Why were liberal or progressive politics so weak in the 1920s? Discuss the strengths and weaknesses of La Follette and Smith as challengers to the Republicans in 1924 and 1928.
5. The three Republican presidents of the 1920s are usually lumped together as essentially identical in outlook. Is that an accurate way to view them? What differences, if any, in style and policy, existed among Harding, Coolidge, and Hoover?
6. What were the economic and social effects of the Great Depression on the American people? Why did so many of the unemployed blame themselves rather than economic forces for their inability to find work?
7. How did President Hoover attempt to balance his belief in rugged individualism with the economic necessities of the time? Why do historians today, more than people of the time, tend to see Hoover as a more tragic figure, rather than a heartless or cruel president?
8. Which economic policies of the 1920s and 1930s helped cause and deepen the Depression. Since the depression soon became worldwide, did the Depression's fundamental causes lie inside or outside the United States?
9. How could the economic and political conservatism of the 1920s coincide with the great cultural and intellectual innovations of the same decade (see Chapter 31)? Was it fitting or ironic that someone as straight-laced and traditional as Calvin Coolidge should preside over an age of jazz, gangsterism, and Hollywood?
10. Why did American intervention in Latin America in the 1920s run contrary to the general turn toward isolationism and indifference to the outside world?

CHAPTER 33

The Great Depression and the New Deal, 1933–1939

PART I: REVIEWING THE CHAPTER

A. Checklist of Learning Objectives

After mastering this chapter, you should be able to:

1. Describe the rise of Franklin Roosevelt to the presidency in 1932 and the important role that Eleanor Roosevelt played in the Roosevelt administration.
2. Describe each of the early New Deal three R goals—relief, recovery, and reform—and indicate what major efforts were made to achieve each goal.
3. Describe the New Deal's effect on labor and labor organizations.
4. Discuss the early New Deal's efforts to organize business and agriculture in the NRA and the AAA, and indicate what directions Roosevelt took after those two agencies were declared unconstitutional.
5. Explain why Roosevelt became so frustrated with the conservative Supreme Court, and how his Court-packing plan backfired and weakened the political momentum of the New Deal.
6. Explain how Roosevelt mobilized a New Deal political coalition that included the South, Catholics, Jews, African Americans, and women.
7. Describe and analyze the arguments presented by both critics and defenders of the New Deal.

B. Glossary

To build your social science vocabulary, familiarize yourself with the following terms.

1. **dispossessed** The economically deprived. ". . . she . . . emerged as a champion of the dispossessed. . . ."
2. **rubberstamp** To approve a plan or law quickly or routinely, without examination. ". . . it was ready to rubberstamp bills drafted by White House advisors. . . ."
3. **blank check** Referring to permission to use an unlimited amount of money or authority. ". . . Congress gave the president extraordinary blank-check powers. . . ."
4. **foreign exchange** The transfer of credits or accounts between the citizens or financial institutions of different nations. "The new law clothed the president with power to regulate banking transactions and foreign exchange. . . ."
5. **hoarding** Secretly storing up quantities of goods or money. "Roosevelt moved swiftly . . . to protect the melting gold reserve and to prevent panicky hoarding."

6. **boondoggling** Engaging in trivial or useless work; any enterprise characterized by such work. "Tens of thousands of jobless were employed at . . . make-work tasks, which were dubbed 'boondoggling.' "

7. **Fascist (Fascism)** A political system or philosophy that advocates a mass-based party dictatorship, extreme nationalism, racism, and the glorification of war. "Fear of Long's becoming a fascist dictator ended. . . ."

8. **parity** Equivalence in monetary value under different conditions; specifically, in the United States, the price for farm products that would give them the same purchasing power as in the period 1909–1914. ". . . this agency was to establish 'parity prices' for basic commodities."

9. **holding company** A company that controls the stocks and securities of another company. "New Dealers . . . directed their fire at public utility holding companies. . . ."

10. **collective bargaining** Bargaining between an employer and his or her organized work force over hours, wages, and other conditions of employment. "The NRA blue eagles, with their call for collective bargaining, had been a godsend. . . ."

11. **jurisdictional** Concerning the proper sphere in which authority may be exercised. ". . . bitter and annoying jurisdictional feuding involving strikes continued. . . ."

12. **checks and balances** In American politics, the interlocking system of divided and counter-weighted authority among the executive, legislative, and judicial branches of government. ". . . Roosevelt was savagely condemned for attempting to break down the delicate checks and balances. . . ."

13. **pinko** Disparaging term for someone who is not completely a "red," or Communist, but is alleged to be sympathetic to communism. "Critics deplored the employment of 'crackpot' college professors, leftist 'pinkos.'. . ."

14. **deficit spending** The spending of public funds beyond the amount of income. "Despite some $20 billion poured out in six years of deficit spending. . . ."

15. **left** (or **left-wing**) In politics, groups or parties that traditionally advocate progress, social change, greater economic and social equality, and the welfare of the common worker. (The **right** or **right-wing** is traditionally groups or parties that advocate adherence to tradition, established authorities, and an acceptance of some degree of economic and social hierarchy.) "He may even have headed off a more radical swing to the left. . . ."

PART II: CHECKING YOUR PROGRESS

A. True-False

Where the statement is true, circle **T**; where it is false, circle **F**.

1. T F Roosevelt's call for a New Deal in the 1932 campaign included attacks on the Hoover deficits and a promise to balance the federal budget.

2. T F Eleanor Roosevelt had little experience with social reform and women's concerns before her husband was elected president.

3. T F Congress rushed to pass many of the early New Deal programs that granted large emergency powers to the president.

4. T F In designing the New Deal, Roosevelt and his advisers avoided drawing on European models that might smack of socialism to Americans.

5. T F The Civilian Conservation Corps (CCC) and the Public Works Administration (PWA) were both designed to reform American business practices.

6. T F Two early New Deal programs, the National Recovery Administration (NRA) and the Agricultural Adjustment Administration (AAA), were both declared unconstitutional by the Supreme Court.

7. T F Even amidst the worst of the Great Depression, most Americans did not worry that the United States would follow Italy or Germany in giving a dictator power to solve the crisis.

8. T F The New Deal opened new opportunities for women through appointment to government offices and the new social sciences.

9. T F The Tennessee Valley Authority (TVA) was designed primarily to aid in conserving water and soil resources in eroded hill areas.

10. T F The Committee for Industrial Organization (CIO) used sympathetic New Deal laws to unionize many unskilled workers previously ignored by the American Federation of Labor (AF of L).

11. T F Roosevelt's political coalition rested heavily on lower-income groups, including African Americans, Jews, Catholics, and southerners.

12. T F After Roosevelt's Court-packing plan failed, the conservative Supreme Court continued to strike down New Deal legislation just as it had before.

13. T F The U.S. Social Security System created by the New Deal provided more comprehensive social welfare insurance than anything available in Europe at the time.

14. T F The New Deal more than doubled the U.S. national debt through deficit spending.

15. T F By 1939, the New Deal had largely solved the major depression problem of unemployment.

B. Multiple Choice

Select the best answer and circle the corresponding letter.

1. Franklin Roosevelt's presidential campaign in 1932
   a. called for large-scale federal spending to reduce unemployment and restore prosperity.
   b. focused primarily on issues of international trade.
   c. promised to aid the "forgotten man" by balancing the federal budget and ending deficits.
   d. emphasized that there were no simple solutions to recovering from the Depression.
   e. declared that curing the Depression would require the president to exercise unprecedented power over the economy.

2. Even before FDR won the White House, Eleanor Roosevelt had become an influential figure in her own right by advocating the causes of
   a. blacks and people with disabilities.
   b. consumer protection and environmentalism.
   c. farmers and ranchers.
   d. immigrant ethnic groups and Roman Catholics.
   e. women and the poorer classes.

3. The Roosevelt landslide of 1932 included the shift into the Democratic camp of traditionally Republican
   a. New Englanders.
   b. African Americans.
   c. labor unions.
   d. southerners.
   e. Hispanics.
4. Roosevelt's first bold action during the Hundred Days was
   a. taking the nation off the gold standard.
   b. taking federal control of the railroads.
   c. legalizing unions and strikes.
   d. doubling relief for the unemployed.
   e. closing all the banks and declaring a national bank holiday.
5. The primary purpose of the Civilian Conservation Corps (CCC) was to
   a. restore unproductive farmland to productive use.
   b. protect wildlife and the environment.
   c. provide better-trained workers for industry.
   d. provide jobs and experience for unemployed young people.
   e. construct public buildings, shelters, and trails in the National Forests.
6. Strong political challenges to Roosevelt came from extremist critics like
   a. Herbert Hoover and Al Smith.
   b. Frances Perkins and Harry Hopkins.
   c. Henry Ford and Mary McLeod Bethune.
   d. John Steinbeck and John L. Lewis.
   e. Father Charles Coughlin and Huey Long.
7. Roosevelt's National Recovery Administration (NRA) ended when
   a. Dr. Francis Townsend attacked it as unfair to the elderly.
   b. Congress refused to provide further funding for it.
   c. it came to be considered too expensive for the results achieved.
   d. the Supreme Court declared it unconstitutional.
   e. it was caught engaging in wasteful and corrupt spending.
8. Roosevelt's Agricultural Adjustment Administration met especially sharp criticism because it
   a. failed to raise farm prices.
   b. actually contributed to soil erosion on the Great Plains.
   c. raised prices by paying farmers to slaughter animals and not grow crops.
   d. relied too much on private bank loans to aid farmers.
   e. favored southern cotton and sugar growers at the expense of Midwestern grain farmers.
9. In addition to the natural forces of drought and wind, the Dust Bowl of the 1930s was also caused by
   a. Roosevelt's AAA farm policies.
   b. excessive use of dry farming and mechanization techniques on marginal land.
   c. southwestern farmers' tendency to plant crops only every other year.
   d. the drying up of underground aquifers used to irrigate the Great Plains.
   e. the repeated failure of large-scale dam projects to bring water to the region.

10. The so-called Indian New Deal included an emphasis on
    a. local tribal self-government and recovery of Indian identity and culture.
    b. the distribution of tribal lands to individual Indian landowners.
    c. the migration of Indians from rural reservations to the cities.
    d. programs to encourage businesses like gambling casinos to locate on Indian lands.
    e. creating a common Indian identity beyond identifying with a particular tribe.
11. The daring New Deal program that attempted simultaneously to provide flood control, electric power, and economic development occurred in the valley of the
    a. Columbia River.
    b. Colorado River.
    c. Hudson River.
    d. Tennessee River.
    e. Missouri River.
12. The Social Security Act of 1935 provided for
    a. electricity and conservation for rural areas.
    b. pensions for the elderly, the blind, and unemployment insurance for workers.
    c. assistance for low-income public housing and social services.
    d. insurance for catastrophic medical expenses.
    e. social welfare protections for the poor whether they were able to work or not.
13. The new labor organization that flourished under Depression conditions with the New Deal's legal backing was the
    a. Knights of Labor.
    b. American Federation of Labor.
    c. National Labor Relations Board.
    d. Committee for Industrial Organization.
    e. United Mine Workers.
14. Among the key groups that made up the powerful Roosevelt coalition in the election of 1936 and for many decades afterward were
    a. African Americans, southerners, and Catholics.
    b. Republicans, New Englanders, and Old Immigrants.
    c. Midwesterners, small-town residents, and Presbyterians.
    d. businessmen, prohibitionists, and Coughlinites.
    e. westerners, farmers, and miners.
15. Roosevelt's attempt to pack the Supreme Court with his supporters proved extremely costly because
    a. the Court members he appointed still failed to support the New Deal.
    b. Congress began proceedings to impeach him.
    c. it revealed that he could not stand up to sharp political opposition.
    d. many of his New Deal supporters turned to back Huey Long.
    e. its failure took away much of the political momentum of the New Deal.

C. Identification

Supply the correct identification for each numbered description.

1. ___________ Phrase used to describe all of Franklin Roosevelt's policies and programs to combat the Great Depression

2. ___________ FDR's reform-minded intellectual advisers, who conceived much of the New Deal legislation

3. __________ Popular term for the special session of Congress in early 1933 that rapidly passed vast quantities of Roosevelt-initiated legislation and handed the president sweeping power
4. __________ The early New Deal agency that worked to solve the problems of unemployment and conservation by employing youth in reforestation and other beneficial tasks
5. __________ Large federal employment program, established in 1935 under Harry Hopkins, that provided jobs in areas from road building to art
6. __________ Widely displayed symbol of the National Recovery Administration (NRA), which attempted to reorganize and reform U.S. industry
7. __________ New Deal farm agency that attempted to raise prices by paying farmers to reduce their production of crops and animals
8. __________ The drought-stricken plains areas from which hundreds of thousands of Okies and Arkies were driven during the Great Depression
9. __________ New Deal agency that aroused strong conservative criticism by producing low-cost electrical power while providing full employment, soil conservation, and low cost housing to an entire region
10. __________ New Deal program that financed old-age pensions, unemployment insurance, and other forms of income assistance
11. __________ The new union group that organized large numbers of unskilled workers with the help of the Wagner Act and the National Labor Relations Board
12. __________ New Deal agency established to provide a public watchdog against deception and fraud in stock trading
13. __________ Organization of wealthy Republicans and conservative Democrats whose attacks on the New Deal caused Roosevelt to denounce them as economic royalists in the campaign of 1936
14. __________ Roosevelt's highly criticized scheme for gaining Supreme Court approval of New Deal legislation
15. __________ Economic theory of British economist who held that governments should run deliberate deficits to aid the economy in times of depression

D. Matching People, Places, and Events

Match the person, place, or event in the left column with the proper description in the right column by inserting the correct letter on the blank line.

1. ___ Franklin D. Roosevelt
2. ___ Eleanor Roosevelt
3. ___ Francis E. Townsend
4. ___ Harry Hopkins
5. ___ Father Coughlin
6. ___ Huey "Kingfish" Long
7. ___ George W. Norris

a. Republican who carried only two states in a futile campaign against "The Champ" in 1936
b. The "microphone messiah" of Michigan whose mass radio appeals turned anti–New Deal and anti-Semitic
c. Writer whose best-selling novel portrayed the suffering of dust bowl Okies in the Thirties
d. As Director of Minority Affairs for the National Youth Administration, the highest black official in the Roosevelt administration

8. ___ Harold Ickes
9. ___ John Steinbeck
10. ___ John L. Lewis
11. ___ Frances Perkins
12. ___ Alfred M. Landon
13. ___ Ruth Benedict
14. ___ John Maynard Keynes
15. ___ Mary McLeod Bethune

e. Presidential wife who became an effective lobbyist for the poor during the New Deal

f. Louisiana senator and popular mass agitator who promised to make "every man a king" at the expense of the wealthy

g. Former New York governor who roused the nation to action against the depression with his appeal to the "forgotten man"

h. Roosevelt's secretary of labor, America's first female cabinet member

i. Prominent 1930s social scientist who argued that each culture produced its own type of personality

j. Former New York social worker who became an influential FDR adviser and head of several New Deal agencies

k. Former bull moose progressive who spent billions of dollars on public building projects while carefully guarding against waste

l. Leader of senior citizen movement who called for the federal government to pay $200 a month to everyone over sixty

m. British economist whose theories helped justify New Deal deficit spending

n. Vigorously progressive senator from Nebraska whose passionate advocacy helped bring about the New Deal's Tennessee Valley Authority

o. Domineering boss of the mine workers' union who launched the CIO

E. Putting Things in Order

Put the following events in correct order by numbering them from 1 to 5.

1. __________ FDR devalues the dollar to about sixty cents in gold in an attempt to raise domestic prices.

2. __________ Congress passes numerous far-reaching laws under the pressure of a national crisis and strong presidential leadership.

3. __________ Republican attempts to attack the New Deal fall flat, and FDR wins reelection in a landslide.

4. __________ FDR's frustration at the conservative Supreme Court's overturning of New Deal legislation leads him to make a drastic proposal.

5. __________ Passage of new federal pro-labor legislation opens the way for a new union group and successful mass labor organizing.

F. Matching Cause and Effect

Match the historical cause in the left column with the proper effect in the right column by writing the correct letter on the blank line.

Cause

1. ___ The lame-duck period from November 1932 to March 1933
2. ___ Roosevelt's leadership during the Hundred Days
3. ___ The Civilian Conservation Corps, the Works Progress Administration, and the Civil Works Administration
4. ___ New Deal farm programs like the AAA
5. ___ The Tennessee Valley Authority
6. ___ The Wagner (National Labor Relations) Act
7. ___ FDR's political appeals to workers, African Americans, southerners, and "New Immigrants"
8. ___ The Supreme Court's conservative rulings against New Deal legislation
9. ___ Roosevelt's attempt to pack the Supreme Court
10. ___ The rapid cutback in federal pump-priming spending in 1937

Effect

a. Succeeded in raising farm prices but met strong opposition from many conservatives

b. Encouraged the CIO to organize large numbers of unskilled workers

c. May have pushed the Court toward more liberal rulings but badly hurt FDR politically

d. Caused a sharp Roosevelt Depression that brought unemployment back up to catastrophic levels

e. Caused a political paralysis that nearly halted the U.S. economy

f. Provided federal economic planning, conservation, cheap electricity, and jobs to a poverty-stricken region

g. Provided federal jobs for unemployed workers in conservation, construction, the arts, and other areas

h. Caused Roosevelt to propose a plan to pack the Supreme Court

i. Pushed a remarkable number of laws through Congress and restored the nation's confidence

j. Forged a powerful political coalition that made the Democrats the majority party

G. Developing Historical Skills

Reading Charts

Charts can classify complex information for ready reference. In this chapter, they are an effective way to present the many New Deal laws, agencies, and programs. The chart dealing with the Hundred Days is on p. 827, and that dealing with the later New Deal on p. 831.

Answer the following questions.

1. Which Hundred Days agency whose primary purpose was recovery also contributed to relief and reform?

2. List three Hundred Days actions that were aimed primarily at recovery.

3. List three later New Deal measures aimed primarily at reform.

4. Which later New Deal law aimed primarily at relief also contributed to recovery and reform?

5. Which was the last of the later New Deal laws aimed primarily at providing relief?

6. Compare the two charts. What can you conclude about the Hundred Days compared to the later New Deal, in relation to their relative emphasis on the three goals of relief, recovery, and reform? In which of the areas do you see the most continuity of purpose?

H. Map Mastery

Map Discrimination

Using the maps and charts in Chapter 34, answer the following questions.

1. *TVA Area*: In which four states was most of the Tennessee Valley Authority located?

2. *TVA Area*: How many major TVA dams were located in (a) Tennessee and (b) Alabama?

3. *Labor Union Membership in Selected Countries, 1913–2001*: Which two major industrialized nations had the lowest percentage of unionized workers before the onset of the Great Depression in 1930? Which two had the highest percentage of unionized workers?

4. *Labor Union Membership in Selected Countries, 1913–2001*: Which two nations had the lowest percentage of unionized workers in 1950, after the Great Depression and World War II. Which two nations had the highest percentage of such workers in 1950?

Map Challenge

Using *Labor Union Membership in Selected Countries, 1913–2001*: Write a brief essay comparing the growth of organized labor during the Depression and the following decade—1930–1950—with the growth of unionization in other industrialized nations. How has the percentage of unionized American workers altered in comparison to other nations since 1950? What might explain such differences?

PART III: APPLYING WHAT YOU HAVE LEARNED

1. What qualities did FDR bring to the presidency, and how did he display them during the New Deal years? What particular role did Eleanor Roosevelt play in FDR's political success?
2. How did the early New Deal legislation attempt to achieve the three goals of relief, recovery, and reform?
3. Which of the New Deal's many programs to reform the economy and alleviate the depression was the most successful, and why? (You may identify and discuss more than one.) Which was least successful, and why?
4. Were direct federal efforts to provide work for the unemployed—such as the Civilian Conservation Corps, the Works Progress Administration, and the Public Works Administration—justified either in terms of their immediate benefits to workers or as means of stimulating the economy. Why or why not?
5. Why did the New Deal arouse such opposition from conservatives, including those on the Supreme Court?
6. Discuss the political components of the Roosevelt coalition, formed in the 1930s. What did the New Deal offer to the diverse elements of this coalition?
7. Was the New Deal essentially a conservative attempt to save American capitalism from collapse, a radical change in traditional American antigovernment beliefs, or a moderate liberal response to a unique crisis?
8. How was the New Deal a culmination of the era of progressive reform, and how did it differ from the pre–World War I progressive era (see Chapters 28 and 29)?
9. One of the strongest arguments that proponents of the New Deal make was that it saved Depression-plagued America from the radical right-wing or left-wing dictatorships that seized power in much of Europe. Was the United States ever in danger of turning to fascism or communism if there had been no New Deal or if Roosevelt and his policies had failed. In what ways did the demagogues of the 1930s, like Coughlin, Long, and Townsend, resemble European radical leaders, and in what ways were they different?
10. Critics of the New Deal have often pointed out that it did not really solve the great Depression problem of unemployment; only World War II did that. Did the New Deal's other positive effects—such as in Social Security, labor rights, and regulation of the stock market—counter-balance its inability to overcome the central problem of unemployment?

CHAPTER 34

Franklin D. Roosevelt and the Shadow of War, 1933–1941

PART I: REVIEWING THE CHAPTER

A. Checklist of Learning Objectives

After mastering this chapter, you should be able to:

1. Describe Franklin Roosevelt's early isolationist policies, and explain their political and economic effects.
2. Explain how American isolationism dominated U.S. policy in the mid-1930s.
3. Explain how America gradually began to respond to the threat from totalitarian aggression, while still trying to stay neutral.
4. Describe Roosevelt's increasingly bold moves toward aiding Britain in the fight against Hitler and the sharp disagreements these efforts caused at home.
5. Indicate how the United States responded to Nazi anti-Semitism in the 1930s, and why it was slow to open its arms to refugees from Hitler's Germany.
6. Discuss the events and diplomatic issues in the growing Japanese-American confrontation that led up to Pearl Harbor.

B. Glossary

To build your social science vocabulary, familiarize yourself with the following terms.

1. **exchange rate** The monetary ratio according to which one currency is convertible into another, for instance, American dollars vis-à-vis German deutschmarks, which determines their value relative to one another. "Exchange-rate stabilization was essential to revival of world trade. . . ."
2. **militarist** Someone who glorifies military values or institutions and extends them into the political and social spheres. "Yet in Tokyo, Japanese militarists were calculating that they had little to fear. . . ."
3. **totalitarianism** A political system of absolute control, in which all social, moral, and religious values and institutions are put in direct service of the state. "Post-1918 chaos in Europe, followed by the Great Depression, fostered the ominous spread of totalitarianism."
4. **quarantine** In politics, isolating a nation by refusing to have economic or diplomatic dealings with it. ". . . they feared that a moral quarantine would lead to a shooting quarantine."
5. **division** The major unit of military organization, usually consisting of about 3,000 to 10,000 soldiers, into which most modern armies are organized. " . . . he sent his mechanized divisions crashing into Poland at dawn on September 1, 1939."
6. **unilateral** In politics, concerning a policy or action undertaken by only one nation. "This ancient dictum [was] hitherto unilateral. . . ."

7. **multilateral** In international diplomacy, referring to a policy or action undertaken by more than one nation. "Now multilateral, [the Monroe Doctrine bludgeon] was to be wielded by twenty-one pairs of American hands. . . ."

8. **steppes** The largely treeless great plains of southeastern Europe and western Asia. "The two fiends could now slit each other's throats on the icy steppes of Russia."

9. **convoy (v.)** To escort militarily, for purposes of protection. The escorting ships or troops are called a **convoy (n.)**. "Roosevelt made the fateful decision to convoy in July 1941."

10. **warlord** An armed leader or ruler who maintains power by continually waging war, often against other similar rulers or local military leaders, without constitutional authority or legal legitimacy. ". . . Roosevelt had resolutely held off an embargo, lest he goad the Tokyo warlords. . . ."

11. ***hara-kiri*** Traditional Japanese ritual suicide. "Japan's *hara-kiri* gamble in Hawaii paid off only in the short run."

PART II: CHECKING YOUR PROGRESS

A. True-False

Where the statement is true, circle **T**; where it is false, circle **F**.

1. T F Roosevelt's policy toward the 1933 London Economic Conference showed his concern for establishing a stable international economic order.

2. T F Roosevelt adhered to his Good Neighbor principle of nonintervention in Latin America, even when Mexico seized American oil companies in 1938.

3. T F American isolationism was caused partly by deep disillusionment with U.S. participation in World War I.

4. T F The Neutrality Acts of the mid-1930s prevented Americans from lending money or selling weapons to warring nations and from sailing on belligerent ships.

5. T F Despite the neutrality laws, the United States government provided assistance and sent unofficial military units to defend the democratic Spanish Loyalist government in its Civil War with rebel fascist General Francisco Franco.

6. T F America's isolationist mood began to swing toward interventionism in response to Roosevelt's Quarantine speech and Japan's attack on the U.S. gunboat *Panay* in 1937.

7. T F The United States attempted to dissuade the Western European democracies from pursuing their policy of appeasing Hitler's aggressive demands at the Munich Conference and after.

8. T F The cash-and-carry Neutrality Act of 1939 allowed America to aid the Allies without making loans or transporting weapons on U.S. ships.

9. T F The fall of France to Hitler in 1940 strengthened U.S. determination to stay neutral.

10. T F Isolationists argued that economic and military aid to Britain would inevitably lead to U.S. involvement in the European war.

11. T F Republican presidential nominee Wendell Willkie joined the isolationist attack on Roosevelt's pro-Britain policy in the 1940 campaign.

12. T F The 1941 Lend-Lease Act marked the effective abandonment of U.S. neutrality and the beginning of naval clashes with Germany.

13. T F The Atlantic Charter was an agreement on future war aims signed by Great Britain, the United States, and the Soviet Union.

14. T F U.S. warships were already being attacked and sunk in clashes with the German navy before Pearl Harbor.

15. T F The focal point of conflict between the United States and Japan in the pre–Pearl Harbor negotiations was Japan's demand that the Philippines be freed from U.S. colonial rule.

B. Multiple Choice

Select the best answer and circle the corresponding letter.

1. Roosevelt torpedoed the international London Economic Conference of 1933 because he
   a. wanted to concentrate primarily on the recovery of the American domestic economy.
   b. saw the hand of Hitler and Mussolini behind the conference's proposals.
   c. was firmly committed to the gold standard.
   d. wanted economic cooperation only between the United States and Britain, not the rest of Europe.
   e. resented the role of European bankers in bringing on the Great Depression and feared their return to influence.
2. Seeking to withdraw from overseas commitments and colonial expense, the United States, in 1934, promised future independence to
   a. Puerto Rico.
   b. the Virgin Islands.
   c. American Samoa.
   d. Cuba.
   e. the Philippines.
3. Roosevelt's Good Neighbor policy toward Latin America included
   a. a substantial program of American economic aid for Latin American countries.
   b. a renunciation of American intervention in Mexico or elsewhere in the region.
   c. an American military presence to block growing German influence in Argentina and Brazil.
   d. an American pledge to transfer the Panama Canal to Panama by the year 2000.
   e. opening American markets to Latin exports of cotton, coffee, and rubber.
4. The immediate response of most Americans to the rise of the fascist dictators Mussolini and Hitler was
   a. a call for a new military alliance to contain aggression.
   b. a focus on political cooperation with Britain and the Soviet Union.
   c. support for the Spanish government against fascist rebels.
   d. a deeper commitment to remain isolated from European problems.
   e. a willingness to aid Italian and German refugees from the totalitarian regimes.
5. The Neutrality Acts of 1935, 1936, and 1937 essentially required that
   a. United States remain neutral in any war between Britain and Germany.
   b. no Americans sail on belligerent ships, sell munitions, or make loans to nations at war.
   c. no belligerent power could conduct propaganda campaigns, sell goods, or make loans within the United States.
   d. the United States as a neutral power intervene to end the wars in China and Ethiopia and the Spanish Civil War.
   e. German Americans, Italian Americans, and Japanese Americans all had to declare their loyalty to the United States and not send aid or give support to the aggressors.

6. The effect of the strict American arms embargo during the civil war between the Loyalist Spanish government and Franco's fascist rebels was to
   a. encourage a negotiated political settlement between the warring parties.
   b. strengthen the Spanish government's ability to resist Franco.
   c. push Britain and the Soviet Union to intervene in the Spanish Civil War.
   d. cripple the democratic Loyalist government while the Italians and Germans armed Franco.
   e. encourage American arms merchants to sell their heaviest weapons to the Soviet Union.
7. The policy of appeasing the Fascist dictators reached its low point in 1938, when Britain and France sold out Czechoslovakia to Hitler in the conference at
   a. Geneva.
   b. Versailles.
   c. Munich.
   d. Prague.
   e. Paris.
8. The cash-and-carry Neutrality Act of 1939 was cleverly designed to
   a. guarantee that American policy would not benefit either side in World War II.
   b. enable American merchants to provide loans and ships to the Allies without violating neutrality laws.
   c. prepare America for involvement in the war.
   d. aid Britain and France by letting them buy supplies and munitions in the United States without involving American loans or ships.
   e. permit American banks to loan cash to Britain and France but not provide credit.
9. The destroyers-for-bases deal of 1940 provided that
   a. the United States would give Britain fifty American destroyers in exchange for eight British bases in North America.
   b. the United States would give Britain new bases in North America in exchange for fifty British destroyers.
   c. if America entered the war, it would receive eight bases in Britain in exchange for American destroyers.
   d. the British would transfer captured French destroyers to the United States in exchange for the use of American bases in East Asia.
   e. American destroyers would have complete access to eight British naval bases around the world.
10. The twin events that precipitated a clear change in American foreign policy from neutrality to active, though nonbelligerent, support of the Allied cause were the
   a. Munich Conference and the invasion of Poland.
   b. Nazis' *Kristallnacht* and Mussolini's backdoor invasion of France.
   c. fall of Poland and the invasion of Norway.
   d. invasion of the Soviet Union and the German submarine attacks on American shipping.
   e. fall of France and the Battle of Britain.
11. In the campaign of 1940, the Republican nominee Willkie essentially agreed with Roosevelt on the issue of
   a. the New Deal.
   b. the third term.
   c. Roosevelt's use of power in office.
   d. foreign policy.
   e. upholding the Neutrality Acts of 1935, 1936, and 1937.

12. The Lend-Lease Act clearly marked
    a. the end of isolationist opposition to Roosevelt's foreign policy.
    b. an end to the pretense of American neutrality between Britain and Germany.
    c. a secret Roosevelt plan to involve the United States in war with Japan.
    d. the beginning of opposition in Congress to Roosevelt's foreign policy.
    e. the American public's realization that a war with Germany was now inevitable.
13. The provisions of the Atlantic Charter, signed by Roosevelt and Churchill in 1941, included
    a. self-determination for oppressed peoples and a new international peacekeeping organization.
    b. a permanent alliance between Britain, the United States, and the Soviet Union.
    c. a pledge to rid the world of dictators and to establish democratic governments in Germany and Italy.
    d. an agreement to oppose Soviet communism, but only after Hitler was defeated.
    e. a joint commitment to end the British Empire and U.S. domination of Latin America through the Monroe Doctrine.
14. By the fall of 1940, over a year before Pearl Harbor, American warships were being regularly attacked by German destroyers near the coast of
    a. Spain.
    b. Ireland.
    c. the southeastern United States.
    d. Canada.
    e. Iceland.
15. The key issue that caused the negotiations between the United States and Japan to fail just before Pearl Harbor was
    a. the refusal of the Japanese to withdraw their navy from Hawaiian waters.
    b. America's insistence on its right to expand naval power in Asia.
    c. the Japanese refusal to withdraw from China.
    d. the Japanese refusal to guarantee the security of the Philippines.
    e. Japan's unwillingness to loosen its harsh rule in Korea.

C. Identification

Supply the correct identification for each numbered description.

1. __________ International economic conference on stabilizing currency that was sabotaged by FDR

2. __________ Nation to which the U.S. promised independence in the Tydings-McDuffie Act of 1934

3. __________ FDR's repudiation of Theodore Roosevelt's Corollary to the Monroe Doctrine, stating his intention to work cooperatively with Latin American nations

4. __________ A series of laws enacted by Congress in the mid-1930s that attempted to prevent any American involvement in future overseas wars

5. __________ Conflict between the rebel fascist forces of General Francisco Franco and the Loyalist government that severely tested U.S. neutrality legislation

6. __________ Roosevelt's 1937 speech that proposed strong U.S. measures against overseas aggressors

7. __________ European diplomatic conference in 1938, where Britain and France yielded to Hitler's demands for Czechoslovakia

8. ____________ Term for the British-French policy of attempting to prevent war by granting German demands

9. ____________ Leading U.S. group advocating American support for Britain in the fight against Hitler

10. ____________ Leading isolationist group advocating that America focus on continental defense and non-involvement with the European war

11. ____________ Controversial 1941 law that made America the arsenal of democracy by providing supposedly temporary military material assistance to Britain

12. ____________ A devastating night of Nazi attacks on Jewish businesses and synagogues that signaled a deepening of anti-Semitism and caused revulsion in the United States

13. ____________ U.S.–British agreement of August 1941 to promote democracy and establish a new international organization for peace

14. ____________ U.S. destroyer sunk by German submarines off the coast of Iceland in October 1941, with the loss of over a hundred men

15. ____________ Major American Pacific naval base devastated in a surprise attack in December 1941

D. Matching People, Places, and Events

Match the person, place, or event in the left column with the proper description in the right column by inserting the correct letter on the blank line.

1. ___ Cordell Hull
2. ___ Adolf Hitler
3. ___ Benito Mussolini
4. ___ Gerald Nye
5. ___ Francisco Franco
6. ___ Abraham Lincoln brigade
7. ___ Czechoslovakia
8. ___ Poland
9. ___ France
10. ___ Charles A. Lindbergh
11. ___ Wendell Willkie
12. ___ Winston Churchill
13. ___ Joseph Stalin
14. ___ Iceland
15. ___ Hawaii

a. Courageous prime minister who led Britain's lonely resistance to Hitler

b. Leader of the America First organization and chief spokesman for U.S. isolationism

c. Young American volunteers who went to fight for Loyalist Spain against Franco's Spanish fascist rebels.

d. Dynamic dark horse Republican presidential nominee who attacked FDR only on domestic policy

e. Fanatical fascist leader of Germany whose aggressions forced the United States to abandon its neutrality

f. Instigator of 1934 Senate hearings that castigated World War I munitions manufacturers as "merchants of death"

g. Nation whose sudden fall to Hitler in 1940 pushed the United States closer to direct aid to Britain

h. Site of a naval base where Japan launched a devastating surprise attack on the United States

i. North Atlantic nation near whose waters U.S. destroyers came under Nazi submarine attack

j. Small East European democracy betrayed into Hitler's hands at Munich

k. The lesser partner of the Rome-Berlin Axis who invaded Ethiopia and joined the war against France and Britain

l. FDR's secretary of state, who promoted reciprocal trade agreements, especially with Latin America

m. Russian dictator who first helped Hitler destroy Poland before becoming a victim of Nazi aggression in 1941

n. East European nation whose September 1939 invasion by Hitler set off World War II in Europe

o. Fascist rebel against the Spanish Loyalist government

E. Putting Things in Order

Put the following events in correct order by numbering them from 1 to 5.

1. __________ FDR puts domestic recovery ahead of international economics, torpedoing a major monetary conference.
2. __________ Western democracies try to appease Hitler by sacrificing Czechoslovakia, but his appetite for conquest remains undiminished.
3. __________ Already engaged against Hitler in the Atlantic, the United States is plunged into World War II by a surprise attack in the Pacific.
4. __________ The fall of France pushes FDR into providing increasingly open aid to Britain.
5. __________ Japan invades China and attacks an American vessel, but the United States sticks to its neutrality principles.

F. Matching Cause and Effect

Match the historical cause in the left column with the proper effect in the right column by writing the correct letter on the blank line.

Cause

1. ___ FDR's refusal to support international economic cooperation in the 1930s
2. ___ Roosevelt's Good Neighbor policy
3. ___ Bad memories of World War I and revelations about arms merchants

Effect

a. prevented Roosevelt and the United States from admitting many Jewish refugees from Nazism into the United States

4. ___ The U.S. Neutrality Acts of the 1930s
5. ___ Japanese aggression against China in 1937
6. ___ Hitler's invasion of Poland
7. ___ The fall of France in 1940
8. ___ Willkie's support for FDR's pro-British foreign policy
9. ___ The U.S. embargo on oil and other supplies to Japan
10. ___ Restrictive immigration laws and the hostility of the State Department and southern Democrats

b. Prompted FDR to make his Quarantine Speech, proposing strong action against aggressors
c. Brought new respect for the United States and for democracy in Latin America
d. Shocked the United States into enacting conscription and making the destroyers-for-bases deal
e. Forced Japan to either accept U.S. demands regarding China or go to war
f. Caused the United States to institute a cash-and-carry policy for providing aid to Britain
g. Deepened the worldwide depression and aided the rise of fascist dictators
h. Actually aided fascist dictators in carrying out their aggressions in Ethiopia, Spain, and China.
i. Promoted U.S. isolationism and the passage of several Neutrality Acts in the mid-1930s
j. Kept the 1940 presidential campaign from becoming a bitter national debate

G. Developing Historical Skills

Reading Text for Sequence and Context

In learning to read for and remember the historical sequence of events, it is often helpful to look for the context in which they occurred.

In the first list below are several major events discussed in the chapter. The second list contains the immediate contexts in which those events occurred. First, link the event to the appropriate context by putting a number from the bottom list to the right of the proper event. Then put the event-with-context in the proper sequence by writing numbers 1 to 7 in the spaces to the left.

Order	Event	Context
_____	Destroyer-for-bases deal	_____
_____	Atlantic Charter	_____
_____	Good Neighbor policy	_____
_____	U.S. Neutrality Acts of 1935–1936	_____
_____	Pearl Harbor	_____
_____	Lend-lease	_____
_____	Munich Conference	_____

Context

1. Failure of U.S.–Japanese negotiations
2. Decline of U.S. investment in Latin America
3. Nye Hearings and Italy's invasion of Ethiopia
4. Britain's near-defeat from German bombing
5. The fall of France
6. Hitler's threats to go to war
7. Hitler's invasion of Russia

H. Map Mastery

Map Discrimination

Using the maps and charts in Chapter 34, answer the following questions.

1. *Presidential Election of 1940*: In the 1940 election, how many electoral votes did Willkie win west of the Mississippi River?

2. *Presidential Election of 1940*: How many electoral votes did Willkie win east of the Mississippi River?

3. *Main Flow of Lend-Lease Aid*: Which continent received the most U.S. lend-lease aid?

4. *Main Flow of Lend-Lease Aid*: Which nation received lend-lease aid by way of both the Atlantic and Pacific oceans?

PART III: APPLYING WHAT YOU HAVE LEARNED

1. How and why did the United States attempt to isolate itself from foreign troubles in the early and mid-1930s?
2. Discuss the effects of the U.S. neutrality laws of the 1930s on both American foreign policy and the international situation in Europe and East Asia.
3. How did the fascist dictators' continually expanding aggression gradually erode the U.S. commitment to neutrality and isolationism?
4. How did Roosevelt manage to move the United States toward providing effective aid to Britain while slowly undercutting isolationist opposition?

5. Why was American so slow and reluctant to aid Jewish and other refugees from Nazi Germany? Would there have been effective ways to have helped European Jews before the onset of World War II?
6. The Spanish Civil War is often called "the dress rehearsal for World War II." To what degree is this description accurate? Could the United States and the other democratic powers have successfully prevented the fall of democratic Spain to Franco? Or might it have drawn them even earlier into a Europe-wide war?
7. Was American entry into World War II, with both Germany and Japan, inevitable? Is it possible the U.S. might have been able to fight either Germany or Japan, while avoiding armed conflict with the other?
8. How did the process of American entry into World War II compare with the way the country got into World War I (see Chapter 30). How were the Neutrality Acts aimed at the conditions of 1914–1917, and why did they prove ineffective under the conditions of the 1930s?
9. Argue for or against: America's foreign policy from 1933 to 1939 was fundamentally shaped by domestic issues and concerns, particularly the Great Depression.
10. Isolationists and hostile critics in 1940–1941, and even after World War II, charged Franklin Roosevelt with deliberately and sometimes deceitfully manipulating events and public opinion so as to lead the United States into war. What factual basis, if any, is there for such a charge? Which of Roosevelt's words and actions tend to refute it?

CHAPTER 35

America in World War II, 1941–1945

PART I: REVIEWING THE CHAPTER

A. Checklist of Learning Objectives

After mastering this chapter, you should be able to:

1. Indicate how America reacted to Pearl Harbor and prepared to wage war against both Germany and Japan.
2. Describe the mobilization of the American economy for war and the mobilization of manpower and womanpower for both the military and wartime production.
3. Describe the war's effects on American society, including regional migration, race relations, and women's roles.
4. Explain the early Japanese successes in East Asia and the Pacific, and the American strategy for countering them.
5. Describe the early Allied invasion of North Africa and Italy, the strategic tensions with the Soviet Union over the Second Front, and the invasion of Normandy in 1944.
6. Discuss FDR's successful 1944 campaign against Thomas Dewey for a fourth term and his controversial choice of a new vice president.
7. Explain the final military efforts that brought Allied victory in Europe and Asia and the significance of the atomic bomb.

B. Glossary

To build your social science vocabulary, familiarize yourself with the following terms.

1. **concentration camp** A place of confinement for prisoners or others a government considers dangerous or undesirable. "The Washington top command . . . forcibly herded them together in concentration camps. . . ."
2. ***bracero*** A Mexican farm laborer temporarily brought into the United States. "The *bracero* program outlived the war by some twenty years. . . ."
3. **U-boat** A German submarine (from the German *Unterseeboot*). "Not until the spring of 1943 did the Allies . . . have the upper hand against the U-boat."
4. **depose(d); deposition** Forcibly remove from office or position. "Mussolini was deposed, and Italy surrendered unconditionally soon thereafter."
5. **beachhead** The first position on a beach secured by an invading force and used to land further troops and supplies. "The Allied beachhead, at first clung to with fingertips, was gradually enlarged, consolidated, and reinforced."
6. **underground** A secret or illegal movement organized in a country to resist or overthrow the government. "With the assistance of the French 'underground,' Paris was liberated. . . ."

7. **acclamation** A general and unanimous action of approval or nomination by a large public body, without a vote. "He was nominated at Chicago on the first ballot by acclamation."

8. **bastion** A fortified stronghold, often including earthworks or stoneworks, that guards against enemy attack. ". . . the 101st Airborne Division had stood firm at the vital bastion of Bastogne."

9. **genocide** The systematic extermination or killing of an entire people. "The Washington government had long been informed about Hitler's campaign of genocide against the Jews. . . ."

10. **bazooka** A metal-tubed weapon from which armor-piercing rockets are electronically fired. "The enemy was almost literally smothered by bayonets, bullets, bazookas, and bombs."

PART II: CHECKING YOUR PROGRESS

A. True-False

Where the statement is true, circle **T**; where it is false, circle **F**.

1. T F America's major strategic decision in World War II was to attack Japan first, while holding off Hitler's Germany until later.

2. T F A substantial minority of Americans, particularly those of German, Japanese, and Italian descent, opposed American entry into World War II.

3. T F Government-run rationing and wage-price controls contributed to America's ability to meet the economic challenges of the war.

4. T F New sources of labor such as women and Mexican *braceros* helped overcome the human-resources shortage during World War II.

5. T F World War II stimulated massive black migration to the North and West and encouraged black demands for greater equality.

6. T F A majority of women who worked in wartime factories stayed in the labor force after the war ended.

7. T F American citizens at home had to endure serious economic deprivations during World War II.

8. T F The Japanese navy established its domination of the Pacific sea-lanes in the 1942 battles of Coral Sea and Midway.

9. T F The American strategy in the Pacific was to encircle Japan by flank movements from Burma and Alaska.

10. T F While their Soviet ally was still reeling from Hitler's invasion in the first years of the war, Britain and the United States bore the heaviest burden of Allied ground fighting and casualties.

11. T F By pushing for complete conquest and total destruction of the German government, the Allied policy of unconditional surrender guaranteed that Germany's economy and society would have to be rebuilt from the ground up after the war.

12. T F At the Teheran Conference in 1943, Stalin, Churchill, and Roosevelt planned the D-Day invasion and developed the final strategy for winning the war.

13. T F Liberal Democrats rallied to dump Vice President Henry Wallace from FDR's ticket in 1944 and replace him with Senator Harry S Truman.

14. T F Franklin Roosevelt's death caused a period of hesitation in the Allied war effort and raised German hopes of a negotiated settlement of the war.

15. T F The United States modified its demand for unconditional surrender by allowing Japan to keep its emperor, Hirohito.

B. Multiple Choice

Select the best answer and circle the corresponding letter.

1. The fundamental American strategic decision of World War II was to
   a. attack Germany and Japan simultaneously with equal force.
   b. concentrate naval forces in the Pacific and ground forces in Europe.
   c. attack Germany first, while using just enough strength to hold off Japan.
   d. attack Germany and Japan from the back door routes of North Africa and China.
   e. secure control of North Africa, the Middle East, and India so Germany and Japan could not unite their forces.
2. The major exception to the relatively good American civil liberties record during World War II was the harsh treatment of
   a. American fascist groups.
   b. native Hawaiians.
   c. Mexican Americans.
   d. German Americans.
   e. Japanese Americans.
3. Wartime inflation and shortages of crucial goods were kept partly in check by
   a. government price controls and rationing.
   b. government takeover of critical factories and railroads.
   c. special bonuses to farmers and workers to increase production.
   d. importation of additional fuel and food from Latin America.
   e. decreasing the money supply and releasing federal emergency stockpiles to the public.
4. The Bracero Program, created by the federal government during World War II, was aimed to
   a. encourage Mexican American women to join the work force by providing government child care.
   b. enable Mexican immigrants to take over the homes and farms of interned Japanese Americans.
   c. relieve the agricultural labor shortage by bringing in temporary workers from Mexico.
   d. counteract the growing tension between Latinos and Anglos in California and the Southwest.
   e. draft Latinos and American Indians into the military.
5. Compared to British and Soviet women during and after World War II, American women
   a. were less likely to work for wages in the wartime economy.
   b. worked more often in heavy-industry war plants.
   c. were a higher percentage of the nation's armed forces.
   d. were more ready to put their children into federally run child care.
   e. more often stayed in paid employment following the war's end.
6. The Fair Employment Practices Commission was designed to
   a. prevent discrimination against blacks in wartime industries.
   b. guarantee all regions of the country an opportunity to compete for defense contracts.
   c. prevent discrimination in employment against women.
   d. guarantee that those who had been unemployed longest would be the first hired.
   e. guarantee the right of workers to organize and strike if necessary.

7. The wartime migration of rural southern African Americans to northern and western urban factories was dramatically accelerated after the war by the invention of
   a. the cotton gin.
   b. the gasoline-powered mechanical combine.
   c. synthetic fibers, such as nylon, that largely replaced cotton cloth.
   d. television.
   e. the mechanical cotton picker.
8. Besides African Americans, another traditionally rural group, which used service in the armed forces as a springboard to postwar urban life was
   a. Scandinavian Americans.
   b. New England farmers.
   c. Indians.
   d. Japanese Americans.
   e. Mexican migrant laborers.
9. The 1942 battles of Bataan and Corregidor in the Philippines marked the beginning of
   a. Japanese conquest of key Pacific islands.
   b. the American comeback from the terrible defeat at Pearl Harbor.
   c. air warfare conducted from the decks of aircraft carriers.
   d. brutal tropical warfare in which atrocities were committed on both sides.
   e. the rebellion of Filipinos and others against cruel Japanese rule.
10. The essential American strategy in the Pacific called for
   a. securing bases in China from which to bomb the Japanese home islands.
   b. carrying the war into Southeast Asia from Australia and New Guinea.
   c. advancing on as broad a front as possible all across the Pacific.
   d. island hopping by capturing only the most strategic Japanese bases and bypassing the rest.
   e. seizing rapid control of islands near Japan so that the Japanese home islands could be bombed.
11. The U.S.–British demand for unconditional surrender of Germany and Japan was
   a. a sign of the Western Allies' confidence in its ultimate victory.
   b. designed to weaken Japan's and Germany's will to resist.
   c. a sign of the Western Allies' eagerness to reassure the Soviets in the absence of a Second Front.
   d. developed in close cooperation with the Soviet Union.
   e. aimed at encouraging German and Japanese dissidents to overthrow their governments.
12. The American conquest of Guam and other islands in the Marianas in 1944 was especially important because it
   a. halted the Japanese advance in the Pacific.
   b. was the first time that the United States had reconquered its own territories from Japanese rule.
   c. paved the way for the American reconquest of the Philippines.
   d. indicated that the Japanese would surrender without an invasion of the home island.
   e. made possible round-the-clock bombing of Japan from land bases.
13. The most difficult and brutal European fighting for American forces through most of 1943 occurred in
   a. France.
   b. Italy.
   c. North Africa.
   d. Belgium.
   e. the Philippines.

14. Hitler's last-ditch effort to stop the British and American advance in the west occurred at the Battle of
    a. Normandy.
    b. Château-Thierry.
    c. Rome.
    d. the Bulge.
    e. El Alamein.
15. The second American atomic bomb was dropped on the Japanese city of
    a. Nagasaki.
    b. Hiroshima.
    c. Kyoto.
    d. Okinawa.
    e. Tokyo.

C. Identification

Supply the correct identification for each numbered description.

1. __________ A U.S. minority that was forced into concentration camps during World War II
2. __________ A federal agency that coordinated U.S. industry and successfully mobilized the economy to produce vast quantities of military supplies
3. __________ __________ Women's units of the army and navy during World War II
4. __________ Government arrangement whereby substantial numbers of Mexican workers were temporarily brought into the United States to provide agricultural labor
5. __________ Symbolic personification of female laborers who took factory jobs in order to sustain U.S. production during World War II
6. __________ The federal agency established to guarantee opportunities for African American employment in World War II industries
7. __________ U.S.–owned Pacific archipelago seized by Japan in the early months of World War II
8. __________ Crucial naval battle of June 1942, in which U.S. Admiral Chester Nimitz blocked the Japanese attempt to conquer a strategic island near Hawaii
9. __________ Controversial U.S.–British demand on Germany and Japan that substituted for a second front
10. __________ Site of 1943 Roosevelt-Churchill conference in North Africa, at which the Big Two planned the invasion of Italy and further steps in the Pacific war
11. __________ Iranian capital where Roosevelt, Churchill, and Stalin met to plan D-Day in coordination with Russian strategy against Hitler in the East
12. __________ The beginning of the Allied invasion of France in June 1944
13. __________ The December 1944 German offensive that marked Hitler's last chance to stop the Allied advance
14. __________ __________ The last two heavily defended Japanese islands conquered by the United States near the end of World War II in 1945
15. __________ The top-secret project to develop the atomic bomb

D. Matching People, Places, and Events

Match the person, place, or event in the left column with the proper description in the right column by inserting the correct letter on the blank line.

1. ___ Henry J. Kaiser
2. ___ John L. Lewis
3. ___ A. Philip Randolph
4. ___ Erwin Rommel
5. ___ Jiang Jieshi (Chiang Kai-shek)
6. ___ Douglas MacArthur
7. ___ Chester W. Nimitz
8. ___ Dwight D. Eisenhower
9. ___ Winston Churchill
10. ___ Joseph Stalin
11. ___ Thomas E. Dewey
12. ___ Henry A. Wallace
13. ___ Harry S Truman
14. ___ Albert Einstein
15. ___ Hirohito

a. Commander of the Allied military assault against Hitler in North Africa and France

b. Japanese emperor who was allowed to stay on his throne, despite unconditional surrender policy

c. FDR's liberal vice president during most of World War II, dumped from the ticket in 1944

d. The Allied leader who constantly pressured the United States and Britain to open a second front against Hitler

e. Top German general in North Africa whose advance was finally halted at El Alamein by British General Montgomery

f. Leading American industrialist and shipbuilder during World War II

g. Commander of the U.S. Army in the Pacific during World War II, who fulfilled his promise to return to the Philippines

h. Inconspicuous former senator from Missouri who was suddenly catapulted to national and world leadership on April 12, 1945

i. Tough head of the United Mine Workers, whose work stoppages precipitated antistrike laws

j. Commander of the U.S. naval forces in the Pacific and brilliant strategist of the island-hopping campaign

k. Allied leader who met with FDR to plan strategy at Casablanca and Teheran

l. German-born physicist who helped persuade Roosevelt to develop the atomic bomb

m. Republican presidential nominee in 1944 who failed in his effort to deny FDR a fourth term

n. Head of the Brotherhood of Sleeping Car Porters whose threatened march on Washington opened job opportunities for blacks during World War II

o. U.S. ally who resisted Japanese advances in China during World War II

E. Putting Things in Order

Put the following events in correct order by numbering them from 1 to 4.

1. __________ The United States and Britain invade Italy and topple Mussolini from power.
2. __________ Japan surrenders after two atomic bombs are dropped.
3. __________ The United States enters World War II and begins to "fight Hitler first."
4. __________ The United States stops the Japanese advance in the Pacific and attacks Germany in North Africa.

F. Matching Cause and Effect

Match the historical cause in the left column with the proper effect in the right column by writing the correct letter on the blank line.

Cause

1. ___ The surprise Japanese attack at Pearl Harbor
2. ___ Fear that Japanese Americans would aid Japan in invading the United States
3. ___ Efficient organization by the War Production Board
4. ___ The mechanical cotton picker and wartime labor demand
5. ___ Women's role in wartime production
6. ___ American resistance in the Philippines and the Battle of the Coral Sea
7. ___ The American strategy of leapfrogging toward Japan
8. ___ The British fear of sustaining heavy casualties in ground fighting
9. ___ Conservative Democrats' hostility to liberal vice president Henry Wallace
10. ___ Japan's refusal to surrender after the Potsdam Conference in July 1945

Effect

a. Kept the Western Allies from establishing a second front in France until June 1944

b. Slowed the powerful Japanese advance in the Pacific in 1942

c. Enabled the United States to furnish itself and its allies with abundant military supplies

d. Enabled the United States to set up key bomber bases while bypassing heavily fortified Japanese-held islands

e. Drew millions of African Americans from the rural South to the urban North

f. Resulted in Senator Harry S Truman's becoming FDR's fourth-term running mate in 1944

g. Created a temporary, but not a permanent, transformation in gender roles for most women

h. Caused innocent American citizens to be rounded up and put in concentration camps

i. Created a strong sense of American national unity during World War II

j. Led the United States to drop the atomic bomb on Hiroshima in August 1945

G. Developing Historical Skills

Reading Maps for Routes and Strategy

In order to understand the events and strategies of war, careful reading of military maps is essential. Attention to the routes and dates of the Allied armies, presented in the map of *World War II in Europe and North Africa, 1939–1945* on p. 893, will help you grasp the essentials of Allied strategy and the importance of the postponement of the second front in the west, as described in the text. Answer the following questions.

1. Where were (a) the Russians and (b) the Western Allies Britain and America each fighting in January and February of 1943?

2. Approximately where were the central Russian armies when the British and Americans invaded Sicily?

3. Approximately where were the central Russian armies when the British and Americans invaded Normandy in June 1944?

4. It took approximately ten months for the British and Americans to get from the Normandy beaches to the Elbe River in central Germany. How long did it take the Russians to get from Warsaw to Berlin?

5. Besides north-central Germany, where else did the British, American, and Russian invasion routes converge? From what two countries were the British and Americans coming? From what country was the southern Russian army coming?

H. Map Mastery

Map Discrimination

Using the maps and charts in Chapter 35, answer the following questions.

1. *Internal Migration in the United States During World War II*: During World War II, what was the approximate net migration of civilian population from the East to the West? (Net migration is the number of westward migrants minus the number of those who moved east.)

2. *Internal Migration in the United States During World War II*: Of the nine fastest-growing cities during the 1940s, how many were located in the West and South? (Consider Washington, D.C., as a southern city.)

3. *Internal Migration in the United States During World War II*: Which were the two fastest-growing cities in the North?

4. *United States Thrusts in the Pacific, 1942–1945*: Which two of the following territories were not wholly or partially controlled by Japan at the height of Japanese conquest: India, the Philippines, Australia, Netherlands Indies, Thailand, and New Guinea?

5. *World War II in Europe and North Africa, 1939–1945*: From which North African territory did the Allies launch their invasion of Italy?

6. *World War II in Europe and North Africa, 1939–1945*: As the Russian armies crossed into Germany from the east, which three Axis-occupied East European countries did they move through?

7. *World War II in Europe and North Africa, 1939–1945*: As the Western Allied armies crossed into Germany from the west, which three Axis-occupied West European countries did they liberate and move through? (Do not count Luxembourg.)

8. *World War II in Europe and North Africa, 1939–1945*: Along which river in Germany did the Western Allied armies meet the Russians?

Map Challenge

Using the maps of both the Pacific (p. 888) and European (p. 893) theaters in World War II, write an essay explaining the principal movements of Allied armies and navies in relation to the principal Allied strategies of the war determined in the ABC–1 agreement and the various wartime exchanges and meetings among American, British, and Soviet leaders.

PART III: APPLYING WHAT YOU HAVE LEARNED

1. What effects did World War II have on the American economy? What role did American industry and agriculture play in the war?
2. What role did American women play during World War II? Why did the war prove to be ultimately less of a turning point in the advancement of women's full equality than some expected or hoped?
3. Most Americans, and the United States government, now regard the internment of Japanese Americans during World War II as an injustice and unnecessary. Why was there so little opposition to it at the time?
4. Ever since World War II, historians and other scholars have commonly spoken of "postwar American society." How was American society different after the war from before? Were these changes all direct or indirect results of the war, or would many have occurred without it?
5. How did the United States and its allies develop and carry out their strategy for defeating Italy, Germany, and Japan?
6. The text says that the American and British demand for unconditional surrender was actually a sign of weakness. Why? What were the effects of this policy, both during and after the war? Would there have been any benefits to permitting the Germany government to survive in some form, without Hitler? Was the agreement to permit Hirohito to remain as emperor of Japan as wise decision?
7. What were the costs of World War II, and what were its effects on America's role in the world?
8. Compare America's role in World War I—domestically, militarily, and diplomatically—with its role in World War II (see Chapter 30). What accounts for the differences in America's participation in the two wars?
9. Examine the controversy over the atomic bomb in the context of the whole conduct of World War II on both sides. Is it correct to say that the bomb did not mark a change in the character of warfare against civilians, but only its scope? Despite the larger casualties in other bombings, why did the bombings of Hiroshima and Nagasaki stir a greater concern?
10. World War II has sometimes been called "the good war." Is this an accurate label? Why or why not?

CHAPTER 36

The Cold War Begins, 1945–1952

PART I: REVIEWING THE CHAPTER

A. Checklist of Learning Objectives

After mastering this chapter, you should be able to:

1. Explain the causes and consequences of the post–World War II economic boom.
2. Describe the large postwar migrations to the Sunbelt and the suburbs.
3. Explain changes in American society and culture brought about by the baby boom.
4. Explain the origin and causes of the emerging conflict between the United States and the Soviet Union after Germany's defeat and Truman's accession to the presidency.
5. Describe the early U.S.-Soviet Cold War conflicts over Germany and Eastern Europe, and explain why the United Nations proved largely ineffectual in addressing them.
6. Discuss the American theory and practice of containment, as reflected in the Truman Doctrine, the Marshall Plan, and NATO.
7. Describe the concern about Soviet spying and communist subversion within the United States and the increasing climate of fear it engendered.
8. Describe the expansion of the Cold War to East Asia, including the Chinese communist revolution and the Korean War.

B. Glossary

To build your social science vocabulary, familiarize yourself with the following terms.

1. **gross national product** The total value of a nation's annual output of goods and services. "Real gross national product (GNP) slumped sickeningly in 1946 and 1947. . . ."
2. **agribusiness** Farming and related activities considered as commercial enterprises, especially large corporate agricultural ventures. ". . . consolidation produced giant agribusinesses able to employ costly machinery."
3. **population curve** The varying size and age structure of a given nation or other group, measured over time. "This boom-or-bust cycle of births begot a bulging wave along the American population curve."
4. **precinct** The smallest subdivision of a city, as it is organized for purposes of police administration, politics, voting, and so on. "He then tried his hand at precinct-level Missouri politics. . . ."
5. **protégé** Someone under the patronage, protection, or tutelage of another person or group. "Though a protégé of a notorious political machine in Kansas City, he had managed to keep his own hands clean."

6. **superpower** One of the two overwhelmingly dominant international powers after World War II—the United States and the Soviet Union. "More specific understandings among the wartime allies—especially the two emerging superpowers—awaited the arrival of peace."

7. **exchange rates** The ratios at which the currencies of two or more countries are traded, which express their values relative to one another. ". . . the International Monetary Fund (IMF) [was established] to encourage world trade by regulating currency exchange rates."

8. **underdeveloped** Economically and industrially deficient. "They also founded the International Bank for Reconstruction and Development . . . to promote economic growth in war-ravaged and underdeveloped areas."

9. **military occupation** The holding and control of a territory and its citizenry by the conquering forces of another nation. ". . . Germany had been divided at war's end into four military occupation zones. . . ."

10. **containment** In international affairs, the blocking of another nation's expansion through the application of military and political pressure short of war. "Truman's piecemeal responses . . . took on intellectual coherence in 1947, with the formulation of the 'containment doctrine.' "

11. **communist-fronter** One who belongs to an ostensibly independent political, economic, or social organization that is secretly controlled by the Communist party. ". . . he was nominated . . . by . . . a bizarre collection of disgruntled former New Dealers . . . and communist-fronters."

12. **Politburo** The small ruling executive body that controlled the Central Committee of the Soviet Communist party, and hence dictated the political policies of the Soviet, Chinese, and other Communist parties (from "Political Bureau"). "This so-called Pied Piper of the Politburo took an apparently pro-Soviet line. . . ."

13. **perimeter** The outer boundary of a defined territory. ". . . Korea was outside the essential United States defense perimeter in the Pacific."

PART II: CHECKING YOUR PROGRESS

A. True-False

Where the statement is true, circle **T**; where it is false, circle **F**.

1. T F The American consumer economy began to grow dramatically as soon as World War II ended, during the years 1945 to 1950.

2. T F The postwar economic boom was especially fueled by military spending and cheap energy.

3. T F The enormous American population migrations of the immediate postwar era strengthened the traditional family and inter-generational forms of child-rearing.

4. T F The economic and population growth of the Sunbelt occurred because the South relied less than the North did on federal government spending for its economic well-being.

5. T F In the decades after World War II most big American cities became heavily populated by minorities, while the new suburbs were almost entirely white.

6. T F Government housing policies played a role in creating a high degree of residential segregation in the cities and new suburbs.

7. T F The inexperienced new president Harry S Truman relied heavily on his advisors and often dodged responsibility for difficult decisions.

8. T F The new United Nations proved more effective than the old League of Nations because its effective power was concentrated in the Security Council, made up of the great powers.

9. T F The Soviet Union wanted to build a strong, neutral German state after World War II, while the Western Allies feared a Nazi revival and sought a weak or divided Germany.

10. T F The Truman Doctrine was initiated in response to threatened Soviet gains in Iran and Afghanistan.

11. T F The Marshall Plan was developed primarily as a response to the possible Soviet military invasion of Western Europe.

12. T F The fundamental purpose of NATO was to end the historical feuds among the European nations of Britain, France, Italy, and Germany.

13. T F The postwar hunt for communist subversion was supposedly aimed at rooting out American communists from positions in government and teaching.

14. T F Truman defeated Dewey in 1948 partly because of the deep splits within the Republican party that year.

15. T F Truman fired General MacArthur because MacArthur wanted to expand the Korean War and publicly criticized the president for refusing to use nuclear weapons against China.

B. Multiple Choice

Select the best answer and circle the corresponding letter.

1. Besides giving educational benefits to returning veterans, the Servicemen's Readjustment Act of 1944 (the GI Bill of Rights) was partly intended to
   a. prevent returning soldiers from flooding the job market.
   b. provide American colleges with a new source of income.
   c. keep the GIs' military skills in high readiness for the Cold War.
   d. help to slow down the inflationary economy that developed at the end of World War II.
   e. make sure that veterans' benefits were spent on education rather than on scarce housing.
2. Perhaps the greatest beneficiaries of the post–World War II economic boom were
   a. the industrial inner cities.
   b. farm laborers.
   c. labor unions.
   d. women.
   e. Mexican Americans.
3. Among the primary causes of the long postwar economic expansion were
   a. foreign investment and international trade.
   b. military spending and cheap energy.
   c. labor's wage restraint and the growing number of small businesses.
   d. government economic planning and investment.
   e. low bank interest rates and foreign investment.

4. The two regions that gained most in population and new industry in the postwar economic expansion were the
   a. Pacific Northwest and New England.
   b. Northeast and South.
   c. Midwest and West.
   d. Southeast and Appalachia.
   e. South and West.
5. The federal government played a large role in the growth of the Sunbelt through
   a. federal subsidies to southern and western agriculture.
   b. its policies supporting civil rights and equal opportunity for minorities.
   c. its lower-costs housing loans to veterans who would settle in that region.
   d. its financial support of the aerospace and defense industries.
   e. its promotion of high energy costs that drove people away from the cold-weather North.
6. Among the federal policies that contributed to the huge postwar migration from the inner cities to the suburbs were
   a. civil rights laws guaranteeing integrated housing in the suburbs.
   b. public housing and Social Security.
   c. military and public-works spending.
   d. direct subsidies to homebuilders for planned suburban communities.
   e. housing-mortgage tax deductions and federally built highways.
7. The postwar baby-boom population expansion contributed to the
   a. sharp rise in elementary school enrollments in the 1970s.
   b. strains on the Social Security system in the 1950s.
   c. popular youth culture of the 1960s.
   d. expanding job opportunities of the 1980s.
   e. more rapid growth of multi-unit rental housing compared with home ownership.
8. Among President Harry Truman's most valuable qualities as a leader was his
   a. considerable experience in international affairs.
   b. personal courage, authenticity, and sense of responsibility for big decisions.
   c. intolerance of pettiness or corruption among his subordinates.
   d. patience and willingness to compromise with honest critics.
   e. willingness to hand over responsibility for big decisions to his cabinet members.
9. Which of the following was *not* among the causes of the Cold War between the United States and the Soviet Union?
   a. The Americans and Soviets had both been relatively isolated from world affairs before World War II.
   b. The U.S. call for an open world clashed with the Soviets' insistence on controlling a sphere of interest in Eastern Europe.
   c. The Soviets supported an end to European colonialism in the Third World, while the Americans helped their Allies put down colonial rebellions.
   d. The Americans and Soviets both had a missionary ideology that tried to spread their ideas to other nations.
   e. The Soviets were resentful of America's slowness in opening a second front and abrupt cancellation of lend-lease.

10. Which of the following was *not* among the successful achievements of the new United Nations?
    a. Preserving peace in Iran, Kashmir, and other world places of crisis
    b. Guiding former European colonies to independence
    c. Creating the new Jewish state of Israel
    d. Controlling atomic energy and containing the spread of nuclear weapons
    e. Promoting international health, science, and education
11. A crucial early development of the Cold War occurred when
    a. Germany was divided into an East Germany under Soviet control and a pro-American West Germany.
    b. American and Soviet forces nearly engaged in armed clashes in Austria.
    c. the Soviets crushed anticommunist rebellions in Poland and Hungary.
    d. the pro-Soviet French and Italian Communist parties attempted revolutions against their own governments.
    e. the Soviet Union announced that it would seek to develop atomic bombs and nuclear missiles.
12. The NATO alliance represented an historic departure from traditional American foreign policy because it
    a. departed from the principles of the Monroe Doctrine.
    b. committed the United States to guaranteeing the permanent subordination of Germany.
    c. gave command of American soldiers to officers from other countries.
    d. meant establishing military bases outside the territory of the continental United States.
    e. committed the United States to a permanent military alliance with other nations.
13. The Truman Doctrine originally developed because of the dangerous communist threat to
    a. Turkey and Greece.
    b. France and West Germany.
    c. Iran and Afghanistan.
    d. Poland and Hungary.
    e. Korea and Japan.
14. Senator Joseph McCarthy's anticommunist crusade was first directed primarily against
    a. Soviet spies inside the United States.
    b. potential internal Communist party takeovers of France and Italy.
    c. the Chinese communists.
    d. the alleged employment of American communists by the United States government.
    e. local school boards that employed atheist and homosexual teachers.
15. President Harry Truman fired General Douglas MacArthur from his command of American forces in East Asia because
    a. MacArthur had bungled the invasion of Inchon.
    b. MacArthur refused to accept the idea of American forces being under United Nations control.
    c. MacArthur wanted to widen the Korean War by bombing Communist China and publicly criticized the president.
    d. MacArthur was effectively seizing power as the military dictator of South Korea.
    e. Truman learned that MacArthur was planning to run against him for the presidency in 1952.

C. Identification

Supply the correct identification for each numbered description.

1. __________ Popular name for the Servicemen's Readjustment Act that provided education and economic assistance to former soldiers

2. __________ Shorthand name for the southern and western regions of the United States that experienced the highest rates of growth after World War II

3. __________ New York suburb where postwar builders pioneered the techniques of mass home construction

4. __________ Term for the dramatic rise in U.S. births that began immediately after World War II

5. __________ Big Three wartime conference that later became the focus of charges that Roosevelt had sold out Eastern Europe to the Soviet communists

6. __________ The extended post–World War II confrontation between the United States and the Soviet Union that stopped just short of a shooting war

7. __________ Meeting of Western Allies during World War II that established the economic structures to promote recovery and enhance FDR's vision of an open world

8. __________ New international organization that experienced some early successes in diplomatic and cultural areas but failed in areas like atomic arms control

9. __________ Allied-organized judicial tribunal that convicted and executed top Nazi leaders for war crimes

10. __________ American-sponsored effort that provided substantial funds for the economic relief and recovery of Western Europe

11. __________ The new anti-Soviet organization of Western nations that ended the long-time American tradition of not joining permanent military alliances

12. __________ Jiang Jieshi's (Chiang Kai-shek's) pro-American forces, which lost the Chinese civil war to Mao Zedong's (Mao Tse-tung's) communists in 1949

13. __________ Key U.S. government memorandum that militarized American foreign policy and indicated national faith in the economy's capacity to sustain large military expenditures

14. __________ U.S. House of Representatives committee that took the lead in investigating alleged procommunist agents such as Alger Hiss

15. __________ The dividing line between North and South Korea, across which the fighting between communists and United Nations forces ebbed and flowed during the Korean War

D. Matching People, Places, and Events

Match the person, place, or event in the left column with the proper description in the right column by inserting the correct letter on the blank line.

1. ___ Benjamin Spock
2. ___ Hermann Goering
3. ___ Joseph Stalin
4. ___ Julius and Ethel Rosenberg
5. ___ Jiang Jieshi (Chiang Kai-shek)
6. ___ George F. Kennan

a. Top Nazi official who committed suicide after being convicted in war-crimes trials

b. Physician who provided advice on child rearing to baby-boomers' parents after World War II

c. Young California congressman whose investigation of Alger Hiss spurred fears of communist influence in

7. ___ Mao Zedong (Mao Tse-tung)
8. ___ George C. Marshall
9. ___ J. Robert Oppenheimer
10. ___ Reinhold Niebuhr
11. ___ Richard Nixon
12. ___ Joseph McCarthy
13. ___ Henry A. Wallace
14. ___ Strom Thurmond
15. ___ Douglas MacArthur

America

d. Chinese Nationalist leader whose corrupt and ineffective government fell to communist rebels in 1949

e. Originator of a massive program for the economic relief and recovery of devastated Europe

f. American military commander in Korea fired by President Harry Truman

g. Former vice president of the United States whose 1948 campaign as a pro-Soviet liberal split the Democratic Party

h. Leading American theologian who advocated Christian realism and the use of force if necessary to maintain justice against Nazi or Stalinist evil

i. Wisconsin senator whose charges of communist infiltration of the U.S. government deepened the anti-red atmosphere of the early 1950s

j. Former scientific director of the Manhattan Project who joined Albert Einstein in opposing development of the hydrogen bomb

k. The tough leader whose violation of agreements in Eastern Europe and Germany helped launch the Cold War

l. Leader of the Chinese Communists whose revolutionary army seized power in China in 1949

m. Americans convicted and executed for spying and passing atomic secrets to the Soviet Union

n. Southern segregationist who led Dixiecrat presidential campaign against Truman in 1948

o. Brilliant U.S. specialist on the Soviet Union and originator of the theory that U.S. policy should be to contain the Soviet Union

E. Putting Things in Order

Put the following events in correct order by numbering them from 1 to 5.

1. ________ The threatened communist takeover of Greece prompts a presidential request for aid and a worldwide effort to stop communism.
2. ________ The collapse of Jiang Jieshi's (Chiang Kai-shek's) corrupt government means victory for Mao Zedong's (Mao Tse-tung's) communists and a setback for U.S. policy in Asia.
3. ________ A new president takes charge of American foreign policy amid growing tension between America and its ally, the Soviet Union.
4. ________ A "give-'em-hell" campaign by an underdog candidate overcomes a three-way split in his own party and defeats his overconfident opponent.
5. ________ Communists go on the offensive in a divided Asian nation, drawing the United States into a brutal and indecisive war.

F. Matching Cause and Effect

Match the historical cause in the left column with the proper effect in the right column by writing the correct letter on the blank line.

Cause

1. ___ Cheap energy, military spending, and rising productivity
2. ___ The mechanization and consolidation of agriculture
3. ___ Job opportunities, warm climates, and improved race relations
4. ___ White flight to the suburbs
5. ___ The post–World War II baby boom
6. ___ The American airlift to West Berlin
7. ___ The British withdrawal from communist-threatened Greece
8. ___ The threat of Soviet invasion or U.S. isolationist withdrawal from Europe
9. ___ General MacArthur's reform-oriented rule of occupied Japan
10. ___ Mao Zedong's (Mao Tse-tung's) defeat of Jiang Jieshi (Chiang Kai-shek)

Effect

a. Caused an era of unprecedented growth in American prosperity from 1950 to 1970
b. Drew millions of white and black Americans to the Sunbelt after World War II
c. Led to the proclamation of the Truman Doctrine and hundreds of millions of dollars in aid for anticommunist governments
d. Led to the organization of the permanent NATO alliance
e. Caused the rise of big commercial agribusiness and spelled the near-disappearance of the traditional family farm
f. Aroused Republican charges that Democrats Truman and Acheson had lost China
g. Broke a Soviet ground blockade and established American determination to resist further Soviet advance

h. Left America's cities heavily populated by racial minorities

i. Led to the firm establishment of Japanese democracy and the beginnings of a great Japanese economic advance

j. Caused much school building in the 1950s, a youth culture in the 1960s, and a growing concern about aging in the 1980s

G. Developing Historical Skills

Reading a Bar Graph

Read the bar graph of *National Defense Budget* on p. 914 and answer the following questions.

1. In what census year, after World War II, did the defense budget first decline as a percentage of the federal budget and a percentage of GNP?

2. In what census year, after 1960, was the defense budget the same fraction of GNP as it was in 1950?

3. Which decade, after World War II, saw the largest increase in actual dollar outlays for defense?

4. By approximately what percentage of the federal budget did the defense budget increase from 1950 to 1960? By roughly what percentage did it decrease from 1970 to 1980? By what percentage did it increase from 1980 to 1990? By about what percentage did it decrease from 1990 to 1999?

H. Map Mastery

Map Discrimination

Using the maps and charts in Chapter 36, answer the following questions.

1. *Postwar Partition of Germany*: Which of the Big Four had the smallest occupation zone in postwar Germany?

2. *Postwar Partition of Germany*: Which of the three Western occupation zones was closest to Berlin?

3. *Postwar Partition of Germany*: Which two other nations did the American occupation zone border on?

4. *The Shifting Front in Korea*: When General MacArthur attacked at Inchon, did he land above or below the thirty-eighth parallel?

5. *The Shifting Front in Korea*: Besides China, what other nation bordering North Korea presented a potential threat to American forces?

6. *The Shifting Front in Korea*: After the armistice—signed on July 27, 1953—which of the two Koreas had made very slight territorial gains in the Korean War?

Map Challenge

Using the map of *Distribution of Population Increase, 1950–2005* on p. 916, write an essay explaining the differences in the regional impact of post–World War II migration and population growth from 1950 to 2005. What states and regions exhibited exceptions to the general patterns of growth?

PART III: APPLYING WHAT YOU HAVE LEARNED

1. Why did the American economy soar from 1950 to 1970? How did this new, widely distributed affluence alter the American way of life?
2. Describe how the population movements from the Northeast to the Sunbelt, and from inner cities to the suburbs, altered major features of American society as well as its center of gravity. Which of these two migrations do you regard as the more significant, and why?
3. What were the immediate conflicts and deeper causes that led the United States and the Soviet Union to go from being allies to bitter Cold War rivals?
4. Explain the steps that led to the long-term involvement of the United States in major overseas military commitments and expenditures, including NATO and the Korean War. How did expanding military power and the Cold War affect American society and its ideas?
5. Discuss President Harry Truman's role as a leader in both international and domestic affairs from 1945 to 1952. Does Truman deserve to be considered a great president? Why or why not?
6. Why did World War II—unlike World War I—lead to a permanent end to American isolationism (see Chapter 30)?

7. Was the spread of nuclear weapons from the United States to the Soviet Union, and then to other nations, simply inevitable once the technology was known? How, if at all, could nuclear proliferation have been prevented?

8. Why did America's growing international struggle against the Soviet Union so quickly lead to a fear of communist subversion within the United States. Would it have been possible to have rationally tried to stop Soviet spying without creating an indiscriminate witch hunt? To what extent was the anticommunist crusade really concerned about American national security, and to what extent was it simply persecuting people perceived as different?

9. Compared to the total victory and unconditional surrender of World War II, the Korean War led to a frustrating stalemate and armed hostile peace. What made Korea a different sort of war? Why was MacArthur's claim that "there is no substitute for victory" problematic in the case of Korea?

10. Was the early Cold War primarily an ideological crusade of democracy against international communism and its totalitarian ideas, or was it essentially an American defense of its national security and economic interests against the direct threat of the Soviet Union? Support your answer by considering some of the key events of the early Cold War, including the Korean War.

CHAPTER 37

The Eisenhower Era, 1952–1960

PART I: REVIEWING THE CHAPTER

A. Checklist of Learning Objectives

After mastering this chapter, you should be able to:

1. Describe the changes in the American consumer economy in the 1950s and their relationship to the rise of popular mass culture.
2. Describe the Republicans' return to power under Eisenhower and the rise and decline of McCarthyism.
3. Trace the emergence of the civil rights movement in the 1950s and its initial impact on American race relations and the nation's image abroad.
4. Describe the practice of Eisenhower Republicanism in the 1950s, including domestic consequences of the Cold War.
5. Outline the Eisenhower-Dulles approach to the Cold War and the nuclear arms race with the Soviet Union.
6. Indicate how Eisenhower's foreign policy was implemented in Vietnam, the Middle East, and Cuba.
7. Describe the issues and outcome of the tight Kennedy-Nixon presidential campaign of 1960.
8. Summarize the major changes in American culture in the 1950s, including the rise of Jewish, southern, and African American writers and playwrights.

B. Glossary

To build your social science vocabulary, familiarize yourself with the following terms.

1. **Pentecostal** A family of Protestant Christian churches that emphasize a "second baptism" of the holy spirit, speaking in tongues, faith healing, and intense emotionalism in worship. "'Televangelists' like the Baptist Billy Graham, the Pentecostal Holiness preacher Oral Roberts."
2. **McCarthyism** The practice of making sweeping, unfounded charges against innocent people with consequent loss of reputation, job, and so on. "But 'McCarthyism' has passed into the English language as a label for the dangerous forces of unfairness. . . ."
3. **universalism** The belief in the fundamental moral and social unity of humankind, and its transcendence of particular national or local cultural differences " . . . published a bestseller in 1943, *One World*, which advocated a new postwar era of racially-blind universalism."
4. **taboo** A social prohibition or rule that results from strict tradition or convention. ". . . Warren shocked the president and other traditionalists with his active judicial intervention in previously taboo social issues."

5. **sheikdom** Small, traditional tribal territory ruled by a **sheik**, an hereditary Arab chieftain. "The poor, sandy sheikdoms increasingly resolved to reap for themselves the lion's share of the enormous oil wealth. . . ."

6. **jury tampering** The felony of bribing, threatening, or otherwise interfering with the autonomous deliberations and decisions of a jury. "Convicted of jury tampering, Hoffa served part of his sentence before disappearing without a trace. . . ."

7. **secondary boycott** A boycott of goods, aimed not at the employer or company directly involved in a dispute but at those who do business with that company. "The new law also prohibited 'secondary boycotts' and certain kinds of picketing."

8. **thermonuclear** Concerning the heat released in nuclear fission; specifically, the use of that heat in hydrogen bombs. "Thermonuclear suicide seemed nearer in July 1958. . . ."

9. **confiscation** The seizure of property by a public authority, often as a penalty. "Castro retaliated with further wholesale confiscations of Yankee property. . . ."

10. **iconoclastic** Literally, a breaking of sacred images; hence, by extension, any action that assaults ideas or principles held in reverence or high regard. "Gore Vidal penned . . . several impish and always iconoclastic works. . . ."

PART II: CHECKING YOUR PROGRESS

A. True-False

Where the statement is true, circle **T**; where it is false, circle **F**.

1. T F The growth of aerospace industries in the 1950s meant the continued expansion of blue collar jobs and a rise in union membership.

2. T F The rise of television and other forms of mass entertainment in the 1950s undermined the cultural influence of religion and religious leaders.

3. T F Senator Joseph McCarthy's great power and capacity to destroy careers finally collapsed when he attacked the U.S. Army.

4. T F The effective use of television by the Eisenhower-Nixon campaign in 1952 demonstrated the power of the new medium to bypass older political structures.

5. T F The Supreme Court ruled in *Brown* v. *Board of Education* that black schools had to receive additional funding in order to guarantee that racially separate education would be truly equal.

6. T F Martin Luther King, Jr., argued that the civil rights movement needed to cast aside the influence of the traditionally conservative African American churches.

7. T F President Eisenhower and Secretary of State John Foster Dulles's Cold War strategy was to expand conventional weapons and troop deployments in Western Europe in order to contain the Soviet Union.

8. T F In the Suez crisis of 1956, the United States backed the French and British invasion of Egypt in order to guarantee the flow of oil from the Middle East.

9. T F The Soviet launch of the Sputnik satellite in 1957 fueled criticism of the American educational system and led to federal funding for advancing the sciences and foreign languages.

10. T F The Paris summit conference of 1960 between President Eisenhower and Soviet premier Khrushchev signaled the first major thaw in the Cold War.

11. T F The strict American embargo on all trade with Cuba was precipitated by Castro's confiscation of American property for his land reform program.

12. T F Senator Kennedy was able to successfully neutralize the issue of his Roman Catholicism during the 1960 campaign.

13. T F In his foreign policies, Dwight Eisenhower attempted to avoid threats to peace without the extensive use of American military power.

14. T F World War II sparked a great literary outpouring of sober, realistic novels about the realities of warfare.

15. T F Post–World War II American literature was enriched by African American novelists like Ralph Ellison and Jewish novelists like Saul Bellow.

B. Multiple Choice

Select the best answer and circle the corresponding letter.

1. A key economic transformation of the 1950s was the
   a. displacement of large corporations by smaller entrepreneurial businesses.
   b. decline in the percentage of women in the paid labor force.
   c. turn from World War II military and defense industries to civilian production.
   d. replacement of mass consumer production by targeted marketing aimed at particular segments of the population.
   e. growth of white collar office jobs that increasingly replaced blue collar factory labor.
2. During the 1950s, a majority of American women were
   a. working in blue-collar factory or service jobs.
   b. married, raising children, and not employed outside the home.
   c. pursuing training and education to prepare them for the new high technology positions.
   d. agitating for federal child care and other assistance to enable them to assume a larger place in the work force.
   e. single, divorced, or widowed.
3. The primary force shaping the new consumerism and mass popular culture of the 1950s was
   a. the computer.
   b. erotic magazines like *Playboy*.
   c. television.
   d. evangelical Protestantism.
   e. sports.
4. In the 1952 Republican presidential campaign, the war hero Dwight Eisenhower stayed above the battle and left the task of attacking Democratic candidate Governor Adlai E. Stevenson as soft on Communism to
   a. Senator Joseph McCarthy.
   b. vice presidential candidate Senator Richard Nixon.
   c. General Douglas MacArthur.
   d. future Secretary of State John Foster Dulles.
   e. Governor Earl Warren of California.

5. As president, Eisenhower enjoyed great popularity by presenting a leadership style of
   a. reassurance, sincerity, and optimism.
   b. aggressiveness, boldness, and energy.
   c. political shrewdness, economic knowledge, and hands-on management.
   d. vision, imagination, and moral leadership.
   e. charisma, vigor, and charm.
6. The Korean War ended with
   a. an agreement to unify and neutralize Korea.
   b. a peace treaty that provided for withdrawal of American and Chinese forces from Korea.
   c. an American and South Korean military victory.
   d. a stalemated armistice and the continued hostile division of North and South Korea.
   e. the withdrawal of all American and Chinese troops from the Korean peninsula.
7. President Eisenhower's fundamental attitude and policy toward Senator Joseph McCarthy was
   a. to tolerate McCarthy's attacks on Democrats, but prevent him from having influence within the Eisenhower administration.
   b. public distance from McCarthyism, but private admiration for McCarthy himself.
   c. to attack McCarthy as a threat to civil liberties and American traditions of fairness.
   d. private loathing, but public unwillingness to challenge McCarthy's power.
   e. to develop a U.S. Army plan to destroy McCarthy's power through televised hearings.
8. The precipitating event that led to the rise of Dr. Martin Luther King, Jr. as the most prominent civil rights leader was the
   a. lynching of Emmett Till.
   b. Little Rock school crisis.
   c. Montgomery bus boycott.
   d. passage of the 1957 Civil Rights Act.
   e. lunch counter sit-in movement.
9. European criticism of widespread American racism and segregation was especially strengthened in the 1950s by
   a. black soldiers' attacks on the U.S. government when stationed in Europe.
   b. Soviet and American Communists' attacks on U.S. racial attitudes.
   c. the Supreme Court's decisions upholding segregated schools.
   d. U.S. government mistreatment of black artists like Paul Robeson and Josephine Baker.
   e. the prohibition on black participation in major league sports.
10. Martin Luther King, Jr.'s own civil rights organization, the SCLC, rested on the institutional foundation of
   a. black businesses.
   b. labor unions.
   c. black colleges.
   d. northern philanthropic foundations.
   e. black churches.
11. President Dwight Eisenhower's basic approach to domestic economic policy was to
   a. seek to overturn the Democratic New Deal.
   b. propose major new federal social programs.
   c. turn most New Deal programs over to the states.
   d. trim back some New Deal programs but keep most in place.
   e. make business and labor equal partners with government in maintaining a strong economy.

12. During the Suez crisis of 1956, President Eisenhower used America's great oil power to
    a. break the power of the new OPEC organization of petroleum-producing states.
    b. force the Arab nationalist Nasser to back down from his seizure of the Suez Canal.
    c. force Britain, France, and Israel to withdraw their troops from Egypt.
    d. guarantee that the United States would not become dependent on Middle Eastern oil.
    e. prop up pro-American Arab monarchies in Saudi Arabia and Iraq.
13. The United States first became involved in Vietnam by
    a. providing economic aid to the democratic Vietnamese government of Ngo Dinh Diem.
    b. providing economic aid to the French colonialists fighting Ho Chi Minh.
    c. providing aid to Ho Chi Minh in his fight against the French colonialists.
    d. sending American bombers to defend the French at Dien Bien Phu.
    e. supporting Chinese Nationalists in their attempt to regain power in China.
14. Senator John F. Kennedy's principal issue against Vice President Richard Nixon in the campaign of 1960 was that
    a. as a Catholic, he would better be able to deal with Catholic Latin America.
    b. the United States should seek a nuclear disarmament agreement with the Soviets.
    c. the United States had fallen behind the Soviet Union in prestige and power.
    d. the Eisenhower administration had failed to work hard enough for desegregation.
    e. Nixon was a cynical political opportunist who might abuse power if he became president.
15. One major breakthrough in American literature in the early post–World War II years was
    a. the realistic depiction of war and industrial poverty.
    b. angry social criticism of the American dream.
    c. satirical and comic novels by Jewish writers.
    d. an optimistic vision of nature and love in the work of American poets and playwrights.
    e. a literary renaissance among Latino writers and playwrights.

C. Identification

Supply the correct identification for each numbered description.

1. __________ Term for making ruthless and unfair charges against opponents, such as those leveled by a red-hunting Wisconsin senator in the 1950s

2. __________ Supreme Court ruling that overturned the old *Plessy* v. *Ferguson* principle that black public facilities could be "separate but equal"

3. __________ The doctrine upon which Eisenhower and Dulles based American nuclear policy in the 1950s

4. __________ Nonviolent direct action, led by Martin Luther King, Jr., that launched the civil rights movement into major prominence

5. __________ The British-and-French-owned waterway whose nationalization by Egyptian President Nasser triggered a major Middle East crisis

6. __________ A soviet scientific achievement that set off a wave of American concern about Soviet superiority in science and education

7. __________ Swedish scholar Gunnar Myrdal's powerful book highlighting the conflict between America's high democratic ideals and its treatment of its black citizens

8. __________ High-flying American spy plane, whose downing in 1960 destroyed a summit and heightened Cold War tensions

9. __________ The Eisenhower administration's massive roundup and deportation of nearly a million illegal Mexican immigrants in 1954

10. __________ Betty Friedan's 1963 book that launched a revolution against the suburban cult of domesticity that reigned in the 1950s

D. Matching People, Places, and Events

Match the person, place, or event in the left column with the proper description in the right column by inserting the correct letter on the blank line.

1. ___ Dwight D. Eisenhower
2. ___ Joseph R. McCarthy
3. ___ Earl Warren
4. ___ Martin Luther King, Jr.
5. ___ Ho Chi Minh
6. ___ Ngo Dinh Diem
7. ___ Betty Friedan
8. ___ Adlai E. Stevenson
9. ___ Billy Graham
10. ___ James R. Hoffa
11. ___ John Foster Dulles
12. ___ Nikita Khrushchev
13. ___ Fidel Castro
14. ___ Richard Nixon
15. ___ John F. Kennedy

a. Eloquent Democratic presidential candidate who was twice swamped by a popular Republican war hero

b. Anticommunist leader who set up a pro-American government to block Ho Chi Minh's expected takeover of all Vietnam

c. Latin American revolutionary who became economically and militarily dependent on the Soviet Union

d. Eisenhower's tough-talking secretary of state who wanted to roll back communism

e. Red-hunter turned world-traveling diplomat who narrowly missed becoming president in 1960

f. Black minister whose 1955 Montgomery bus boycott made him the leader of the civil rights movement

g. The soldier who kept the nation at peace for most of his two terms and ended up warning America about the military-industrial complex

h. Popular religious evangelical who effectively used the new medium of television

i. Youthful politician who combined television appeal with traditional big-city Democratic politics to squeak out a victory in 1960

j. Blustery Soviet leader who frequently challenged Eisenhower with both threats and diplomacy

k. Reckless and power-hungry demagogue who intimidated even President Eisenhower before his bubble burst

l. A Vietnamese nationalist and communist whose defeat of the French led to calls for American military intervention in Vietnam

m. Writer whose 1963 book signaled the beginnings of more extensive feminist protest

n. Tough Teamster-union boss whose corrupt actions helped lead to passage of the Landrum-Griffin Act

o. Controversial jurist who led the Supreme Court into previously off-limits social and racial issues

E. Putting Things in Order

Put the following events in correct order by numbering them from 1 to 5.

1. __________ Major crises in Eastern Europe and the Middle East create severe challenges or Eisenhower's foreign policy.
2. __________ An American plane is downed over the Soviet Union, disrupting a summit and rechilling the Cold War.
3. __________ Eisenhower refuses to use American troops to prevent a communist victory over a colonial power in Asia.
4. __________ Eisenhower orders federal troops to enforce a Supreme Court ruling over strong resistance from state officials.
5. __________ Eisenhower's meeting with Soviet leader Khrushchev marks the first real sign of a thaw in the Cold War.

F. Matching Cause and Effect

Match the historical cause in the left column with the proper effect in the right column by writing the correct letter on the blank line.

Cause

1. ___ Joseph McCarthy's attacks on the U.S. Army
2. ___ *Brown* v. *Board of Education*
3. ___ Governor Orval Faubus's use of the National Guard to prevent integration
4. ___ The 1956 Hungarian revolt
5. ___ The Communist Vietnamese victory over the French in 1954
6. ___ Nasser's nationalization of the Suez Canal

Effect

a. Set off massive resistance to integration in most parts of the Deep South

b. Led to continuing nuclear tests and the extension of the arms race

c. Caused the United States to begin backing an anticommunist regime in South Vietnam

d. Created widespread resentment of the United States in parts of the Western Hemisphere

7. ___ The fears of both the United States and the Soviet Union that the other nation was gaining a lead in rocketry and weapons
8. ___ The mistreatment of American black artists like Paul Robeson and Josephine Baker and their own protests
9. ___ American intervention in Latin America and support for anti-communist dictators in that region
10. ___ Kennedy's television glamour and traditional political skills

e. Forced Secretary of State Dulles to abandon his plans to roll back communism
f. Exposed the senator's irresponsibility and brought about his downfall
g. Forced President Eisenhower to send federal troops to Little Rock
h. Led to increasingly harsh international criticism of America's racial policies.
i. Enabled the Democrats to win a narrow electoral victory in 1960
j. Led to the 1956 British-French-Israeli invasion of Egypt

G. Developing Historical Skills

Comparing and Interpreting Election Maps

Carefully read and compare the maps for the elections of 1952 (p. 949) and 1960 (p. 965). Answer the following questions.

1. Which was the only non-southern (border) state to vote for both the Democrats Stevenson in 1952 and Kennedy in 1960?

2. Which three southern states (states of the old Confederacy) voted for Republicans, Eisenhower in 1952 and Nixon in 1960?

3. Which was the only southern (former Confederate) state to switch from Republican (Eisenhower) in 1952 to Democratic (Kennedy) in 1960? Which was the only border state to switch from Republican in 1952 to Democratic in 1956?

4. How many more electoral votes did Kennedy get in the West (counting Hawaii, but not counting Texas) in 1960 than Stevenson got in the same region in 1952?

5. How many electoral votes did Kennedy win in 1960 from southern states that Stevenson also carried in 1952? (Note the divided electoral vote in one state.)

PART III: APPLYING WHAT YOU HAVE LEARNED

1. In what ways was the Eisenhower era a time of caution and conservatism, and in what ways was it a time of dynamic economic, social, and cultural change?
2. American blacks had suffered and often protested segregation and discrimination since the end of Reconstruction, but without result. Why did the civil rights movement finally began to gain public attention and influence in the 1950s?
3. Besides *Brown* v. *Board of Education* and the Montgomery bus boycott, which were the most important breakthroughs in civil rights and race relations of the late 1940s and 1950s?
4. How did Eisenhower balance assertiveness and restraint in his foreign policies in Vietnam, Europe, and the Middle East?
5. How did such an irresponsible figure as Senator Joseph McCarthy gain enormous power for a brief period of time in the early 1950s, and then rapidly fall into powerlessness and disgrace? Was McCarthy a unique phenomenon of that time playing on Americans' Cold Wars fears, or could such a witch-hunting atmosphere return with another such leader?
6. What were the dynamics of the Cold War with the Soviet Union in the 1950s, and how did Eisenhower and Khrushchev combine confrontation and conversation in their relationship?
7. How did America's far-flung international responsibilities shape the U.S. economy and society in the Eisenhower era? Was the American way of life fundamentally altered by the nation's new superpower status, or did it remain largely sheltered from world affairs?
8. How did television and other innovations of the consumer age affect American politics, society, and culture in the 1950s?
9. Despite widespread power and affluence, the 1950s were often described as an "age of anxiety." What were the major sources of anxiety and conflict that stirred beneath the surface of the time? Could they have been addressed more effectively by Eisenhower and other national leaders? Why or why not?
10. Argue for or against: American politics, society, and culture in the 1950s were all stagnant and narrow, and did not address the real social problems facing the country.

CHAPTER 38

The Stormy Sixties, 1960–1968

PART I: REVIEWING THE CHAPTER

A. Checklist of Learning Objectives

After mastering this chapter, you should be able to:

1. Describe the high expectations stirred by Kennedy's New Frontier and his limited success in achieving his domestic objectives.
2. Analyze the theory of Kennedy's doctrine of flexible response to communist challenges around the world and its dangerous application in Vietnam.
3. Describe Johnson's succession to the presidency in 1963, his electoral landslide over Goldwater in 1964, and his Great Society successes of 1965.
4. Discuss the course of the black movement of the 1960s, from civil rights to Black Power.
5. Outline the steps by which Johnson led the United States deeper into the Vietnam quagmire.
6. Explain how the Vietnam War brought turmoil to American society and eventually drove Johnson and the divided Democrats from power in 1968.
7. Describe the youthful cultural rebellions of the 1960s in the United States and around the world, and indicate which of their features quickly faded and which endured.

B. Glossary

To build your social science vocabulary, familiarize yourself with the following terms.

1. **free world** During the Cold War, the noncommunist democracies of the Western world, as opposed to the communist states. "But to the free world the 'Wall of Shame' looked like a gigantic enclosure around a concentration camp."
2. **nuclear proliferation** The spreading of nuclear weapons to nations that have not previously had them. "Despite the perils of nuclear proliferation or Soviet domination, de Gaulle demanded an independent Europe. . . ."
3. **exile** A person who has been banished or driven from her or his country by the authorities. "He had inherited . . . a CIA-backed scheme to topple Fidel Castro from power by invading Cuba with anticommunist exiles."
4. **peaceful coexistence** The principle or policy that communists and noncommunists—specifically, the United States and the Soviet Union—ought to live together without trying to dominate or destroy each other. "Kennedy thus tried to lay the foundations for a realistic policy of peaceful coexistence with the Soviet Union."
5. **détente** In international affairs, a period of relaxed agreement in areas of mutual interest. "Here were the modest origins of the policy that later came to be known as 'détente.' "

6. **sit-in** A demonstration in which people occupy a facility for a sustained period to achieve political or economic goals. "Following the wave of sit-ins that surged across the South. . . ."

7. **establishment** The ruling inner circle of a nation and its principal institutions. "Goldwater's forces had . . . rid[den] roughshod over the moderate Republican 'eastern establishment.'"

8. **literacy test** A literacy examination that a person must pass before being allowed to vote. "Ballot-denying devices like the poll tax, literacy tests, and barefaced discrimination still barred black people from the political process."

9. **ghetto** The district of a city where members of a religious or racial minority are forced to live, either by legal restriction or by informal social pressure. (Originally, ghettoes were enclosed Jewish districts in Europe.) ". . . a bloody riot exploded in Watts, a black ghetto in Los Angeles."

10. **black separatism** The doctrine that blacks in the United States ought to separate themselves from whites, either in separate institutions or in a separate political territory. ". . . Malcolm X trumpeted black separatism. . . ."

11. **hawk** During the Vietnam War, someone who favored vigorous prosecution or escalation of the conflict. "If the United States were to cut and run from Vietnam, claimed prowar 'hawks,' other nations would doubt America's word. . . ."

12. **dove** During the Vietnam War, someone who opposed the war and favored de-escalation or withdrawal by the United States. "New flocks of antiwar 'doves' were hatching daily."

13. **militant** In politics, someone who pursues political goals in a belligerent way, often using paramilitary means. "Other militants . . . shouted obscenities. . . ."

14. **dissident** Someone who dissents, especially from an established or normative institution or position. ". . . Spiro T. Agnew [was] noted for his tough stands against dissidents and black militants."

15. **coattails** In politics, the ability of a popular candidate at the top of a ticket to transfer some of his or her support to lesser candidates on the same ticket. "Nixon was . . . the first president-elect since 1848 not to bring in on his coattails at least one house of Congress. . . ."

PART II: CHECKING YOUR PROGRESS

A. True-False

Where the statement is true, circle **T**; where it is false, circle **F**.

1. T F Kennedy's pledge to land a man on the moon by the end of the 1960s was primarily an attempt to restore America's damaged prestige in the missile-and-space race with the Soviet Union.

2. T F The Kennedy doctrine of flexible response was applied primarily to the effort to contain potential Soviet expansion into central and western Europe.

3. T F The successful U.S.-supported coup against the corrupt Diem regime in South Vietnam enabled a more democratic South Vietnamese government to take a stronger role in defeating the Communist Viet Cong.

4. T F Kennedy financed and trained the Cuban rebels involved in the Bay of Pigs invasion, but refused to intervene directly with American troops or planes when their invasion failed.

5. T F The Soviets' humiliation in the Cuban missile crisis resulted in Khrushchev's ouster and a new round of military competition between the United States and the Soviet Union.

6. T F Even after Martin Luther King's civil rights demonstrators were viciously attacked in Birmingham in 1963, President Kennedy stayed aloof and urged restraint and caution by African American leaders.

7. T F Johnson passed his major Great Society legislation like Medicare and Medicaid only by compromising with Republicans and conservative southern Democrats in Congress.

8. T F The Gulf of Tonkin Resolution authorized the president to respond to naval attacks but kept the power to make war in Vietnam firmly in the hands of Congress.

9. T F Johnson's Great Society immigration reforms ended the discriminatory quotes in place since the 1920s and opened America's doors to millions of immigrants from Asia and Latin America.

10. T F The culmination of the nonviolent civil rights movement was the passage of the Civil Rights Act of 1964 and the Voting Rights Act of 1965.

11. T F The urban riots of the late 1960s demonstrated that the South had vehemently resisted the civil rights movement's efforts to integrate southern schools and neighborhoods.

12. T F The insurgent antiwar campaigns of Senators Eugene McCarthy and Robert Kennedy forced Johnson to withdraw as a presidential candidate and de-escalate the Vietnam War.

13. T F The bitter Democratic divisions over Vietnam enabled Richard Nixon to win the presidency with a minority of popular votes and no clear policy mandate.

14. T F The youth rebellion of the 1960s and the political crisis of 1968 were caused by the unique events and conditions in the United States at that time.

15. T F One major American institution largely unaffected by the cultural upheaval of the 1960s was the conservative Roman Catholic Church.

B. Multiple Choice

Select the best answer and circle the corresponding letter.

1. President Kennedy's New Frontier proposals for increased federal educational aid and medical assistance to the elderly
   a. succeeded because of his skill in legislative bargaining.
   b. were traded away in exchange for passage of the bill establishing the Peace Corps.
   c. were stalled by strong opposition in Congress from Republicans and southern Democrats.
   d. were strongly opposed by business interests.
   e. were essentially abandoned because of Kennedy's concentration on foreign policy.
2. The industry that engaged in a bitter conflict with President Kennedy over price increases was the
   a. airline industry.
   b. health care industry.
   c. steel industry.
   d. oil industry.
   e. banking industry.

3. The fundamental strategic and military policy pursued by the Kennedy administration was to
    a. develop a flexible response to fighting brushfire wars in the Third World.
    b. threaten massive nuclear retaliation against any communist advances.
    c. build up heavy conventional armed forces in Western Europe against the threat of a Soviet invasion.
    d. provide military assistance to client states in the Third World so that they could fight proxy wars without the need of American forces.
    e. arm and train rebels to overthrow the Soviet puppet regimes in Eastern Europe.
4. The Kennedy administration suffered a major foreign policy disaster when
    a. Middle East governments sharply raised the price of imported oil.
    b. American-backed Cuban rebels were defeated by Castro's Cuban army at the Bay of Pigs.
    c. Khrushchev forced the United States to remove its missiles from Turkey during the Cuban missile crisis.
    d. American Green Beret guerrilla forces began suffering heavy casualties in the jungles of Vietnam.
    e. Britain and France both withdrew from NATO and developed their own nuclear forces.
5. The Cuban missile crisis ended when
    a. the American-backed Cuban invaders were defeated at the Bay of Pigs.
    b. the United States agreed to allow Soviet missiles in Cuba as long as they were not armed with nuclear weapons.
    c. Nikita Khrushchev was overthrown, and the new Soviet leader Brezhnev called for an end to the nuclear arms race.
    d. the United States and the Soviet Union agreed that Cuba should become neutral in the Cold War.
    e. the Soviets agreed to pull all missiles out of Cuba and the United States agreed not to invade Cuba.
6. The Kennedy administration was pushed into taking a stronger stand on civil rights by
    a. the civil rights movement, led by the Freedom Riders and Martin Luther King, Jr.
    b. realizing the political advantages of enabling blacks to vote.
    c. pressure from foreign governments and the United Nations.
    d. the threat of violent race riots in northern cities.
    e. civic and business leaders who saw racial conflict as disruptive to the economy.
7. One major reason why Lyndon Johnson won an overwhelming landslide victory in the 1964 election was that
    a. he repudiated many of the policies of the unpopular Kennedy administration.
    b. he promised to take a tough stand in opposing communist aggression in Vietnam.
    c. he successfully portrayed Republican candidate Senator Barry Goldwater as a trigger-happy extremist.
    d. Johnson had achieved considerable personal popularity with the electorate.
    e. his economic plans promised to deliver the nation from hard economic times.
8. President Johnson was more successful than President Kennedy in pushing economic and civil rights reforms through Congress because
    a. he was better at explaining the purposes of the laws in his speeches.
    b. the Democrats gained overwhelming control of Congress in the landslide of 1964.
    c. Republicans were more willing to cooperate with Johnson than with Kennedy.
    d. Johnson was better able to swing southern Democrats behind his proposals.
    e. he was not distracted by foreign policy crises in Vietnam and Latin America.

9. The Civil Rights Act of 1965 guaranteed
   a. desegregation in interstate transportation.
   b. job opportunities for African Americans.
   c. desegregation of high schools and colleges.
   d. voting rights for African Americans.
   e. equal opportunity in housing and an end to discriminatory real estate practices.
10. Which of the following was *not* among Lyndon Johnson's Great Society achievements?
   a. Federal aid to education
   b. Civil rights and voting rights for blacks
   c. Federally funded medical care for the elderly and the poor
   d. Clean water and clean air legislation
   e. Immigration liberalization and reform
11. Which of the following was *not* among the political problems that the Johnson administration faced in waging the Vietnam War?
   a. Growing doubts among some within the administration itself about the wisdom of the war
   b. Strong opposition from world opinion and many of America's allies
   c. Political opposition and draft resistance inside the United States
   d. The weakness and corruption of frequently changing South Vietnamese governments
   e. The threat that some South Vietnamese government would simply ask the Americans to leave
12. Opposition to the Vietnam War in Congress was centered in the
   a. House Foreign Affairs Committee.
   b. Senate Armed Services Committee.
   c. Republican leadership of the House and Senate.
   d. Senate Foreign Relations Committee.
   e. New York congressional delegation led by Senator Robert Kennedy.
13. The two antiwar candidates whose strong political showing forced Johnson to withdraw from the 1968 presidential race were
   a. Nelson Rockefeller and Ronald Reagan.
   b. Eugene McCarthy and Robert Kennedy.
   c. J. William Fulbright and George McGovern.
   d. George Wallace and Curtis LeMay.
   e. Richard Nixon and Spiro Agnew.
14. Which of the following was *not* among the political upheavals and crises that occurred around the world in 1968?
   a. The anticommunist uprising against Fidel Castro's rule in Cuba.
   b. The Prague spring revolt in Czechoslovakia and its crushing by Soviet tanks
   c. French student and worker revolts that nearly overthrew the French government
   d. The student rebellions at Columbia University and many other American campuses
   e. The antiwar political campaigns of Senators Eugene McCarthy and Robert Kennedy
15. One dominant theme of the 1960s youth culture that had deep roots in American history was
   a. conflict between the generations.
   b. distrust and hostility toward authority.
   c. the widespread use of mind-altering drugs.
   d. a positive view of sexual experimentation.
   e. interracial collaboration and marriage.

C. Identification

Supply the correct identification for each numbered description.

1. __________ Kennedy administration program that sent youthful American volunteers to work in underdeveloped countries
2. __________ High barrier between East and West, erected during the 1961 Berlin crisis
3. __________ Shorthand term for Kennedy administration's policies aimed at "getting America moving again"
4. __________ An attempt to provide American aid for democratic reform in Latin America that met with much disappointment and frustration
5. __________ Site where anti-Castro guerrilla forces failed in their U.S.-sponsored invasion
6. __________ Tense confrontation between Kennedy and Khrushchev that nearly led to nuclear war in October 1962
7. __________ Civil rights demonstrators who sought to desegregate public facilities like bus stations by traveling through the South
8. __________ LBJ's broad program of welfare legislation and social reform that swept through Congress in 1965
9. __________ The 1964 congressional action that became a blank check for the Vietnam War
10. __________ Law, spurred by Martin Luther King, Jr.'s march from Selma to Montgomery, that guaranteed rights originally given blacks under the Fifteenth Amendment
11. __________ Racial slogan that signaled a growing challenge to King's nonviolent civil rights movement by militant younger blacks
12. __________ The Vietnamese New Year celebration, during which the communists launched a heavy offensive against the United States in 1968
13. __________ Brief, dramatic war between Israel and neighboring Arab states that led to Israeli conquest and control of the Palestinian West Bank and Gaza
14. __________ Student organization that moved from nonviolent protest to underground terrorism within a few years
15. __________ Site of an off-duty police raid in 1969 that spurred gay and lesbian activism

D. Matching People, Places, and Events

Match the person, place, or event in the left column with the proper description in the right column by inserting the correct letter on the blank line.

1. ___ John F. Kennedy
2. ___ Robert S. McNamara
3. ___ Nikita Khrushchev
4. ___ Martin Luther King, Jr.
5. ___ Lyndon B. Johnson
6. ___ Barry M. Goldwater
7. ___ James Meredith

a. First black student admitted to the University of Mississippi, shot during a civil rights march in 1966

b. Cabinet officer who promoted flexible response, but came to doubt the wisdom of the Vietnam War he had presided over

8. ___ Malcolm X
9. ___ J. William Fulbright
10. ___ Eugene J. McCarthy
11. ___ Robert F. Kennedy
12. ___ Richard M. Nixon
13. ___ George C. Wallace
14. ___ Hubert Humphrey
15. ___ Allen Ginsberg

c. New York senator whose antiwar campaign for the presidency was ended by an assassin's bullet in June 1968

d. Former vice president who staged a remarkable political comeback to win presidential election in 1968

e. Charismatic Black Muslim leader who promoted separatism in the early 1960s

f. Minnesota senator whose antiwar Children's Crusade helped force Johnson to alter his Vietnam policies

g. Chair of the Senate Foreign Relations Committee and leader of congressional opposition to the Vietnam War

h. Nonviolent black leader whose advocacy of peaceful change came under attack from militants after 1965

i. Vice president whose loyalty to LBJ's Vietnam policies sent him down to defeat in the 1968 presidential election

j. Charismatic president whose brief administration experienced domestic stalemate and foreign confrontations with communism

k. Third-party candidate whose conservative, hawkish 1968 campaign won 9 million votes and carried five states

l. Aggressive Soviet leader whose failed gamble of putting missiles in Cuba cost him his job

m. Beat poet of the 1950s whose hostility to materialism and establishment values helped lay groundwork for 1960s counterculture

n. Conservative Republican whose crushing defeat opened the way for the liberal Great Society programs

o. Brilliant legislative operator whose domestic achievements in social welfare and civil rights fell under the shadow of his Vietnam disaster

E. Putting Things in Order

Put the following events in correct order by numbering them from 1 to 5.

1. ___________ A southern Texas populist replaces a Harvard-educated Irish American in the White House.
2. ___________ An American-sponsored anticommunist invasion of Cuba fails.
3. ___________ Kennedy successfully risks nuclear confrontation to thwart Khrushchev's placement of Russian missiles in Cuba.
4. ___________ A candidate running on a peace platform obtains a congressional blank check for subsequent expanded military actions against the Communist Vietnamese.
5. ___________ Communist military assaults, political divisions between hawks and doves, and assassinations of national leaders form the backdrop for a turbulent election year.

F. Matching Cause and Effect

Match the historical cause in the left column with the proper effect in the right column by writing the correct letter on the blank line.

Cause

1. ___ Kennedy's unhappiness with the corrupt Diem regime
2. ___ Khrushchev's placement of missiles in Cuba
3. ___ Johnson's landslide victory over Goldwater in 1964
4. ___ The Gulf of Tonkin Resolution
5. ___ Martin Luther King, Jr.'s civil rights marches
6. ___ Angry discontent in northern black ghettos
7. ___ American escalation of the Vietnam War
8. ___ The communist Vietnamese Tet Offensive in 1968
9. ___ Senator Eugene McCarthy's strong antiwar campaign
10. ___ The deep Democratic Party divisions over Vietnam

Effect

a. Pushed Johnson into withdrawing as a presidential candidate in 1968

b. Brought ever-rising American casualties and a strengthened will to resist on the part of the communist Vietnamese

c. Led to a U.S.-encouraged coup and greater political instability in South Vietnam

d. Helped push through historic civil rights legislation in 1964 and 1965

e. Brought along huge Democratic congressional majorities that passed a fistful of Great Society laws

f. Helped Nixon win a minority victory over his divided opposition

g. Became the questionable legal basis for all of Johnson's further escalation of the Vietnam War

h. Led to a humiliating defeat when Kennedy forced the Soviet Union to back down

i. Sparked urban riots and the growth of the militant Black Power movement

j. Led to an American military request for 200,000 more troops as well as growing public discontent with the Vietnam War

G. Developing Historical Skills

Interpreting Line Graphs

Read the line graph of *Poverty in the United States* on p. 987 carefully and answer the following questions.

1. In what year did the number of people below the poverty line return to approximately the same level it had been at in 1964?

2. In what two years did the percentage of the American population below the poverty line reach its lowest point since 1960?

3. Between what years did the absolute numbers of people below the poverty line rise slightly at the same time those in poverty declined slightly as a percentage of the total population? What would explain this difference?

4. The number of people in poverty in 1966 was about the same as the number in poverty in which subsequent year?

H. Map Mastery

Map Discrimination

Using the maps and charts in Chapter 38, answer the following questions.

1. *Vietnam and Southeast Asia*: Besides North Vietnam, which two other Southeast Asian countries bordered on South Vietnam?

2. *Presidential Election of 1964*: How many electoral votes did Barry Goldwater win outside the Deep South in 1964?

3. *Presidential Election of 1968*: What four northeastern states did Nixon carry in 1968?

4. *Presidential Election of 1968*: Which five states outside the Northeast did Humphrey carry in 1968? (One of them is not in the continental United States.)

Map Challenge

After pushing through Congress the Civil Rights Act of 1964 and the Voting Rights Act of 1965, President Lyndon Johnson is said to have remarked that as a result "the Democratic party will lose the South for at least an entire generation." Using the electoral maps of the five elections of 1952, 1960, 1964, and 1968 (pp. 949, 965, 986, and 996 in Chapters 37 and 38), write a brief essay describing the changing fortunes of the Republican and Democratic parties in different regions of the country from 1952 to 1968. To what extent did the emerging pattern of dramatically shifting party loyalties in 1964 and 1968 suggest that Johnson may have been right. Are there any other factors that may help explain these changes?

PART III: APPLYING WHAT YOU HAVE LEARNED

1. What successes and failures did Kennedy's New Frontier experience at home and abroad?
2. President Kennedy's pledge to "land a man on the moon in this decade," which was successfully fulfilled by the Apollo moon landing in 1969, was a dramatic assertion of America's global power and technological leadership of the world. How important was the space program to the New Frontier, and to America's image of itself? Did the Apollo project and the moon landing still retain its luster after Vietnam and the social upheavals of the 1960s?
3. Compare and contrast Kennedy and Johnson as presidential leaders in the 1960s. Why did Kennedy come to be remembered so fondly by many Americans, and Johnson not, even though Kennedy's accomplishments in office were very slim compared to Johnson's enormous Great Society achievements?
4. What led the United States to become so deeply involved in the Vietnam War? (See Chapters 36 and 37 for background on the Cold War, anticolonialism, and earlier events in Vietnam.)
5. How did the civil rights movement move from its difficult beginnings in the 1950s and early 1960s to great successes in 1964–1965. Why did it encounter increasing criticism and opposition from both black militants and the forces of white backlash (represented by George C. Wallace) so soon after its greatest triumphs?
6. Compare and contrast Martin Luther King, Jr., and Malcolm X as black leaders. Was the emphasis on black pride and self-determination that Malcolm represented really opposed to King's ideals, or did it just address a different set of problems more deeply rooted in northern ghettos than in southern segregation? Why did so many blacks—and whites—begin to criticize King's emphasis on absolute nonviolence in the freedom struggle?
7. Why did the Vietnam War, and the domestic opposition to it, come to dominate American politics in the 1960s?

8. In later decades, many historians came to interpret the upheavals of 1968, in the United States and elsewhere around the world, as the end of the postwar era. Is this an accurate interpretation? Why did authority of all kinds—and not just political authority—come under assault in this period?

9. When the Democratic party tore itself apart over the Vietnam War and other issues in the late 1960s, the winner proved to be the forces of an emerging conservatism led by Richard Nixon and George Wallace. How and why did conservatism emerge so rapidly from the seemingly devastating Goldwater defeat in the election of 1964?

10. What, if anything, was valuable about the radical social movements of the 1960s, such as those led by Students for a Democratic Society? What was most destructive and negative? Did such movements have any long-term impact?

11. How was the cultural upheaval of the 1960s related to the political and social changes of the decade? Is the youth rebellion best seen as a response to immediate events, or as a consequence of such longer-term forces as the population bulge and economic prosperity? What were the long-term results of the counterculture in all its varieties?

CHAPTER 39

The Stalemated Seventies, 1968–1980

PART I: REVIEWING THE CHAPTER

A. Checklist of Learning Objectives

After mastering this chapter, you should be able to:

1. Describe Nixon's foreign policy in relation to Vietnam, the Soviet Union, and Communist China.
2. Analyze Nixon's domestic policies, his opposition to the "Warren Court," his southern strategy, and his landslide victory against George McGovern in 1972.
3. Examine the political and economic tensions created by the secret bombing of Cambodia, the American withdrawal from Vietnam, and the first Arab oil embargo.
4. Discuss the Watergate scandals, Nixon's resignation, and Ford's unelected presidency.
5. Explain the closely intertwined economic, energy, and Middle East crises of the 1970s and why both Republican and Democratic administrations were unable to address them successfully.
6. Describe the racial tensions of the 1970s, especially over school busing and affirmative action.
7. Discuss the rise of second-wave feminism in the United States and elsewhere, and the conservative resistance to it that blocked the Equal Rights Amendment.
8. Indicate how Jimmy Carter's outsider presidency fell into political disarray, culminating in the Iranian hostage crisis humiliation.

B. Glossary

To build your social science vocabulary, familiarize yourself with the following terms.

1. **moratorium** A period in which economic or social activity is suspended, often to achieve certain defined goals. "Antiwar protestors staged a massive national Vietnam moratorium in October 1969. . . ."
2. **Marxism** The doctrines of Karl Marx, advocated or followed by worldwide communist parties and by some democratic socialists. "The two great communist powers . . . were clashing bitterly over their rival interpretations of Marxism."
3. **anti-ballistic missile** A defensive missile designed to intercept and destroy an offensive missile in flight. "The first major achievement was an anti-ballistic missile (ABM) treaty. . . ."
4. **devaluation** In economics, steps taken to reduce the purchasing power of a given unit of currency in relation to foreign currencies. " . . . he next stunned the world by taking the United States off the gold standard and devaluing the dollar."
5. **foray** a single, defined movement or attack by a military unit. "The most disturbing feature of these sky forays. . . ."

6. **Kremlin** The extensive palace complex in Moscow that houses the Soviet (Russian) government; hence, a shorthand term for the Soviet or Russian government. "Believing that the Kremlin was poised to fly combat troops to the Suez area. . . ."

7. **attorney general** The presidentially appointed head of the Department of Justice and chief legal officer of the federal government. ". . . firing his own special prosecutor . . . as well as his attorney general and deputy attorney general. . . ."

8. **executive privilege** In American government, the claim that certain information known to the president or the executive branch of government should be unavailable to Congress or the courts because of the principle of separation of powers. " . . . the Supreme Court unanimously ruled that "executive privilege" gave him no right to withhold evidence. . . ."

9. **recession** A moderate and short-term economic downturn, less severe than a depression. (Economists define a recession as two consecutive quarters: that is, six months, of declining gross domestic product.) "Lines of automobiles at service stations lengthened as tempers shortened and a business recession deepened."

10. **born-again** The evangelical Christian belief in a spiritual renewal or rebirth, involving a personal experience of conversion and a commitment to moral transformation. ". . . this born-again Baptist touched many people with his down-home sincerity."

11. **balance of payments** The net ratio, expressed as a positive or negative sum, of a nation's exports in relation to its imports. (It may be calculated in relation to one particular foreign nation, or to all foreign states collectively.) "The soaring bill for imported oil plunged America's balance of payments deeply into the red. . . ."

12. **commando** Member of a small, elite military force trained to carry out difficult missions, often inside territory controlled by the enemy. "A highly trained commando team penetrated deep into Iran's sandy interior."

PART II: CHECKING YOUR PROGRESS

A. True-False

Where the statement is true, circle **T**; where it is false, circle **F**.

1. T F Nixon's Vietnamization policy was aimed at bringing an immediate negotiated end to the Vietnam War.

2. T F The roaring inflation of the 1970s was fundamentally caused by President Johnson's decision to fight the Vietnam War and fund the Great Society programs without raising taxes to pay for them.

3. T F Nixon's 1970 invasion of Cambodia provoked vehement domestic protests and intensified political clashes between hawks and doves.

4. T F Nixon's and Kissinger's diplomacy attempted to play the Soviet Union and China off against each other in order to enhance America's position in Vietnam and elsewhere.

5. T F The Warren Supreme Court's decisions on sexual freedom, rights of accused criminals, and school prayer stirred fierce attacks by President Nixon and political conservatives.

6. T F Nixon consistently opposed a greater federal government role in environmental protection and worker safety issues.

7. T F The burning issue in the 1972 Nixon-McGovern campaign was inflation and the management of the economy.

8. T F Congress initially supported President Nixon's bombing campaign against Cambodia as the only way to save South Vietnam from defeat.

9. T F The 1973 Paris agreement on Vietnam provided for a cease-fire and American withdrawal but did not really end the civil war among the Vietnamese.

10. T F The 1973 Arab-Israeli War and OPEC-led rise in the price of oil greatly accelerated the inflation that began in the wake of the Vietnam War.

11. T F Republican leaders in Congress strenuously opposed Nixon's resignation and urged him to fight to stay in office even after the Watergate tapes were released.

12. T F President Gerald Ford immediately set out to reverse the Nixon-Kissinger policy of détente toward the Soviet Union.

13. T F The feminist movement's successes in advancing women's economic and educational opportunities culminated in the passage of the Equal Rights Amendment (ERA).

14. T F President Carter's declaration that America's problems were due to a "moral and spiritual crisis" aroused strong public support for his proposals to decrease dependency on Middle Eastern oil.

15. T F The Iranian revolution against the pro-American shah brought the United States into a bitter confrontation with the new, militant Muslim leaders of that country.

B. Multiple Choice

Select the best answer and circle the corresponding letter.

1. Which of the following was *not* a cause of the growing economic slowdown and crises of the 1970s?
   a. Lyndon Johnson's refusal to raise taxes to pay for the Vietnam War and the Great Society
   b. The declining productivity of the average American worker
   c. The growth in tariffs and trade barriers between the United States and Europe
   d. Sharply rising oil prices and the end of America's energy independence
   e. The competitive advantage of modern German and Japanese manufacturers compared to older American technologies
2. The essential principle of President Nixon's Vietnamization policy was that
   a. the United States would accept a unified but neutral Vietnam.
   b. the United States would escalate the war in Vietnam but withdraw from Cambodia and Laos.
   c. the United States would gradually withdraw ground troops, while supporting the South Vietnamese war effort.
   d. the United States would seek a negotiated settlement of the war.
   e. China would restrain North Vietnamese aggression, while the United States withdrew from South Vietnam.
3. The antiwar movement exploded dramatically in 1970 when
   a. the massacre of civilians at My Lai by some U.S. soldiers was revealed.
   b. Nixon ordered further bombing of North Vietnam.
   c. the communist Vietnamese staged their Tet Offensive against American forces.
   d. Nixon ordered an invasion of Cambodia.
   e. several U.S. army units refused to continue fighting.

4. President Nixon and Secretary of State Kissinger successfully pressured the Soviet Union into making diplomatic deals with the United States by
   a. playing the China card by opening U.S. diplomacy and trade with the Soviets' rival communist power.
   b. using American economic aid as an incentive for the Soviets.
   c. threatening to attack Soviet allies such as Cuba and Vietnam.
   d. drastically increasing spending on nuclear weapons and missiles.
   e. building an anti-ballistic missile system that effectively neutralized the Soviet nuclear threat.
5. The Supreme Court came under sharp political attack in the 1970s, especially because of its rulings on
   a. antitrust laws and labor rights.
   b. voting rights and election laws.
   c. foreign trade and business regulation.
   d. environmental laws and immigrants' rights.
   e. criminal defendants' rights and prayer in public schools.
6. The most controversial element of Nixon's Philadelphia Plan was
   a. its guarantees of women's equal right to employment in the construction trades.
   b. the extension of affirmative action to promote the employment of minorities and women as social groups rather than individuals.
   c. its insistence that employers and labor provide financial compensation to individuals who had suffered discrimination.
   d. its attempt to get around Supreme Court decisions prohibiting racial and sexual discrimination by business and labor.
   e. its requirement that private businesses had to hire based on affirmative action, while government was exempt.
7. The two areas where President Nixon created powerful new federal agencies that directly impinged on business operations were
   a. workforce education and training and private pension policies.
   b. automobile safety and urban planning.
   c. civil rights and women's rights.
   d. environmental protection and occupational health and safety.
   e. workplace child care and executive compensation.
8. The War Powers Act was passed by Congress specifically in response to
   a. the Watergate scandal.
   b. President Nixon's secret bombing of Cambodia.
   c. the continuing war in Vietnam.
   d. Nixon's willingness to send U.S. troops to support Israel in the Six-Day War.
   e. the use of American troops for peacekeeping in the Middle East.
9. The most serious of the many corrupt Nixon administration practices, exposed by the Senate Watergate Committee, was
   a. the acceptance of illegal payments by foreign governments.
   b. bribes to congressmen and senators.
   c. the illegal use of the Federal Bureau of Investigation and the Central Intelligence Agency to cover up White House crimes and harass Nixon's enemies.
   d. the illegal use of the Environmental Protection Agency and the Occupational Safety and Health Administration to force businesses to contribute to Nixon's election campaign.
   e. the payment of kickbacks from businesses awarded federal contracts.

10. The Arab oil embargo of 1973–1974 and its aftermath dramatically affected the American economy by
    a. forcing America to turn to alternative energy sources.
    b. leading the United States to expand oil drilling in Alaska and in offshore oil fields.
    c. increasing American investment in the Middle East.
    d. ending the era of cheap energy and igniting a raging inflation.
    e. enabling Arab governments to gain substantial control of major American businesses.
11. President Gerald Ford's most controversial decision in the White House was
    a. appointing New York Governor Nelson Rockefeller as his new vice president.
    b. imposing federal wage and price controls to dampen double-digit inflation.
    c. signing the third basket of human rights guarantees in the Helsinki accords.
    d. refusing to send American ground troops back into South Vietnam.
    e. granting a complete pardon to Richard Nixon for all crimes he may have committed.
12. Despite numerous successes for women in the 1970s, the feminist movement suffered a severe setback when
    a. the Supreme Court began to oppose the extension of women's rights.
    b. the Equal Rights Amendment failed to achieve ratification by the states.
    c. Congress refused to extend women's right to an equal education to the area of athletics.
    d. moderate and radical feminists began to attack each other over whether gender differences should be totally eradicated.
    e. the declining economy created a growing gap between men's and women's earning power.
13. The conservative antifeminist movement attacked the Equal Rights Amendment by arguing that it would
    a. lead to the establishment of nongendered dress codes.
    b. force an end to women-only colleges.
    c. require equal pay for equal work by men and women.
    d. make abortion rights the law of the land.
    e. end traditional workplace protections for women and undermine the family.
14. President Jimmy Carter's political support plummeted when he
    a. supported Iranian militants in their overthrow of the Shah of Iran.
    b. called for the use of alternative energy to end America's dependence on Middle Eastern oil.
    c. told Americans in a speech that their excessive concern for material goods had led to a moral and spiritual crisis.
    d. negotiated a peace treaty between Israel and Egypt.
    e. established full diplomatic relations with Communist China.
15. President Carter's greatest foreign policy failure was his
    a. negotiation of the Panama Canal treaties.
    b. inadequate response to the Soviet invasion of Afghanistan.
    c. inability to get other Arab states besides Egypt to make peace with Israel.
    d. reinstitution of registration of all young men for the military draft.
    e. inability to end the Iranian revolutionaries' seizure of American hostages.

C. Identification

Supply the correct identification for each numbered description.

1. __________ Nixon's policy of withdrawing American troops from Vietnam, while providing aid for the South Vietnamese to fight the war

2. __________ The Ohio university where four students were killed during protests against the 1970 invasion of Cambodia

3. __________ Top-secret documents, published by the *New York Times* in 1971, that showed the blunders and deceptions that led the United States into the Vietnam War
4. __________ Site of massacre by American soldiers of Vietnamese civilians.
5. __________ Nixon's regionally-focused plan to win reelection by curbing the Supreme Court's judicial activism and soft-pedaling civil rights
6. __________ Term for the new group-oriented affirmative action policy promoted by the Nixon administration
7. __________ A Washington office complex whose name was applied to the widespread corruption and crimes of the Nixon administration
8. __________ The law, passed in reaction to the secret Cambodia bombing, that restricted presidential use of troops overseas without congressional authorization
9. __________ Powerful new federal agency established to enforce the Clean Air Act, the Clean Water Act, and other similar laws.
10. __________ Nixon-Ford-Kissinger policy of seeking relaxed tensions with the Soviet Union through trade and arms limitation
11. __________ International agreement of 1975, signed by President Ford, that settled postwar European boundaries and attempted to guarantee human rights in Eastern Europe
12. __________ Proposed constitutional amendment promoting women's rights that fell short of ratification
13. __________ Supreme Court decision that declared women's right to choose abortion.
14. __________ President Jimmy Carter's 1979 speech that blamed Americans' excessive materialism for causing a national "moral and spiritual crisis"
15. __________ The action by Iranian revolutionary militants that aroused worldwide outrage and further crippled Jimmy Carter's presidency

D. Matching People, Places, and Events

Match the person, place, or event in the left column with the proper description in the right column by inserting the correct letter on the blank line.

1. ___ Richard Nixon
2. ___ Spiro Agnew
3. ___ Rachel Carson
4. ___ Daniel Ellsberg
5. ___ Henry Kissinger
6. ___ Earl Warren
7. ___ George McGovern
8. ___ Phyllis Schlafly
9. ___ Gerald Ford
10. ___ John Dean

a. Nixon appointee as Chief Justice of the Supreme Court who failed to overturn earlier liberal Court decisions as Nixon hoped
b. The first appointed vice president of the United States who became the first unelected president
c. Supreme Court justice whose judicial activism came under increasing attack by conservatives
d. Nixon's tough-talking conservative vice president, who was forced to resign in 1973 for taking bribes and kickbacks

11. ___ James Earl Carter
12. ___ Warren Burger
13. ___ Allen Bakke
14. ___ Shah of Iran
15. ___ Anwar Sadat

e. Talented diplomatic negotiator and leading architect of détente with the Soviet Union during the Nixon and Ford administrations

f. Egyptian leader who signed the Camp David accords with Israel

g. California medical school applicant whose case led a divided Supreme Court to uphold limited forms of affirmative action for minorities

h. Environmental writer whose book, *Silent Spring*, helped encourage laws like the Clean Water Act and the Endangered Species Act

i. South Dakota senator whose antiwar campaign was swamped by Nixon

j. Former Georgia governor whose presidency was plagued by economic difficulties and a crisis in Iran

k. Former Pentagon official who leaked the Pentagon Papers

l. Winner of an overwhelming electoral victory who was forced from office by the threat of impeachment

m. White House lawyer whose dramatic charges against Nixon were validated by the Watergate tapes

n. Conservative activist who led a successful movement to stop ratification of the Equal Rights Amendment

o. Repressive pro-Western ruler whose 1979 overthrow precipitated a crisis for the United States

E. Putting Things in Order

Put the following events in correct order by numbering them from 1 to 6.

1. __________ The overthrow of a dictatorial shah leads to an economic and political crisis for President Carter and the United States.

2. __________ An impeachment-threatened president resigns, and his appointed vice president takes over the White House.

3. __________ A U.S. president travels to Beijing (Peking) and Moscow, opening a new era of improved diplomatic relations with the communist powers.

4. __________ The American invasion of a communist stronghold near Vietnam creates domestic turmoil in the United States.

5. __________ The signing of an agreement with North Vietnam leads to the final withdrawal of American troops from Vietnam.

6. __________ A plainspoken former governor becomes president by campaigning against F. Matching Cause and Effect

F. Matching Cause and Effect

Match the historical cause in the left column with the proper effect in the right column by writing the correct letter on the blank line.

Cause

1. ___ Nixon's Vietnamization policy
2. ___ The U.S. invasion and bombing of Cambodia
3. ___ Nixon's trips to Beijing (Peking) and Moscow
4. ___ The Warren Court's judicial activism
5. ___ Pressure on Moscow and renewed bombing of North Vietnam
6. ___ The growing successes of the women's movement in areas of employment and education
7. ___ Nixon's tape-recorded words ordering the Watergate cover-up
8. ___ The communist Vietnamese offensive in 1975
9. ___ The Soviet invasion of Afghanistan
10. ___ The 1979 revolution in Iran

Effect

a. Spawned a powerful backlash that halted federal day care efforts and the Equal Rights Amendment

b. Caused Senate defeat of the SALT II treaty and the end of détente with Moscow

c. Brought about gradual U.S. troop withdrawal but extended the Vietnam War for four more years

d. Prompted conservative protests and Nixon's appointment of less activist justices

e. Led to the taking of American hostages and new economic and energy troubles for the United States

f. Brought about a cease-fire and the withdrawal of American troops from Vietnam in 1973

g. Caused protests on U.S. campuses and congressional attempts to restrain presidential war powers

h. Brought an era of relaxed international tensions and new trade agreements

i. Caused the collapse of South Vietnam and the flight of many refugees to the United States

j. Proved the president's guilt and forced him to resign or be impeached

G. Developing Historical Skills

Understanding Political Cartoons

The more controversial a major political figure, the more likely he or she is to be the subject of political cartoons. Richard Nixon was such a controversial figure, and the cartoons in this chapter show several views of him. Answer the following questions.

1. What is the view of Nixon's diplomacy in the cartoon *Balancing Act* on p. 1007? What is the significance of his unusual balance bar?

2. In the cartoon of *Nixon, the "Law-and-Order-Man"* on p. 1014, what aspect of Nixon's earlier career is satirized? What details suggest the cartoonist's view of Nixon's Watergate strategy?

3. In the cartoon *Who Lost Vietnam* on p. 1016, Nixon is satirized, but less harshly than in the other cartoons. What changes the perspective on him here?

PART III: APPLYING WHAT YOU HAVE LEARNED

1. Was the Nixon-Kissinger foreign policy of détente with the Soviet Union and engagement with Communist China fundamentally a great success? What were its major accomplishments, and what were its limitations?
2. In what ways did Nixon's domestic policies appeal to Americans' racial and economic fears, and in what ways did he positively address problems like inflation, discrimination, environmental degradation, and worker safety?
3. What were Nixon's fundamental goals in waging the Vietnam War from 1969 to 1973? Did he achieve them? Why did the secret bombing and invasion of Cambodia cause such a furious reaction by Congress and the public?
4. How did Nixon fall from the political heights of 1972 to his forced resignation in 1974? What were the political consequences of Watergate?
5. How did both Republican and Democratic administrations of the 1970s attempt to cope with the interrelated problems of energy, economics, and the Middle East? Why were they so largely unsuccessful in addressing these concerns?
6. How and why did the United States become increasingly involved in the political and economic affairs of the Middle East during the 1970s?
7. Why did the American public eventually become so disillusioned with the policy of détente toward the Soviet Union? Was the policy itself fundamentally flawed from the beginning, or was it Soviet misbehavior and aggression that destroyed an originally wise policy?

8. The American public had high hopes for Jimmy Carter as an honest and well-intentioned president who could clean up Washington after the corruption of Watergate. Why did Carter's presidency come to be seen as such a failure? Was Carter largely a victim of events he could not control, or did his own outlook and policies contribute to his failures in the White House?

9. In what ways were the foreign policy and economic issues of the 1970s similar to those of the whole post–World War II era, and in what ways were they different (see Chapters 36, 37, and 38)?

10. It is sometimes said that the recent American disillusionment and even cynicism about politics dates to the paired tribulations of Vietnam and Watergate. Why were these two events so deeply unsettling to traditional American views of democracy and government? Is the linking of the two events accurate, or were there fundamental differences between them?

CHAPTER 40

The Resurgence of Conservatism, 1981–1992

PART I: REVIEWING THE CHAPTER

A. Checklist of Learning Objectives

After mastering this chapter, you should be able to:

1. Describe the rise of Reagan and the New Right in the 1980s, including their effective use of social issues like abortion, affirmative action, and homosexuality.
2. Explain the Reagan revolution in economic policy, and indicate its immediate and long-term consequences.
3. Describe the revival of the Cold War in Reagan's first term and the consequences of Reagan's tough stands toward the Soviet Union.
4. Discuss the growing American entanglement in Central American and Middle Eastern troubles in the 1980s, including the Iran-Contra Affair.
5. Describe the change in Soviet policies initiated by Mikhail Gorbachev and Reagan's second-term turn to negotiation with the Soviets.
6. Analyze the growing power of the religious right in American politics and the battles over abortion and other issues before the Supreme Court.
7. Describe the end of the Cold War and its complex consequences for America's foreign relations and domestic economy.
8. Explain America's growing involvement in the Middle East, including the First Persian Gulf War and its aftermath.

B. Glossary

To build your social science vocabulary, familiarize yourself with the following terms.

1. **neoconservatives (neoconservatism)** Political activists and thinkers, mostly former liberals, who turned to a defense of traditional social and moral values and a strongly anticommunist foreign policy in the 1970s and 1980s. "Though Reagan was no intellectual, he drew on the ideas of a small but influential group of thinkers known as 'neoconservatives.'"
2. **supply side** In economics, the theory that investment incentives such as lowered federal spending and tax cuts will stimulate economic growth and increased employment. "But at first 'supply-side' economics seemed to be a beautiful theory mugged by a gang of brutal facts. . . ."
3. **red ink** Referring to a deficit in a financial account, with expenditures or debts larger than income or assets. "Ironically, this conservative president thereby plunged the government into a red-ink bath of deficit spending. . . ."
4. **oligarchs** A small, elite class of authoritarian rulers. ". . . the aging oligarchs in the Kremlin. . . ."

5. **welfare state** The political system, typical of modern industrial societies, in which government assumes responsibility for the economic well-being of its citizens by providing social benefits. "They achieved, in short, Reagan's highest political objective: the containment of the welfare state."

6. **leveraged buy-out** The purchase of one company by another using money borrowed on the expectation of selling a portion of assets after the acquisition. "A wave of mergers, acquisitions, and leveraged buy-outs washed over Wall Street. . . ."

7. **logistical (adj.) (logistics (n.)**Relating to the organization and movement of substantial quantities of people and material in connection with some defined objective. "In a logistical operation of astonishing complexity, the United States spearheaded a massive international military deployment on the sandy Arabian peninsula."

PART II: CHECKING YOUR PROGRESS

A. True-False

Where the statement is true, circle **T**; where it is false, circle **F**.

1. T F Ronald Reagan successfully attacked big government as the enemy rather than the friend of the common man.

2. T F Reagan's landslide victory over Carter in 1980 did not have the coattails to bring his fellow Republicans into office.

3. T F Once in office, Reagan backed away from most of his ideologically conservative election promises and concentrated on practical management of the economy and relations with the Russians.

4. T F The fact that Reagan's supply-side economic proposals bogged down in Congress demonstrated the continuing stalemate between Congress and the executive branch.

5. T F Reagan's vigorous free-market economic and hard-line stance against the Soviet Union was opposed by all of America's traditional European allies.

6. T F Part of Reagan's strategy in confronting the Soviet Union was to raise U.S. military expenditures to enormous heights that he believed the Soviets could not match.

7. T F Reagan pursued a tough policy of military intervention and aid in opposition to leftist governments in Central America and the Caribbean.

8. T F Soviet leader Mikhail Gorbachev's policies of *glasnost* and *perestroika* helped reduce Soviet-American conflict in Reagan's second term.

9. T F The Iran-Contra Affair involved the secret exchange of weapons to Iran in exchange for the release of American hostages and the illegal transfer of the profits to Nicaraguan rebels.

10. T F The failure of Reaganomics to deliver a balanced federal budget actually served Reagan's political goal of curbing the liberal welfare state.

11. T F The powerful new religious right borrowed many of its tactics and organizing methods from the new left of the 1960s.

12. T F The Supreme Court cases of *Webster* v. *Reproductive Health Services* and *Casey* v. *Planned Parenthood* carved out compromises that softened the conflict between pro-life and pro-choice forces.

13. T F The collapse of the Soviet Communist government led to the overthrow of the puppet communist regimes throughout Eastern Europe.

14. T F The overthrow of communism in Eastern Europe and the Soviet Union led to vicious fighting among previously repressed ethnic groups.

15. T F The First Persian Gulf War achieved its primary goal of liberating Kuwait but left Saddam Hussein in power in Iraq.

B. Multiple Choice

Select the best answer and circle the corresponding letter.

1. In the 1980 national elections
   a. Ronald Reagan declared that as a conservative he would not seek drastic changes in American foreign or domestic policy.
   b. Ronald Reagan won the presidency, but both houses of Congress retained Democratic party majorities.
   c. third-party candidate John Anderson nearly forced the election into the House of Representatives.
   d. Ronald Reagan won the presidency by the closest margin since the Kennedy-Nixon election of 1960.
   e. Senator Edward Kennedy's primary challenge to incumbent President Carter revealed the divisions and weakness of the Democratic party.
2. Ronald Reagan was similar to Franklin D. Roosevelt in that both presidents
   a. disliked big business.
   b. championed the common person against vast impersonal menaces.
   c. came from privileged backgrounds and family wealth.
   d. favored social engineering by the government.
   e. emphasized hands-on management skills rather than ideology.
3. Ronald Reagan differed from Franklin D. Roosevelt because Reagan
   a. said big business was the enemy of the common person, while Roosevelt declared that the problem was big government.
   b. appealed to the working class, while Roosevelt appealed primarily to the rich.
   c. advocated a populist political philosophy and Roosevelt did not.
   d. branded big government as the enemy of the common person, while Roosevelt said that big business was the major foe.
   e. was effective in using the media to appeal directly to the American people, while Roosevelt was less successful as a media communicator.
4. Conservative Democrats who helped Ronald Reagan pass his budget and tax-cutting legislation were called
   a. boll weevils.
   b. Sagebrush rebels.
   c. scalawags.
   d. neoconservatives.
   e. Contras.
5. The one area of the federal government activity that Ronald Reagan spent lavishly on was
   a. farm programs.
   b. social security.
   c. defense.
   d. education.
   e. environmental protection.

6. Reagan's fundamental principle in negotiating with the Soviet Union was to
   a. trade America's minor interests for major concessions from the Soviets.
   b. negotiate only from a position of overwhelming military superiority.
   c. negotiate only in cooperation with the Western European allies.
   d. insist on greater human rights and economic freedoms as conditions of the negotiations.
   e. demand that the Soviets tear down the Berlin Wall in exchange for nuclear arms agreements.
7. President Reagan formed a strong personal and political partnership with British Prime Minister Margaret Thatcher based upon
   a. Reagan's admiration and support for the idea of female leadership in high office.
   b. their belief in cultivating support for Western policies from Third World countries.
   c. their common devotion to protecting the social safety net for those left behind by technological change.
   d. their shared support for a stronger role for religion in public and political life.
   e. their mutual support for vigorous free-market economics and tough confrontation with the Soviet Union.
8. Reagan's key agreements with Soviet leader Mikhail Gorbachev provided for
   a. the eventual end of communism inside the Soviet Union.
   b. a major reduction in both Soviet and American nuclear weapons and intercontinental missiles.
   c. the opening of Soviet markets to American businesses.
   d. an end to Soviet and American sponsorship of governments and rebels in the Third World.
   e. the banning of all intermediate-range nuclear missiles from Europe.
9. In the bitter 1980s war between Islamic revolutionary Iran and Iraqi dictator Saddam Hussein, the United States
   a. maintained strict neutrality and an arms embargo on both sides.
   b. secretly supported the Iranians in hopes that they could overthrow Saddam Hussein.
   c. ended up supplying weapons to both sides.
   d. tried to negotiate a peaceful settlement of the war.
   e. threatened the use of military force to prevent a victory by Saddam Hussein.
10. The religious right movement of the 1980s adopted many ideas and tactics from the 1960s new left such as
    a. advertising in newspapers and television.
    b. practicing identity politics, consciousness raising, and civil disobedience.
    c. taking over traditional political party machines from within.
    d. wearing Native American clothing and hairstyles.
    e. relying on charismatic personal leaders rather than ideology.
11. Among the issues that many religious right activists were most concerned about were
    a. abortion and gay rights.
    b. taxation and economic development.
    c. U.S. foreign policy in the Middle East.
    d. Medicare and Social Security.
    e. energy and environmental protection.
12. The 1989 Supreme Court decision that upheld some state restrictions on a woman's right to have an abortion was
    a. *Roe* v. *Wade*.
    b. *Webster* v. *Reproductive Health Services*.
    c. *Brown* v. *Board of Education*.
    d. the *Miranda* decision.
    e. *Martin* v. *Wilks*.

13. In which of the following communist nations did mass protests, demanding liberty and democracy, in the years 1989–1991 completely fail?
    a. The Soviet Union
    b. East Germany
    c. China
    d. Poland
    e. Cuba
14. The great success achieved by American and Allied forces in the 1991 Persian Gulf War was the
    a. overthrow of Saddam Hussein.
    b. liberation of Kuwait from Iraqi rule.
    c. freeing of the Kurds from Iraqi oppression.
    d. achievement of an enduring peace in the Middle East.
    e. formation of a strong American-Arab alliance against Islamic extremism.
15. The bitter hearings over the confirmation of Clarence Thomas to the U.S. Supreme Court revealed
    a. the continuing strong appeal of the antipornography issue.
    b. the continued American public fear of interracial sexual relations.
    c. President George H.W. Bush's attempt to steer the Supreme Court in a moderate direction.
    d. the American public's disgust at hearing public testimony about sexual harassment.
    e. a growing gender gap, with more women turning away from Republican social policies.

C. Identification

Supply the correct identification for each numbered description.

1. __________ Influential group of intellectuals, led by Irving Kristol and Norman Podhoretz, who provided key ideas for the Reagan Revolution

2. __________ California ballot initiative of 1978 that set the stage for the tax revolt that Reagan rode to victory in 1980

3. __________ The economic theory of Reaganomics that emphasized cutting taxes and government spending in order to stimulate investment, productivity, and economic growth by private enterprise

4. __________ Term for young urban professionals of the 1980s who flaunted their wealth through conspicuous consumer spending

5. __________ Conservative southern Democrats who supported Reagan's economic policies in Congress

6. __________ Polish labor union crushed by the communist-imposed martial-law regime in 1983

7. __________ __________ The twin policies of openness and restructuring by which Soviet leader Mikhail Gorbachev attempted to reform the Communist system

8. __________ The leftist revolutionary rulers of Nicaragua, strongly opposed by the Reagan administration

9. __________ Right-wing rebels against radical Nicaraguan government, secretly funded by profits of U.S. arms sales to Iran

10. __________ The scandal, carried out by Reagan administration officials, in which weapons were sold to Iran in exchange for the release of American hostages, the profits used to fund Nicaraguan rebels

11. ___________ Reagan's proposed space-based nuclear defense system, nicknamed "Star Wars"

12. ___________ Leading organization of the new religious right, led by Reverend Jerry Falwell

13. ___________ Physical symbol of the Cold War and divided Europe that came down in 1989

14. ___________ The central location in Beijing, China, where demonstrators demanding greater freedom and democracy were brutally crushed by government tanks in spring 1989

15. ___________ Code name for the military operation of the hundred-hour war that drove Saddam Hussein out of Kuwait

D. Matching People, Places, and Events

Match the person, place, or event in the left column with the proper description in the right column by inserting the correct letter on the blank line.

1. ___ Jimmy Carter
2. ___ Edward Kennedy
3. ___ Ronald Reagan
4. ___ Margaret Thatcher
5. ___ Sandra Day O'Connor
6. ___ Mikhail Gorbachev
7. ___ George H. W. Bush
8. ___ Norman Podhoretz
9. ___ Saddam Hussein
10. ___ Anita Hill
11. ___ Walter Mondale
12. ___ Geraldine Ferraro
13. ___ Jerry Falwell
14. ___ Norman Schwartzkopf
15. ___ Clarence Thomas

a. Prominent evangelical minister, leader of the Moral Majority

b. University of Oklahoma law professor who charged Clarence Thomas with sexual harassment during bitter 1991 Supreme Court hearings

c. Soviet leader whose summit meetings with Reagan achieved an arms-control breakthrough in 1987

d. Jimmy Carter's vice president who lost badly to Ronald Reagan in the 1984 election

e. Iraqi dictator defeated by the United States and its allies in the Persian Gulf War

f. Brilliant legal scholar appointed by Reagan as the first woman justice on the Supreme Court

g. Well-meaning president who was swamped by the 1980 Reagan landslide but later won the Nobel Peace Prize

h. Leading neoconservative intellectual who attacked excesses of 1960s liberalism and provided ideological support for Ronald Reagan

i. First woman to be nominated to a major party ticket as Democratic vice-presidential candidate in 1984

j. Successful commander of American forces in the First Persian Gulf War

k. Liberal Democratic senator whose opposition to Carter helped divide the Democrats in 1980

l. Long-time Republican political figure who defeated Dukakis for the presidency in 1988

m. Controversial Supreme Court justice who narrowly won confirmation despite charges of sexual harassment

n. British Prime Minister of the 1980s whose support of free-market economics and tough anticommunism made her Ronald Reagan's closest partner

o. Political darling of Republican conservatives who won landslide election victories in 1980 and 1984

E. Putting Things in Order

Put the following events in correct order by numbering them from 1 to 6.

1. __________ Reagan easily wins reelection by overwhelming divided Democrats.
2. __________ The United States and its allies defeat Iraq in the Persian Gulf War.
3. __________ President Jimmy Carter loses in a landslide to former actor and California governor Ronald Reagan.
4. __________ Reagan's supply-side economic programs pass through Congress, cutting taxes and federal spending.
5. __________ George Herbert Walker Bush defeats Michael Dukakis in a "referendum on Reaganism."
6. __________ The Soviet Union dissolves into Russia and other new nations, many plagued by fierce ethnic conflicts

F. Matching Cause and Effect

Match the historical cause in the left column with the proper effect in the right column by writing the correct letter on the blank line.

Cause

1. ___ The intellectual movement called neoconservatism
2. ___ Reagan's crusade against big government and social spending
3. ___ By 1983, Reagan's supply-side economic policies

Effect

a. Led to a break-off of arms-control talks, U.S. economic sanctions against Poland, and growing anxiety in Western Europe

b. Brought about an overwhelming Republican victory in the 1984 presidential election

4. ___ The revival of the Cold War in the early eighties
5. ___ Continued political turmoil and war in Lebanon
6. ___ Reagan's hostility to leftist governments in Central America and the Caribbean
7. ___ Reagan's personal popularity and Democratic divisions
8. ___ Reagan's "Star Wars" plan for defensive missile systems in space
9. ___ The huge federal budget deficits of the 1980s
10. ___ Reagan's and Bush's appointments of conservative justices to the Supreme Court
11. ___ The Reagan administration's frustration with hostages and bans on aid to Nicaraguan rebels
12. ___ Dissident movements like that of Solidarity in Poland
13. ___ The widespread student protests in China's Tiananmen Square in 1989
14. ___ Saddam Hussein's invasion of Kuwait
15. ___ Anita Hill's charges of sexual harassment against Supreme Court nominee Clarence Thomas

c. Resulted in the failure of the American marines' peacekeeping mission in 1983

d. Helped curb affirmative action and limit the right to abortion

e. Led to sharp cuts in both taxes and federal social programs in 1981

f. Strained relations with America's European allies

g. Curbed inflation and spurred economic growth but also caused sky-high deficits and interest rates

h. Prompted Congress to pass the Gramm-Rudman-Hollings Act calling for automatic spending cuts and a balanced budget by 1991

i. Helped fuel Ronald Reagan's successful presidential campaign in 1980

j. Caused the U.S. invasion of Grenada and the CIA-engineered mining of Nicaraguan harbors

k. Led to the overthrow of communist puppet governments in Eastern Europe

l. Brought the killing of many people by tanks and machine guns and a re-assertion of harsh Communist Party rule

m. Brought a large American army to the Arabian peninsula and naval forces to the Persian Gulf

n. Caused a bitter Senate hearing and a growing gender gap between Republicans and Democrats

o. Led to the Iran-contra affair

G. Developing Historical Skills

Using Chronologies

Properly read, chronologies provide handy tools for understanding not only the sequence of events but also their historical relations.

Examine the Chronology for this chapter (p. 1053), and answer the following questions.

1. In which year did a number of events indicate deep Soviet-American tension and a revived Cold War?

2. How many years did it take after the first Reagan-Gorbachev summit to reach agreement on the INF treaty?

3. List three events prior to the Persian Gulf War in 1991 that reflect growing American involvement in the Middle East.

4. List three events between the imposition of sanctions against Poland (1981) and the dissolution of the Soviet Union (1991) that show the progress in easing Cold War tensions.

PART III: APPLYING WHAT YOU HAVE LEARNED

1. What caused the rise of Reagan and the new right in the 1980s, and how did their conservative movement fundamentally reshape American politics?
2. What were the goals of Reagan's supply-side economic policies, and what were those policies' short-term and long-term effects?
3. What led to the revival of the Cold War in the early 1980s, and how did Ronald Reagan turn the conflict with the Soviet Union to American advantage?
4. Why did the Reagan administration pursue its policy of opposing leftists in Central America and the Caribbean so fervently, to the point of funding the Nicaraguan Contras with arms sale profits from Iran? Was this primarily motivated by ideological anticommunism, or by fear of the Soviet Union gaining a strategic foothold in the Americas?
5. How and why did religious and moral issues rather suddenly jump to the forefront of American politics and law in the 1980s?
6. Many historians have compared the Reagan revolution with Franklin Roosevelt's New Deal because of the way it seemed to transform radically American economics and politics. Is this a valid comparison? Is it correct to see the Reagan legacy as a complete reversal of the New Deal, or of the Great Society of Lyndon Johnson?

7. Trace the evolution of the Supreme Court from the dominant days of the Warren Court in the 1960s (see Chapter 39) to the more conservative Court of the late 1980s. Why did Supreme Court decisions and judicial appointments become such focal points of political controversy in this period? In what ways did the Supreme Court "follow the election returns." In what ways did it resist narrowly political pressures?

8. To what extent were American policies responsible for the overthrow of communism in Eastern Europe and the Soviet Union in 1989–1991.

9. Was the first Persian Gulf War fundamentally based on America's Wilsonian foreign policy of promoting democracy, liberty, and self-determination for small nations (in this case, Kuwait), or was it primarily a defense of national self-interest, such as in protecting oil supplies and strengthening America's allies in the Middle East? Use evidence from the chapter to support your answer.

10. What were the opportunities and problems created by America's new status as the sole superpower after the end of the Cold War and the dissolution of the Soviet Union?

CHAPTER 41

America Confronts the Post-Cold War Era, 1992–2009

PART I: REVIEWING THE CHAPTER

A. Checklist of Learning Objectives

After mastering this chapter, you should be able to:

1. Describe the major domestic developments of the Clinton administration, including Clinton's attempts to govern as a New Democrat and the fierce partisan warfare against him conducted by Gingrich Republicans.
2. Discuss the causes and consequences of the violence that plagued American society in the 1990s.
3. Discuss America's challenges in developing a foreign policy in the post–Cold War environment, including the U.S. intervention in the Balkans and the continuing failure to achieve peace in the Middle East.
4. Describe the disputed 2000 election between Albert Gore, Jr. and George W. Bush, and indicate how and why American politics remained sharply polarized the first decade of the twenty-first century.
5. Discuss the impact of the September 11 terrorist attacks on American society and global involvements, including the wars in Afghanistan and Iraq.
6. Describe President George Bush's domestic and foreign policies, and explain why they met increasing opposition after Bush's victory in the 2004 election.
7. Indicate how both Democrats and Republicans attempted to respond to the concerns about the economy and the Iraq War, and identify each nominated presidential candidate strongly advocating change from the Bush administration.

B. Glossary

To build your social science vocabulary, familiarize yourself with the following terms.

1. **sect** A separatist religious group that claims for itself exclusive knowledge of truth and a superior method of salvation over all other religious organizations. "That showdown ended in the destruction of the sect's compound and the deaths of many Branch Davidians. . . ."
2. **paramilitary** Unauthorized or voluntary groups that employ military organization, methods, and equipment outside the official military system of command and organization. "These episodes brought to light a lurid and secretive underground of paramilitary private 'militias.' . . ."
3. **protectionism (protectionists)** The policy of promoting high tariff taxes on imported goods or services in order that domestic producers can sell at lower prices than foreign manufacturers or service providers. " . . . he reversed his own stand in the 1992 election campaign and bucked the opposition of protectionists in his own party. . . . "

4. **vouchers** Officially granted certificates for benefits of a particular kind, redeemable by a designated agency or service provider. "Bush championed private-sector initiatives, such as school vouchers. . . ."

5. **junta** From Latin America politics: a small armed group, usually military officers, who seize power and rule as a collective dictatorship. " . . . surely it was better to have the buck stop with the judges, not with a junta."

6. **autocratic (autocracy)** Relating to authoritarian or repressive government or institutional practices. "There was little evidence that Saddam's downfall might topple other autocratic regimes in the region."

PART II: CHECKING YOUR PROGRESS

A. True-False

Where the statement is true, circle **T**; where it is false, circle **F**.

1. T F Bill Clinton's presentation of himself as a New Democrat was designed to emphasize his commitment to reversing past Democratic party positions on civil rights.
2. T F After victory in the 1994 congressional elections, the militant conservatism of Speaker Newt Gingrich stumbled when it shut down the federal government for a time.
3. T F Clinton's liberal reforms put conservative Republicans on the defensive and led to substantial Democratic gains in the 1994 mid-term Congressional elections.
4. T F The Oklahoma City bombing of 1995, the Columbine High School shootings of 1999, and the Virginia Tech killings of 2007 led Congress to pass strong restrictions on handguns and other weapons.
5. T F The struggling economy of the 1990s led President Clinton to support increased protectionism and restrictions on the export of American jobs overseas.
6. T F The Clinton administration's major foreign policy success came in negotiating a peace settlement between Israelis and Palestinians in the Middle East.
7. T F The two charges on which President Clinton was impeached and then acquitted were perjury before a grand jury and obstruction of justice.
8. T F In the 2000 election, George W. Bush defeated Albert Gore in the Electoral College but not in the popular vote.
9. T F Once in office, President George W. Bush pursued strongly conservative policies on abortion, the environment, and taxes.
10. T F Osama bin Laden, the mastermind of the September 11 terrorist attacks, was an Afghan Taliban leader who had originally fought the Soviet invasion of his country.
11. T F The United Nations, in 1993, declined to authorize the use of force against Iraq to compel compliance with its resolutions.
12. T F The USA-Patriot Act, passed in response to September 11, authorized the detention and deportation of immigrants suspected of terrorism.
13. T F President George Bush's second-term proposal to privatize Social Security received strong support from liberals and senior citizens' groups.

14. T F A major source of President George Bush's declining popular approval rating came from the federal government's inadequate response to the devastation of Hurricane Katrina.

15. T F The primary cause of the Democrats' strong showing in the 2006 mid-term election was discontent with Bush's education and trade policies.

B. Multiple Choice

Select the best answer and circle the corresponding letter.

1. Bill Clinton defeated incumbent President George Bush in 1992 by focusing especially on the issue of
   a. women's rights and gay rights.
   b. the environment.
   c. the economy.
   d. health care.
   e. education
2. In 1992, businessman H. Ross Perot made the strongest showing of any third-party presidential candidate since Theodore Roosevelt by winning approximately _____ percent of the popular vote.
   a. 5
   b. 10
   c. 20
   d. 40
   e. 50
3. Two areas where President Clinton's initial attempts at liberal reform failed badly were
   a. free trade and welfare reform.
   b. the environment and consumer protection.
   c. health care and gay service in the military.
   d. affirmative action and education funding.
   e. gun control and deficit reduction.
4. Two areas where the Clinton administration achieved success in domestic affairs were
   a. health care and gay rights.
   b. political campaign reform and term limits.
   c. gun control and deficit reduction.
   d. immigration reform and improved race relations.
   e. environmental protection and stock market regulation.
5. The assault on the Branch Davidian compound in Waco, Texas, and the bombing of the Oklahoma City federal building were both extreme, violent expressions of a wider 1990s atmosphere of
   a. religious belief in the imminent end of the world.
   b. disillusionment with government and hostility to politicians.
   c. hostility to free market capitalism.
   d. anger toward ethnic minorities and immigrants.
   e. tolerance for foreign terrorist assaults on the United States.

6. The new Republican congressional majority, led by House Speaker Newt Gingrich, caused a severe backlash in favor of President Clinton in 1995 when it
   a. restricted unfunded mandates imposed on state and local governments.
   b. supported the Welfare Reform Act, cutting welfare benefits and requiring recipients to seek employment.
   c. tried to restrict illegal immigration.
   d. attempted to prohibit sex education in the public schools.
   e. shut down the federal government for a time and proposed sending children on welfare to orphanages.
7. Despite the great prosperity of the 1990s economy, President Clinton experienced controversy and strong opposition to his policy of
   a. expanding global free trade and supporting the World Trade Organization.
   b. reducing the power and benefits of American unions.
   c. imposing regulations on the highly speculative dot.com Internet businesses and their stock offerings.
   d. demanding that China allow full human rights in exchange for greater American trade.
   e. increasing the minimum wage for lower income workers.
8. The Democratic minority's fundamental defense of the impeachment charges against President Clinton was that
   a. Clinton had not committed the acts with which he was charged.
   b. Clinton's actions were personal failings that did not rise to the constitutional level of high crimes and misdemeanors.
   c. Newt Gingrich and other leading Republicans had also engaged in sexual misconduct.
   d. the nation could not afford to remove an incumbent president during a time of international crisis.
   e. the special prosecutor Kenneth Starr did not understand the changes in contemporary Americans' attitudes toward sexuality.
9. Victory in the 2000 presidential election was eventually awarded to George W. Bush when
   a. the Florida legislature awarded that state's electoral votes to Bush.
   b. the Supreme Court ruled in Bush's favor that Florida's hand counting of ballots was illegal.
   c. Al Gore conceded that it was impossible for him to win.
   d. a joint session of Congress declared Bush the winner.
   e. a thorough recount showed that Bush had won the state.
10. One of George W. Bush's first vigorously conservative and nationalistic actions in office was to repudiate American participation in the
    a. International Atomic Energy Agency.
    b. United Nations World Health Organization.
    c. International Criminal Court and the Geneva Conventions on the treatment of prisoners.
    d. Kyoto Global Warming Treaty.
    e. international Law of the Sea Treaty.
11. The fundamentalist Islamic party that ruled Afghanistan and shielded Osama bin Laden prior to the September 11 attacks was
    a. the Party of God.
    b. Al Qaeda.
    c. Hamas.
    d. the Baath Party.
    e. the Taliban.

12. Which of the following was *not* among the reasons offered by President George W. Bush for America's 1993 invasion of Iraq?
    a. Possible Iraqi involvement in the September 11 attacks
    b. The need for the U.S. to control Iraqi oil supplies
    c. Saddam Hussein's possession of weapons of mass destruction
    d. The idea that the creation of a peaceful, democratic Iraq would inspire hope and reform throughout the Middle East
    e. Saddam Hussein's cruel oppression of his own people
13. Which of the following was *not* among the controversial Bush administration actions that led to increased polarization between supporters and opponents of the administration?
    a. Attorney General Ashcroft's zealous enforcement of the USA-Patriot Act
    b. Bush's strong anti-abortion policies
    c. The reduction of benefits for Gulf War veterans
    d. Approaches to gay and lesbian rights
    e. Bush's response to the devastation caused by Hurricane Katrina.

C. Identification

Supply the correct identification for each numbered description.

1. __________ Centrist Democratic organization that promoted Bill Clinton's candidacy as a New Democrat
2. __________ Shorthand phrase for compromise policy that emerged after Clinton's failed attempt to end ban on gays and lesbians in the military
3. __________ Fundamentalist group whose compound in Waco, Texas, was assaulted by federal agents in 1993
4. __________ Colorado high school where a deadly shooting in 1999 stirred a national movement against guns and gun violence
5. __________ Conservative campaign platform that led to a sweeping Republican victory in the 1994 mid-term elections
6. __________ Controversial free trade agreement between the United States, Mexico, and Canada that virtually eliminated trade barriers between the three nations.
7. __________ International trade organization that prompted strong protests from antiglobal trade forces in the late 1990s.
8. __________ Caribbean nation where Clinton sent twenty thousand American troops to restore ousted President Jean-Bertrand Aristide to power
9. __________ The sexual scandal involving a young White House intern that led to impeachment but not conviction of President Clinton
10. __________ Third party, led by environmentalist Ralph Nader, that took votes from Democratic presidential nominee Albert Gore in 2000 election
11. __________ Constitutional institution for choosing presidents that came under severe criticism after the 2000 popular vote winner failed to win the office
12. __________ The other site of direct attack by terrorists on September 11, 2001, besides the twin towers of the World Trade Center
13. __________ The international terrorist network headed by Osama bin Laden

14. __________ Controversial law restricting civil liberties, passed in the immediate aftermath of the September 11 attacks

15. __________ Iraqi prison where alleged American abuse of Iraqi prisoners inflamed anti-American sentiment in Iraq and beyond

D. Matching People, Places, and Events

Match the person, place, or event in the left column with the proper description in the right column by inserting the correct letter on the blank line.

1. _____ William J. Clinton
2. _____ H. Ross Perot
3. _____ Hillary Rodham Clinton
4. _____ Robert Dole
5. _____ Newt Gingrich
6. _____ John McCain
7. _____ Slobodan Milosevic
8. _____ Monica Lewinsky
9. _____ William Rehnquist
10. _____ Al Gore
11. _____ George W. Bush
12. _____ Richard Cheney
13. _____ Osama bin Laden
14. _____ Saddam Hussein
15. _____ Barack Obama

a. Young White House intern whose sexual affair with President Clinton led to his impeachment

b. President Clinton's loyal vice president who won the most popular votes but lost the election of 2000

c. George W. Bush's vice president who vigorously promoted conservative domestic policies and the invasion of Iraq

d. Texas billionaire who won nearly 20 percent of the popular vote as third-party candidate in 1992

e. Illinois senator who became the first African American to be elected president, in 2008

f. Serbian president who conducted vicious ethnic cleansing campaigns and was eventually forced from office

g. Son of a former president whose narrow election as president in 2000 did not prevent him from pursuing a strong conservative agenda in office

h. The first baby boomer president who was the first Democrat elected to two full terms since Franklin Roosevelt

i. Long-time Iraqi dictator who was overthrown by invading American armies in 2003

j. First presidential spouse to be given major policy responsibilities and to win election to the United States Senate

k. Fiery Republican Speaker of the House who led his party to great victory in 1994 but resigned after Republican losses in 1998

l. Wealthy Saudi Arabian exile who formed a global terrorist network that assaulted the United States

m. Veteran reform-minded senator who won the Republican Party presidential nomination in 2008

n. 1996 Republican presidential nominee who was soundly defeated by Bill Clinton

o. Chief Justice of the United States who presided at the impeachment trial of President Clinton

E. Putting Things in Order

Put the following events in correct order by numbering them from 1 to 5

1. __________ George W. Bush loses the popular vote but wins the presidency with a majority of the Electoral College.
2. __________ Republicans win a majority in the House of Representatives after Newt Gingrich promotes the strongly conservative Contract with America.
3. __________ Arkansas Governor Bill Clinton defeats incumbent President George H. W. Bush.
4. __________ With authorization from the U.S. Congress, but not the United Nations, President George Bush launches a preemptive American invasion of Iraq.
5. __________ Terrorists conduct the first major attack on American soil in two hundred years.

PART III: APPLYING WHAT YOU HAVE LEARNED

1. Was Bill Clinton's election in 1992 a positive mandate for change, or was it primarily a repudiation of the first Bush administration's record on the economy?
2. How did the antigovernment mood of the 1990s affect both Bill Clinton and his Republican opponents? In what ways did Clinton attempt to uphold traditional Democratic themes, and in what ways did he serve to consolidate the conservative Bush-Reagan era?
3. What new foreign policy challenges did the United States face after the end of the Cold War?
4. What were the greatest foreign policy successes and failures of the Clinton administration in the 1990s?
5. Why was there so much antigovernment rhetoric, political action, and even violence in the 1990s? To what extent did the Clinton administration attempt to counter this mood, and to what extent did it bend to it?

6. Argue for or against: the presidential election of 2000, despite its controversies, demonstrated the strength and resiliency of America's democracy.

7. What was the impact of the September 11, 2001, terrorist attacks on America's national priorities and foreign policies? Is it true that everything changed after September 11, or were there significant areas in which America's global aims remained essentially the same?

8. What caused the increased polarization in American politics in the early 2000s? Is it appropriate to align this polarization with the two political parties and their respective strengths in red states and blue states? Are there significant issues that have not been affected by this political polarization?

9. What were the Bush administration's primary justifications for the Iraq War? Why did Americans find the military and political environment in Iraq so much more difficult than expected?

10. How did President Bush spend the political capital that he said he had accumulated through his victory in the 2004 election.

CHAPTER 42

The American People Face a New Century

PART I: REVIEWING THE CHAPTER

A. Checklist of Learning Objectives

After mastering this chapter, you should be able to:

1. Describe the changing shape of the American economy and work force and the new social and ethical challenges facing the United States in a global economy dominated by high technology and scientific innovation.
2. Explain the impact of the feminist revolution on women's roles and on American society as a whole.
3. Analyze the changing structure and character of American families, and explain the social consequences of the aging of America.
4. Describe the impact of the great wave of immigration from Asia and Latin America since the 1970s and the challenge it posed to the traditional ideals of the melting pot.
5. Describe the difficulties and challenges facing American cities, including the increasing split between central cities and outer suburbs.
6. Describe the changing condition of African Americans in American politics and society, including the impact of economic differences within the African American community.
7. Describe the impact of the information technology revolution on American economics, communications, and culture.
8. Discuss the major developments in American thought, culture, and the arts since the 1970s.

B. Glossary

To build your social science vocabulary, familiarize yourself with the following terms.

1. **biosphere** The earth's entire network of living plants and organisms, conceived as an interconnected whole. ". . . the fragile ecological balance of the wondrous biosphere in which human-kind was delicately suspended."
2. **nuclear family** A parent or parents and their immediate offspring. "The nuclear family, once prized as the foundation of society. . . ."
3. **undocumented** Lacking official certification of status as a legal immigrant or resident alien. ". . . attempted to choke off illegal entry by penalizing employers of undocumented aliens. . . ."
4. **amnesty** An official governmental act in which some general category of offenders is declared immune from punishment. ". . . by granting amnesty to many of those already here."

5. **civil trial** A trial before a judge or jury instigated by a private lawsuit in which one party seeks relief, compensation, or damages from another. A **criminal trial** is instigated by an indictment for criminal law violations brought by a state prosecutor on behalf of the government ("the people"); it may result in fines, imprisonment, or execution. "In a later civil trial, another jury found Simpson liable for the 'wrongful deaths' of his former wife and another victim."

6. **blogosphere** Term for the collective dynamic, environment and interaction of all those who produce information and opinion by writing Internet "weblogs," or **blogs.** "As the 'blogosphere' grew, it posed a major challenge to the traditional media. . . ."

PART II: CHECKING YOUR PROGRESS

A. True-False

Where the statement is true, circle **T**; where it is false, circle **F**.

1. T F The communications and genetics revolutions in postwar America created new social and moral dilemmas as well as widespread economic growth.
2. T F After World War II, America's leading research universities concentrated on basic research and scholarship, while scientists in private industry focused on applied research and product development.
3. T F The gap between America's wealthiest citizens and its poorest continued to grow in the 1990s and early 2000s.
4. T F By the year 2006, almost all women without children at home were employed, but a majority of mothers with small children remained outside the workplace.
5. T F One of the greatest issues affecting the character of American families in the 1990s and after was the growing poverty of the nation's elderly.
6. T F One factor that made Hispanic immigration to the United States unique was the close proximity of Mexican Americans to their former homeland across the border.
7. T F Immigrants contributed more in federal income and excise taxes than they consumed in benefits.
8. T F By the mid-1990s, a majority of Americans lived in suburbs rather than central cities or rural areas.
9. T F Reactions to the O.J. Simpson case and the controversial 2000 election in Florida demonstrated that both whites and blacks were increasingly able to make political judgments without considering race.
10. T F African Americans attained considerable success in being elected to both local and national political leadership positions in the late twentieth and early twenty-first centuries.
11. T F President George Bush's plan to provide a path to citizenship for illegal aliens received strong support from Democrats and Republicans alike.
12. T F The rise of television and rock music caused a sharp decline in the number of Americans who patronized the high culture of museums and symphony orchestras.
13. T F The tradition of fictional and nonfiction writing about the American West declined sharply in the late twentieth century.

14. T F The center of the American and international art world after World War II was San Francisco.

15. T F The greatest challenge to American values posed by the terrorist attacks of September 11, 2001, was how to maintain national security without eroding traditional freedoms and isolating the United States in the world.

B. Multiple Choice

Select the best answer and circle the corresponding letter.

1. The flagship business of the heavy industrial economy of the early twentieth century was the
   a. International Business Machines Company.
   b. Microsoft Corporation.
   c. U.S. Steel Corporation.
   d. General Mills Corporation.
   e. Union Pacific Railroad.
2. The primary engine driving the U.S. economy of the early twenty-first century is
   a. alternative energy development.
   b. corporate mergers and acquisitions.
   c. scientific research.
   d. international investment in American companies.
   e. labor union activism.
3. An example of ethical controversy surrounding fundamental scientific research in the first decade of the twenty-first century concerned
   a. stem cell research using human embryos.
   b. biological research on increasing plant yields.
   c. artificial computer aids to human intelligence.
   d. artificial insemination and organ transplants.
   e. pharmaceutical drugs designed to treat depression.
4. One of the greatest concerns regarding the continuing success of American science and engineering was that
   a. America's research universities were being crippled by antiscientific ideologies.
   b. American industry no longer sought to take advantage of scientific breakthroughs.
   c. women and minorities were still largely unable to pursue scientific careers.
   d. the United States was no longer producing enough scientists or even attracting top scientists from abroad.
   e. there were few remaining frontiers where fundamental scientific advance could occur.
5. The most striking development in the American economic structure in the 1990s and 2000s was the
   a. growing inequality between rich and poor.
   b. slow general decline in the American standard of living.
   c. growing reliance on investments and real estate rather than jobs for income.
   d. increasing concentration of wealth in certain regions and affluent suburbs.
   e. concentration of high tech investment in the older cities of the Northeast and Midwest.
6. Which of the following was *not* among the causes of the income gap in the United States?
   a. Intensifying global economic competition
   b. The shrinkage in manufacturing jobs for unskilled and semiskilled labor
   c. The decline of labor unions
   d. The entry of large numbers of women into the work force
   e. The increasing tendency of educated workers to marry one another

7. The most dramatic change in the patterns of women's employment from the 1950s to the 2000s was
   a. the end of heavy occupational segregation in certain female-dominated job categories.
   b. that the majority of mothers with young children went to work outside the home.
   c. that women made greater employment gains when they were educated in all-female schools and colleges.
   d. that married women worked at a higher rate than single women.
   e. that women made greater economic gains when they operated small businesses from their homes than when they were employed in the workforce.
8. Perhaps the most significant sign of the pressures on the traditional American family in the late twentieth century was that
   a. television no longer accurately portrayed family situations.
   b. a majority of children no longer lived with their birth parents.
   c. immigrant families were less stable than those of traditional old stock Americans.
   d. the elderly were no longer likely to live with their adult children.
   e. families were increasingly slow to form at all.
9. The increasingly longer lives of America's senior citizens were often eased by the
   a. ability of the potent elderly lobby to obtain government benefits for seniors.
   b. willingness of younger generations to provide income support for aged parents.
   c. large-scale migration of senior citizens to the West Coast.
   d. more positive portrayals of the elderly in movies and television.
   e. growing equality of income among seniors caused by private pension programs.
10. The most serious problem caused by federal programs like Social Security and Medicare in the twenty-first century was likely to be that
   a. benefits could not keep up with rising inflation.
   b. the Social Security and Medicare trust funds would exercise too great a control over the economy.
   c. benefits for large numbers of retiring baby boomers would create generational conflict with younger workers.
   d. the health care system could no longer meet the rising demand for services to the elderly.
   e. American businesses would no longer contribute to retirement or health care accounts.
11. The new immigrants of the late twentieth and early twenty-first centuries came to the United States primarily because they
   a. wanted jobs and economic opportunities unavailable in their homelands.
   b. were fleeing religious and political repression.
   c. admired American cultural and intellectual achievements.
   d. wanted to strengthen the minority voting bloc in the United States.
   e. regarded national borders as increasingly irrelevant in the global economy.
12. The largest group of the new immigrants came from
   a. East Asia.
   b. Mexico and other Latin American countries.
   c. Africa and the Middle East.
   d. South Asia.
   e. the Caribbean.

13. Which of the following was *not* a significant result of the Internet revolution in early twenty-first century?
    a. An economic boom in high-tech dot.com companies
    b. A democratization of information and communication
    c. The weakening of traditional, mainstream print media
    d. The rapid dispersal of both information and misinformation through the "blogosphere"
    e. A decline of visual media in favor of electronic reading and writing
14. The primary goals of modern multiculturalists was to
    a. end traditional American national literature and culture.
    b. make Spanish an official American language equal to English.
    c. preserve and promote distinct ethnic and racial cultures in the United States rather than emphasize a common American identity and culture.
    d. emphasize the human rights and human values common to all people regardless of nationality.
    e. promote minority education and media as a means of bringing about radical social change.
15. The most striking development in American literature in the past two decades has been the
    a. importance of the literature of fantasy, absurdism and black comedy.
    b. rise of writers from once-marginal regions and ethnic groups.
    c. focus on themes of nostalgia and lost innocence.
    d. rise of social realism and attention to working-class stories.
    e. avoidance of attention to sensitive sexual and racial issues.

C. Identification

Supply the correct identification for each numbered description.

1. ____________ The computer corporation that symbolized the U.S. economy in the 1990s much as U.S. Steel did in 1900
2. ____________ Health care program for the elderly, enacted in 1965, that created large economic demands on the American economy by the 1990s
3. ____________ Law of 1986 that granted amnesty to past illegal immigrants and penalized employers of future illegal workers
4. ____________ The largest of the new immigrant groups
5. ____________ Organization, headed by César Chavez, that worked to improve conditions for migrant workers
6. ____________ City where major racial disturbance erupted in 1992
7. ____________ American region that saw a particularly rich literary revival beginning in the 1980s
8. ____________ Tax-funded federal agency, created in 1965, that provided support for American art and artists
9. ____________ Avant-garde painting movement pioneered by Jackson Pollock and others in the 1940s and 1950s
10. ____________ Oil tanker whose 1989 spill off the coast of Alaska sparked deep concern over oil drilling and transportation on the world's oceans

D. Matching People, Places, and Events

Match the person, place, or event in the left column with the proper description in the right column by inserting the correct letter on the blank line.

1. ___ O. J. Simpson
2. ___ L. Douglas Wilder
3. ___ Barack Obama
4. ___ Larry McMurtry
5. ___ Norman MacLean
6. ___ August Wilson
7. ___ Toni Morrison
8. ___ N. Scott Momaday
9. ___ David Mamet
10. ___ Eve Ensler
11. ___ Jackson Pollock
12. ___ Frank Gehry

a. Leading Indian writer, author of *House Made of Dawn*

b. Pioneer artistic creator of abstract expressionism in the 1940s and 1950s

c. The first African American state governor

d. Leading twenty-first century American architect whose works, like the Disney Concert Hall, used fanciful metallic forms

e. Feminist playwright whose *Vagina Monologues* blended comedy and sharp social commentary

f. Playwright who deployed gritty American slang in socially critical dramas like *Glengarry Glen Ross*

g. Former football star whose murder trial became a focus of racial tension

h. Author of *Beloved* and winner of the Nobel Prize for Literature

i. Western writer who portrayed small towns in *Last Picture Show* and the cattle-drive era in *Lonesome Dove*

j. First African American elected president of the United States

k. African American playwright who portrayed the psychological costs of the northern migration

l. Former English professor who wrote memorable tales of his Montana boyhood

E. Putting Things in Order

Put the following events in correct order by numbering them from 1 to 5.

1. __________ F. Douglas Wilder is elected the first African American governor.
2. __________ Congress passes the Immigration Reform and Control Act to try to thwart illegal immigration.

3. __________ Jackson Pollock and others pioneer abstract expressionism and the leading form of modern American painting.

4. __________ Los Angeles experiences a major riot as the result of a racial incident involving police brutality.

5. __________ California voters approve Proposition 209 in an attempt to overturn affirmative-action policies.

F. Matching Cause and Effect

Match the historical cause in the left column with the proper effect in the right column by writing the correct letter on the blank line.

Cause

1. ___ Decline of manufacturing jobs and higher pay for educated workers
2. ___ The computer revolution and the new trend toward genetic engineering
3. ___ Expanding economic opportunities for women
4. ___ Rise of the median age of the population since the 1970s
5. ___ Growing numbers and political power for Hispanic Americans
6. ___ The growth of the African American middle class and their migration to the suburbs
7. ___ Poverty and economic upheavals in Latin America and Asia
8. ___ The resentment against many affirmative action measures
9. ___ The reaction against integration and the rise of multiculturalism
10. ___ The success of modernist American art movements since the 1940s

Effect

a. Made the American southwest increasingly a bicultural zone
b. Changed both child-rearing patterns and men's social roles
c. Led to sharp attacks on Eurocentrism in American education
d. Contributed to sharply increased income inequality in the United States
e. Made the elderly a powerful political force
f. Further isolated the poverty-stricken lower class in the inner cities
g. Made New York City the art capital of the world
h. Created the highest rates of immigration to the United States since the early 1900s
i. Led California voters to pass measures restricting the use of racial categories
j. Expanded the economy but threatened many traditional jobs while creating new ethical dilemmas for society

PART III: APPLYING WHAT YOU HAVE LEARNED

1. What were the consequences of the dramatically changed American economy as the United States advanced into the early twenty-first century?
2. What caused the rapidly increasing gap between rich and poor in America? Was this disparity a direct result of economic and social policies, or was it a largely unavoidable consequence of the changes in business, education, and social structure in the period 1980–2007?
3. How did women's new economic opportunities affect American society? What barriers to women's complete economic equality proved most difficult to overcome?

4. How did the new immigration and the rise of ethnic minorities transform American society by the beginning of the twenty-first century? Were the effects of the new immigration similar to that of earlier waves of immigration or fundamentally different?
5. How were the changes in American society reflected in literature and the arts in the late twentieth and early twenty-first centuries?
6. What is the central social and moral challenge America faces in the first half of the twenty-first century? How is the way the nation approaches that challenge shaped by American history, and how does understanding that history contribute to addressing that challenge in productive ways?
7. How did the Internet revolution transform the American economy, communications, and education? What were the most positive results of the explosion of Internet communication? What were some of its problems and dangers?
8. How does the relative uniqueness of America's history and culture affect its relationship to such increasingly international issues as economic development, the environment, immigration, and terrorism?

Answer Key to Volume II of the Guidebook

CHAPTER 22

II. A.

1. True
2. False. Most white Southerners believed that secession had been right and strongly resented being forced back into the Union.
3. True
4. True
5. False. The Freedmen's Bureau largely failed to enhance black economic and social opportunity, though it did make some gains in education.
6. True
7. False. Johnson's rapid pardoning of Confederate leaders angered all Republicans.
8. True
9. False. The Black Codes were extremely harsh laws that gave blacks almost no rights, except for their formal freedom from slavery.
10. True
11. False. Redistribution of land was opposed by moderate Republicans, and never became part of Reconstruction.
12. False. Blacks controlled only one house of one state legislature—South Carolina.
13. True
14. False. The federal government eventually acted with force to suppress the Ku Klux Klan.
15. True

II. B.

1. c
2. c
3. b
4. e
5. c
6. a
7. a

8. e
9. c
10. b
11. c
12. c
13. a
14. e
15. d

II. C.

1. Freedmen's Bureau
2. African Methodist Episcopal Church; Baptist Church
3. 10 percent plan
4. Wade-Davis Bill
5. Black Codes
6. Fourteenth Amendment
7. Military Reconstruction Act (of 1867)
8. Redeemers
9. Union League
10. *Ex parte Milligan*
11. scalawags
12. carpetbaggers
13. Fifteenth Amendment
14. Ku Klux Klan

II. D.

1. h
2. k
3. c
4. m
5. b
6. j
7. o
8. i
9. f
10. g

11. e
12. a
13. l
14. n
15. d

II. E.

4

1

5

3

2

II. F.

1. d
2. e
3. j
4. c
5. i
6. f
7. h
8. b
9. a
10. g

II. G.

1. Eight whites, three blacks; the white woman seated in the center; they are in the rear and partly hidden, suggesting that they might hold subordinate positions on the staff.
2. The shabby clothes of the boy and young woman; the crude log cabin dwelling. The people seem weary but hopeful: at least three of them have partial smiles.
3. The men in the line appear to be working people—perhaps farmers in their best clothes. The voting officials, black and white, appear more affluent and well-dressed. The drawing shows the new voters as somewhat hesitant and uncertain, perhaps being manipulated by the more politically knowledgeable officials.

CHAPTER 23

II. A.

1. False. Grant's lack of political experience hurt, and he did engage in Republican party politics.
2. True

3. False. The political mistakes of the Liberal Republicans caused them to fail.
4. True
5. False. The parties agreed on national issues; their disagreements were at the local level.
6. True
7. False. The Republicans got the presidency and the Democrats got other political and economic concessions.
8. True
9. True
10. True
11. True
12. False. The campaign was based on personal mudslinging rather than issues.
13. True
14. True
15. False. The gold deal made Cleveland extremely unpopular among Democrats and Populists.

II. B.

1. c
2. c
3. b
4. b
5. e
6. d
7. c
8. a
9. a
10. e
11. d
12. b
13. b
14. a
15. d

II. C.

1. (waving the) bloody shirt
2. Credit Mobilier
3. Liberal Republican party

4. silver
5. Greenback Labor party
6. Gilded Age
7. Grand Army of the Republic
8. Stalwarts
9. Half-Breeds
10. Compromise of 1877
11. Chinese
12. civil service
13. McKinley Tariff
14. Populists (People's party)
15. grandfather clause

II. D.

1. d
2. b
3. a
4. n
5. j
6. h
7. i
8. k
9. o
10. c
11. g
12. e
13. l
14. f
15. m

II. E.

3

1

5

2

4

II. F.

1. g
2. e
3. c
4. i
5. a
6. j
7. b
8. f
9. d
10. h

II. G.

1. The fundamental difference was in their ethnic and religious composition. The Republicans were based on morally-oriented groups with Puritan backgrounds; the Democrats on immigrant ethnic groups of Catholic or Lutheran background.
2. Most of the controversial issues existed at the state or local level.
3. The two parties each had well-mobilized machines that got out the vote no matter who the candidates were.
4. Winning elections was crucial for patronage—passing out jobs to party supporters.

II. H.

1. none
2. Connecticut, New Jersey, New York, and Indiana
3. four
4. Texas
5. none

CHAPTER 24

II. A.

1. False. The railroads received subsidies and land grants to build the rail lines.
2. True
3. True
4. True.
5. True
6. False. The description applies to Carnegie's technique of vertical integration. Rockefeller's horizontal integration meant consolidating with competitors in the same market.

7. True
8. True
9. False. The South remained poor and dependent, despite the New South.
10. True
11. False. Most American manufacturers succeeded by producing great volumes of standardized goods for the vast domestic U.S. market.
12. True
13. True
14. True
15. False. The AFL did not even attempt to organize these categories of workers.

II. B.

1. b
2. d
3. b
4. d
5. c
6. d
7. c
8. d
9. d
10. b
11. e
12. d
13. e
14. c
15. b

II. C.

1. land grants
2. Union Pacific Railroad
3. Central Pacific Railroad
4. Pullman palace cars
5. stock watering
6. *Wabash* case
7. Mesabi Iron Range

8. telephone
9. Standard Oil Company
10. United States Steel Corporation
11. New South
12. Social Darwinism
13. Knights of Labor
14. Gibson girls
15. American Federation of Labor (or AF of L)

II. D.

1. j
2. h
3. m
4. g
5. f
6. o
7. a
8. i
9. e
10. b
11. d
12. l
13. n
14. c
15. k

II. E.

5

4

3

2

1

II. F.

1. i
2. d
3. e

4. h
5. a
6. b
7. j
8. f
9. g
10. c

II. G.

1. The family of pieceworkers is in their own home; each concentrates on their own single tasks, but they are able to relate to one another and perhaps offer advice and assistance around the table. The black textile workers are at separate posts, but the women and children can also probably converse and assist one another. In both these two cases, the children and adult workers are mingled and performing the same tasks. By contrast, the adult male Westinghouse workers are dwarfed by their industrial machinery and serve its demands. In the final photo, the child textile workers are by themselves and almost encased by the machines. They are evidently without adult assistance or supervision, and plainly in danger of industrial accident.
2. The scene takes place in front of the owner's house. The men have evidently come directly from the factory. There appears to have been some conflict over wages or working conditions.
3. The owner and the woman—evidently his wife—are very well dressed. The workers, and worker's family on the left, are shabbily dressed. The painting illustrates the considerable class difference between the owner and his immigrant work force.
4. The workers are conversing with the owner and his wife, and also with one another. The first conversation is probably about the grievance. The second may be about what the workers should do next—whether to strike or resort to violence (as the one worker seems about to do).

CHAPTER 25

II. A.

1. True
2. False. Other cities in Europe and elsewhere around the world grew just as rapidly.
3. True
4. True
5. True
6. True
7. False. A large proportion of American Protestants rejected Darwinism and adhered to literal biblical interpretation.
8. False. Secondary education was increasingly carried out in public schools.
9. False. Washington advocated practical, technical education for blacks, not academic rigor or education for political leadership.
10. True

11. True
12. False. They favored social realism in their fiction.
13. True
14. True
15. False. American urban planners adopted many of the grand City Beautiful ideas from European cities.

II. B.

1. c
2. c
3. c
4. c
5. e
6. b
7. d
8. d
9. e
10. d
11. e
12. a
13. a
14. d
15. c

II. C.

1. dumbbell tenement
2. New Immigration
3. America fever
4. social gospel
5. Hull House
6. social work
7. American Protective Association
8. Fundamentalists
9. Tuskegee Institute
10. National Association for the Advancement of Colored People (or NAACP) (Niagara Movement less preferable but OK)
11. *Progress and Poverty*

12. Comstock Law
13. pragmatism
14. the City Beautiful
15. Women's Christian Temperance Union (or WCTU)

II. D.

1. m
2. e
3. j
4. n
5. d
6. f
7. l
8. g
9. a
10. o
11. b
12. h
13. k
14. i
15. c

II. E.

4

2

3

5

1

II. F.

1. g
2. b
3. e
4. i
5. h
6. c
7. f

8. a
9. j
10. d

II. G.

1. Five peaks: end of Civil War, anti-Jewish pogroms, early twentieth-century prosperity, the end of World War I, and the end of World War II and the quota system

   Four valleys: Panic of 1873, Panic of 1893, World War I, and the introduction of quotas
2. Each major period lasted 15–20 years. The most recent growth period has lasted for 40 years.
3. Sharpest rise: 1900–1905; sharpest decline: 1915–1920
4. 800,000: approximately 1882, 1910, and 1923

   200,000: about 1867, 1875, 1880, 1898–99, 1917, 1932, and 1948–49
5. About a million fewer (1.2 million to 200,000)

   About 350,000 to 400,000 more (about 225,000 to 600,000)

CHAPTER 26

II. A.

1. True
2. False. The Indians were defeated only slowly and with difficulty.
3. True
4. False. Humanitarian reformers did not respect the Indians' culture and tried to destroy their tribal way of life.
5. True
6. True
7. False. The Homestead Act was frequently abused and manipulated, and only a minority of ordinary farmers benefited from it.
8. True
9. True
10. False. Farmers in the West and South were highly individualistic, very hard to organize, and continued to suffer economic disadvantages.
11. True
12. True
13. False. Hanna had no difficulty raising large sums of money for McKinley's campaign.
14. True
15. True

II. B.

1. e
2. a
3. e
4. b
5. d
6. d
7. c
8. c
9. b
10. e
11. b
12. a
13. a
14. b
15. c

II. C.

1. Sioux
2. Apaches
3. reservations
4. Ghost Dance
5. Dawes Severalty Act
6. Comstock Lode
7. long drive
8. Homestead Act
9. Frontier Thesis
10. Oklahoma
11. Populists (People's Party)
12. Coin's Financial School
13. Pullman strike
14. Cross of Gold speech
15. "goldbugs"

II. D.

1. j
2. l

3. f
4. b
5. i
6. k
7. g
8. m
9. n
10. c
11. n
12. d
13. e
14. o
15. a

II. E.

4

2

1

3

5

II. F.

1. j
2. e
3. i
4. d
5. h
6. c
7. g
8. b
9. a
10. f

II. G.

1. Wheat
2. Wheat and rice

3. Hogs
4. Beef cattle

II. H.

1. Six (Minnesota, Iowa, North Dakota, South Dakota, Oregon, California)
2. 17 (only Missouri)
3. Bryan
4. None

CHAPTER 27

II. A.

1. False. America was unconcerned and isolated from international affairs in those decades.
2. False. It nearly resulted in a war with Britain.
3. True
4. True
5. True
6. True
7. True
8. True
9. False. The peace treaty was very controversial.
10. False. It ruled that the constitution and bill of rights did not apply to American colonies.
11. True
12. False. The Open Door policy was a unilateral American initiative; neither the Chinese nor the Europeans were consulted.
13. False. Roosevelt believed in a strong, assertive American role in the world, though without bluster ("Speak softly, and carry a big stick")
14. True
15. True
16. True

II. B.

1. b
2. e
3. a
4. e
5. c

6. c
7. b
8. b
9. e
10. b
11. c
12. c
13. c
14. b
15. c

II. C.

1. Samoa (Samoan Islands)
2. Chile
3. Monroe Doctrine
4. yellow journalism or yellow press
5. *Maine*
6. Manila Bay
7. Rough Riders
8. Puerto Rico
9. insular cases
10. Open Door notes
11. Boxer Rebellion
12. Hay-Pauncefote-Treaty
13. Colombia
14. Roosevelt Corollary (to the Monroe Doctrine)
15. Gentlemen's Agreement

II. D.

1. j
2. f
3. k
4. d
5. n
6. c
7. h

8. l
9. g
10. a
11. o
12. e
13. b
14. m
15. i

II. E.

1

3

2

4

5

II. F.

1. f
2. c
3. e
4. g
5. b
6. d
7. a
8. i
9. j
10. h

II. G.

1. The Philippines, Puerto Rico, and Guam
2. American Samoa
3. Luzon
4. San Juan Hill
5. Puerto Rico

CHAPTER 28

II. A.

1. False. Progressives favored the growth of government power over the economy and society.
2. True
3. False. There were large numbers of progressives in both major parties.
4. True
5. False. He threatened the owners with federal intervention, saying he would seize their mines.
6. True
7. False. He believed that there were good trusts and bad trusts, and that only the bad trusts should be broken up.
8. False. It was intended to focus attention on the plight of the meat-packing workers.
9. True
10. True
11. True
12. False. Taft was an unskilled politician and an inept campaigner.
13. False. Progressives grew angry over his tariff and conservation policies, and his alliance with reactionaries.
14. True
15. True

II. B.

1. e
2. a
3. c
4. e
5. d
6. b
7. e
8. c
9. b
10. a
11. d
12. a
13. e
14. c
15. c

II. C.

1. progressivism
2. muckrakers
3. initiative
4. recall
5. Square Deal
6. Hepburn Act
7. Triangle Shirtwaist Fire
8. *The Jungle*
9. Women's Christian Temperance Union
10. Roosevelt panic (Panic of 1907)
11. dollar diplomacy
12. Standard Oil Company

II. D.

1. g
2. l
3. h
4. n
5. e
6. i
7. d
8. b
9. k
10. f
11. m
12. c
13. a
14. o
15. j

II. E.

5

1

4

2

3

II. F.

1. i
2. b
3. g
4. c
5. j
6. d
7. a
8. f
9. h
10. e

II. G.

1. D
2. B
3. A
4. B
5. A
6. C
7. C
8. A
9. B
10. B
11. D
12. B

CHAPTER 29

II. A.

1. True
2. False. The reverse is true: Wilson's New Freedom favored small enterprise and antitrust activities; Roosevelt's New Nationalism favored federal regulation and social activism.
3. True
4. True
5. False. Wilson's policies were unfavorable to blacks.
6. True
7. False. Wilson sent troops to Haiti and Santo Domingo.

8. True
9. True
10. False. It was sent in response to Villa's raids into New Mexico and the killing of United States citizens.
11. False. Most Americans sympathized with Britain from the beginning.
12. True
13. False. The reverse is true: the East was ready to go to war; the Midwest and West largely favored attempts at negotiation.
14. True
15. True

II. B.

1. e
2. b
3. c
4. b
5. e
6. a
7. b
8. c
9. b
10. a
11. e
12. d
13. c
14. d
15. d

II. C.

1. bull moose
2. Socialist Party
3. New Freedom
4. Federal Reserve Board
5. Federal Trade Commission
6. Clayton Anti-Trust Act
7. Jones Act
8. Haiti

9. ABC Powers
10. Central Powers
11. Allies
12. submarine
13. *Lusitania*
14. *Sussex* pledge
15. California

II. D.

1. i
2. k
3. d
4. l
5. j
6. e
7. o
8. m
9. c
10. b
11. h
12. g
13. a
14. n
15. f

II. E.

5

2

1

4

3

II. F.

1. d
2. b
3. i
4. e

5. j
6. g
7. h
8. a
9. f
10. c

II. G.

1. German policy was that they would not try to sink neutral shipping, but they warned that mistakes might occur.
2. America was an important neutral, and Germany had no reason to want American civilians to be killed. The warning could be used to take the burden of responsibility off Germany and put it on those passengers who chose to travel anyway.
3. Germany knew that the *Lusitania* was in fact carrying 4200 cases of ammunition.
4. America claimed a complete right of neutral and unarmed civilian travel on the high seas. Issuing a warning did nothing to affect that.

CHAPTER 30

II. A.

1. False. Germany responded by resuming unrestricted submarine warfare.
2. True
3. True
4. True
5. False. The primary targets were antiwar Socialists and members of the Industrial Workers of the World (IWWs).
6. True
7. True
8. True
9. False. Several nations in Europe and elsewhere had granted women the right to vote before the United States did so.
10. True
11. True
12. True
13. False. Wilson was unable to prevent several Allied nations from imposing imperialistic solutions.
14. True
15. False. The reverse is true: Cox supported the League, while Harding tried to evade the issue or straddle both sides.

II. B.

1. b
2. c
3. c
4. c
5. d
6. a
7. e
8. e
9. e
10. e
11. e
12. c
13. b
14. e
15. b

II. C.

1. Zimmerman note
2. Fourteen Points
3. Committee on Public Information (CPI)
4. Industrial Workers of the World (IWWs)
5. War Industries Board
6. Nineteenth Amendment (Women's Suffrage Amendment OK)
7. Liberty Loans
8. doughboys
9. Big Four
10. League of Nations
11. Treaty of Versailles
12. (Senate) Foreign Relations Committee
13. irreconcilables (or "battalion of death")
14. Lodge reservations
15. "solemn referendum"

II. D.

1. e
2. o

3. n
4. h
5. k
6. i
7. c
8. g
9. a
10. m
11. d
12. b
13. j
14. l
15. f

II. E.

2

5

1

3

4

II. F.

1. e
2. h
3. g
4. j
5. a
6. c
7. f
8. i
9. d
10. b

II. G.

1. The message to "Remember Belgium" is reinforced by the cruel, mustached German soldier dragging away a young girl, who is a kind of personification of Belgium and Belgians; he may even be intending to assault her. In general, the image of Germany as a militaristic violator of the

innocent reinforces that America is fighting a righteous war to restore virtue, justice, and liberty (hence "liberty loans") where they have been violated.

2. Both the flag, symbolizing patriotism, and the soldiers marching in solidarity are on the other side of the window from the young civilian, who is evidently isolated and alone. The fine dress and manner of the potential recruit suggests the poster is targeted at the affluent and educated.
3. It portrays the garden vegetables going "over the top," just as soldiers did; the caption suggests that food will produce not only an Allied victory but peace as well.

CHAPTER 31

II. A.

1. False. The red scare focused on alleged communists and radicals inside the United States; there was no threat of war with Communist Russia.
2. True
3. False. The KKK faded as a political power in the late 1920s, before the Great Depression.
4. True
5. True
6. True
7. False. Scopes was found guilty, and Tennessee's anti-evolution law was upheld.
8. True
9. True
10. False. *The Birth of a Nation* was a racist film that presented blacks in an extremely negative light.
11. False. The decade saw a further loosening of sexual behavior, especially by women.
12. True
13. False. Most prominent writers of the 1920s criticized or mocked small-town life and celebrated urban sophistication.
14. False. Those who became expatriates migrated primarily to France (Paris).
15. True

II. B.

1. c
2. a
3. b
4. d
5. a
6. c
7. d
8. e

9. e
10. e
11. b
12. d
13. e
14. d
15. c

II. C.

1. red scare
2. Ku Klux Klan
3. Immigration Act of 1924
4. cultural pluralism
5. prohibition
6. Scopes trial
7. Model T
8. *The Birth of a Nation*
9. radio
10. birth control
11. jazz
12. Universal Negro Improvement Association (UNIA)
13. *American Mercury*
14. *This Side of Paradise*
15. Harlem Renaissance

II. D.

1. e
2. c
3. g
4. l
5. h
6. d
7. j
8. a
9. m
10. o

11. k
12. f
13. n
14. b
15. i

II. E.

4

1

5

2

3

II. F.

1. c
2. a
3. j
4. e
5. f
6. i
7. b
8. h
9. d
10. g

II. G.

1. Hollywood's movies, like Henry Ford's cars, were mass-produced consumer products created by industry.
2. New products helped free women from the home and from their traditional roles.
3. Fitzgerald's novels idealized the moral and sexual liberation of youth from the past and suggested that personal freedom and pleasure were goals of the new affluent American society.
4. These writers all endorsed new moral and social values at odds with those of the American past. Before the 1920s, most Americans lived on farms or in small towns, and such values were widely shared. Now there was an audience ready to hear what such writers were saying.

CHAPTER 32

II. A.

1. False. The corrupt cabinet officers were the secretary of the interior and the attorney general (Fall and Doherty).
2. False. The antitrust laws were generally not enforced.
3. False. Their isolationism included disarmament policies and reduced military spending.
4. True
5. True
6. True
7. False. The main source of La Follette's support was farmers in the Midwest.
8. True
9. True
10. True
11. False. The Hawley-Smoot Tariff represented a policy of economic isolationism and helped undercut international trade.
12. True
13. True
14. False. Hoover modified his policies somewhat and provided some federal funds for relief and recovery to business.
15. True

II. B.

1. d
2. e
3. b
4. c
5. c
6. e
7. b
8. b
9. e
10. a
11. e
12. b
13. a
14. c
15. e

II. C.

1. Ohio Gang
2. *Adkins* v. *Children's Hospital*
3. American Legion
4. Five-Power Naval Treaty
5. Kellogg-Briand Pact
6. Teapot Dome
7. McNary-Haugen Bill
8. Dawes plan
9. Hoovercrats
10. Hawley-Smoot Tariff
11. Black Tuesday
12. Hoovervilles
13. Reconstruction Finance Corporation
14. Bonus Army (Bonus Expeditionary Force)
15. Manchuria

II. D.

1. i
2. g
3. h
4. m
5. e
6. d
7. f
8. o
9. l
10. k
11. c
12. a
13. b
14. n
15. j

II. E.

5

3

1

4

2

II. F.

1. b
2. e
3. i
4. f
5. d
6. j
7. a
8. c
9. g
10. h

II. G.

1. Americans were private investors in Germany. America also collected allied war debts from France and Britain.
2. France and Britain collected war reparations from Germany.
3. Britain and France both owed war debts to the United States.
4. Credit from U.S. bankers was the only thing that enabled the whole international financial system to function. When Wall Street collapsed in 1929, Europe and the whole financial system collapsed with it.

CHAPTER 33

II. A.

1. True
2. False. Eleanor Roosevelt had been actively involved in social reform and women's causes before her husband's election to the White House.
3. True
4. False. The New Deal drew some of its ideas from European social welfare models.
5. False. They were designed primarily to provide employment for those out of work.

6. True
7. False. There was genuine public concern that the United States could fall into totalitarian dictatorship if the Depression was not addressed.
8. True
9. False. It was also designed to provide jobs, electricity, and low-income housing to residents of the area.
10. True
11. True
12. False. The Court did not remain so hostile to the New Deal.
13. False. Compared to European pension and social welfare systems, America's Social Security System was limited and regressive.
14. True
15. False. Unemployment remained quite high until World War II, despite the New Deal (though lower than it had been in 1933).

II. B.

1. c
2. e
3. b
4. e
5. d
6. e
7. d
8. c
9. b
10. a
11. d
12. b
13. d
14. a
15. e

II. C.

1. New Deal
2. brain(s) trust
3. Hundred Days
4. Civilian Conservation Corps

5. Works Progress Administration (WPA)
6. blue eagle
7. Agricultural Adjustment Administration (AAA)
8. Dust Bowl
9. Tennessee Valley Authority (TVA)
10. Social Security
11. Committee for Industrial Organization (CIO) (Congress of Industrial Organizations OK)
12. Securities and Exchange Commission (SEC)
13. American Liberty League
14. court packing plan
15. Keynesianism

II. D.

1. g
2. e
3. l
4. j
5. b
6. f
7. n
8. k
9. c
10. o
11. h
12. a
13. i
14. m
15. d

II. E.

2

1

4

5

3

II. F.

1. e
2. i
3. g
4. a
5. f
6. b
7. j
8. h
9. c
10. d

II. G.

1. National Recovery Administration (NRA)
2. Any three of the following:
    a. FDR closes banks
    b. Emergency Banking Relief Act
    c. FDR orders gold surrender and abandons gold standard
    d. Gold-payment clause repealed
3. Securities Exchange Commission, Social Security Act, and Public Utilities Holding Company Act
4. National Housing Act creating the FHA
5. Second Agricultural Adjustment Act
6. The Hundred Days was aimed primarily at recovery; the later New Deal was aimed at relief and reform. The most continuity was seen in measures aimed at relief.

II. H.

1. Tennessee, Alabama, North Carolina, and Virginia
2.
    a. five
    b. three
3. France and the United States; Sweden and Germany
4. The United States and Germany; Sweden and Japan

CHAPTER 34

II. A.

1. False. It showed that he put domestic recovery ahead of establishing a stable international economic order.
2. True

3. True
4. True
5. False. The United States adhered to its neutrality laws and refused to help the Loyalist government.
6. False. There was a strong isolationist reaction to both Roosevelt's speech and the *Panay* incident.
7. False. The United States did not object to the appeasement policy and, in effect, endorsed it.
8. True
9. False. It strengthened the movement to give aid to Britain.
10. True
11. False. Willkie agreed with Roosevelt's pro-British stance and did not attack him on foreign policy.
12. True
13. False. It was an agreement between Britain and the United States only.
14. True
15. False. The crucial point of conflict was Japan's refusal to withdraw from China.

II. B.

1. a
2. e
3. b
4. d
5. b
6. d
7. c
8. d
9. a
10. e
11. d
12. b
13. a
14. e
15. c

II. C.

1. London Conference
2. Philippines
3. Good Neighbor policy

4. Neutrality Acts
5. Spanish Civil War
6. Quarantine Speech
7. Munich
8. appeasement
9. Committee to Defend America by Aiding the Allies
10. America First
11. lend-lease
12. *kristallnacht*
13. Atlantic Charter
14. *Reuben James*
15. Pearl Harbor

II. D.

1. l
2. e
3. k
4. f
5. o
6. c
7. j
8. n
9. g
10. b
11. d
12. a
13. m
14. i
15. h

II. E.

1

3

5

4

2

II. F.

1. g
2. c
3. i
4. h
5. b
6. f
7. d
8. j
9. e
10. a

II. G.

Order	Context
4	4
6	7
1	2
2	3
7	1
5	5
3	6

II. H

1. forty-one
2. forty-one
3. Europe
4. Soviet Union

CHAPTER 35

II. A.

1. False. The reverse is true: the decision was to fight Hitler first and then Japan.
2. False. Nearly all Americans supported World War II, including those whose forebears came from enemy nations.
3. True
4. True
5. True

6. False. Most women left the labor force after the war.
7. False. Americans enjoyed economic prosperity during World War II.
8. False. The battles of the Coral Sea and Midway enabled the United States to block Japanese domination of the Pacific sea-lanes.
9. False. The American strategy in the Pacific involved island hopping toward the Japanese home islands.
10. False. The Soviet Union bore the heaviest burden of casualties; U.S. and British casualties were comparatively light.
11. True
12. True
13. False. Conservative Democrats were opposed to Henry Wallace.
14. False. The Allies pushed on for total victory over Germany, despite Roosevelt's death.
15. True

II. B.

1. c
2. e
3. a
4. c
5. a
6. a
7. e
8. c
9. d
10. d
11. c
12. e
13. b
14. d
15. a

II. C.

1. Japanese Americans
2. War Production Board
3. WAACS and WAVES
4. Bracero Program
5. "Rosie the Riveter"

6. Fair Employment Practices Commission (FEPC)
7. Philippines
8. Battle of Midway
9. Unconditional Surrender
10. Casablanca
11. Teheran
12. D-Day
13. Battle of the Bulge
14. Iwo Jima and Okinawa
15. Manhattan Project

II. D.

1. f
2. i
3. n
4. e
5. o
6. g
7. j
8. a
9. k
10. d
11. m
12. c
13. h
14. l
15. b

II. E.

3

4

1

2

II. F.

1. i
2. h

3. c
4. e
5. g
6. b
7. d
8. a
9. f
10. j

II. G.

1.
   a. Russians: Leningrad and Stalingrad
   b. Americans and British: Tunisia, North Africa
2. Driving the Germans out of Russia
3. In Poland
4. About ten months (July 1944 to May 1945)
5. Southern Germany (Austria). The British and Americans were coming from Italy and France, the Russians from Hungary.

II. H.

1. 116,000
2. seven
3. Detroit and New York
4. India and Australia
5. Tunisia
6. Poland, Hungary, and Romania
7. France, Netherlands, and Belgium
8. Elbe

CHAPTER 36

II. A.

1. False. The economy struggled from 1945 to 1950, and only began to grow dramatically after 1950.
2. True
3. False. The large-scale postwar migrations tended to disrupt traditional extended family relationships and limit childrearing assistance and advice from grandparents or others beyond the nuclear family.

4. False. Federal dollars accounted for much of the Sunbelt's prosperity.
5. True
6. True
7. False. Truman relied on his own judgment, and took complete responsibility for his decisions ("The buck stops here").
8. False. The United Nations was not dramatically more effective than the League of Nations, because the Security Council gave a veto to the five Great Powers, who quickly fell to quarreling.
9. False. The reverse is true; the Western Allies wanted a united Germany, while the Soviets endorsed a separate East Germany.
10. False. The threat was to Greece and Turkey.
11. False. It was developed in response to the economic weakness and threat of domestic communism in Western Europe.
12. False. The fundamental purpose of NATO was to defend Europe against the Soviets.
13. True
14. False. Truman defeated Dewey despite splits in his own Democratic party.
15. True

II. B.

1. a
2. d
3. b
4. e
5. d
6. e
7. c
8. b
9. c
10. d
11. a
12. e
13. a
14. d
15. c

II. C.

1. GI Bill of Rights
2. Sunbelt

3. Levittown
4. baby boom
5. Yalta
6. Cold War
7. Bretton Woods
8. United Nations
9. Nuremberg trials
10. Marshall Plan
11. North Atlantic Treaty Organization (NATO)
12. Nationalists
13. NSC-68
14. House Un-American Activities Committee
15. 38th parallel

II. D.

1. b
2. a
3. k
4. m
5. d
6. o
7. l
8. e
9. j
10. h
11. c
12. i
13. g
14. n
15. f

II. E.

2

4

1

3

5

II. F.

1. a
2. e
3. b
4. h
5. j
6. g
7. c
8. d
9. i
10. f

II. G.

1. 1970
2. 1980
3. 1980–1990
4.

1950–1960:	+20%
1970–1980:	–20%
1980–1990:	+5%
1990–1999:	–10%

II. H.

1. France
2. British
3. Austria and Czechoslovakia
4. below
5. U.S.S.R.
6. South Korea

CHAPTER 37

II. A.

1. False. Blue-collar jobs began to decline, and unions slowly lost membership in the 1950s.
2. False. Religious leaders, especially evangelicals, thrived on spreading their message through television.
3. True
4. True.

5. False. It held that segregated schools were inherently unequal and had to be integrated.
6. False. King made the African American churches the basis of his movement.
7. False. The reverse is true: they relied more on nuclear weapons than on conventional forces.
8. False. The United States opposed the British-French invasion of Suez.
9. True
10. False. The summit was never held, and its collapse deepened Cold War tensions.
11. True
12. True
13. True
14. False. Most of the World War II novels were not realistic but absurdist in tone.
15. True

II. B.

1. e
2. b
3. c
4. b
5. a
6. d
7. d
8. c
9. d
10. e
11. d
12. c
13. b
14. c
15. c

II. C.

1. McCarthyism
2. *Brown* v. *Board of Education*
3. massive retaliation
4. Montgomery bus boycott
5. Suez Canal
6. *Sputnik*

7. *An American Dilemma*
8. U-2
9. Operation Wetback
10. *The Feminine Mystique*

II. D.

1. g
2. k
3. o
4. f
5. l
6. b
7. m
8. a
9. h
10. n
11. d
12. j
13. c
14. e
15. i

II. E.

3

5

1

4

2

II. F.

1. f
2. a
3. g
4. e
5. c
6. j
7. b

8. h
9. d
10. i

II. G.

1. Missouri
2. Virginia, Florida, and Tennessee
3. Texas and Louisiana
4. ten: Nevada: 3, Hawaii: 3, New Mexico: 4
5. 60

CHAPTER 38

II. A.

1. True
2. False. It was applied mostly to struggles with communism in the underdeveloped world—Asia and Latin America.
3. False. The coup brought military dictatorships and political instability in South Vietnam.
4. True
5. True
6. False. It was the civil rights movement in Birmingham and elsewhere that encouraged Kennedy to become more outspoken in endorsing civil rights.
7. False. Johnson had such large Democratic majorities in Congress that he did not need Republicans' or southern Democrats' support.
8. False. The Gulf of Tonkin Resolution gave the president a blank check for the whole war in Vietnam.
9. True
10. True
11. False. Most of the riots were in the North, which showed that race was a national and not just a southern problem.
12. True
13. True
14. False. There were similar political upheavals and youth rebellions in many countries in the 1960s.
15. False. The Catholic Church also underwent major change and upheaval.

II. B.

1. c
2. c
3. a

4. b
5. e
6. a
7. c
8. b
9. d
10. d
11. e
12. d
13. b
14. a
15. b

II. C.

1. Peace Corps
2. Berlin Wall
3. New Frontier
4. Alliance for Progress
5. Bay of Pigs
6. Cuban missile crisis
7. Freedom Riders
8. Great Society
9. Gulf of Tonkin Resolution
10. Voting Rights Act of 1965
11. Black Power
12. Tet
13. Six-Day War
14. Students for a Democratic Society (SDS)
15. Stonewall Inn raid

II. D.

1. j
2. b
3. l
4. h
5. o

6. n
7. a
8. e
9. g
10. f
11. c
12. d
13. k
14. i
15. m

II. E.

3

1

2

4

5

II. F.

1. c
2. h
3. e
4. g
5. d
6. i
7. b
8. j
9. a
10. f

II. G.

1. 1974 (1973 or 1975 are acceptable answers)
2. 1973 and 1978
3. From about 1974 to 1976. The difference would be explained by a rise in the total U.S. population.
4. 1980

II. H.

1. Laos and Cambodia
2. five
3. Vermont, New Hampshire, New Jersey, and Delaware
4. Michigan, Minnesota, Washington, Texas, and Hawaii

CHAPTER 39

II. A.

1. False. It sought to transfer the burden of the war to the South Vietnamese, while Americans withdrew.
2. True
3. True
4. True
5. True
6. False. Nixon supported both environmental (EPA) and worker health and safety (OSHA) legislation.
7. False. The burning issue was Vietnam.
8. False. The bombing campaign was conducted in complete secrecy; Congress strongly opposed it when it became known.
9. True
10. True
11. False. Conservative Republicans joined in calling for Nixon's resignation.
12. False. Ford continued to pursue the Nixon-Kissinger policy of détente.
13. False. The Equal Rights Amendment was defeated.
14. False. Carter's "malaise speech" cost him badly in public support and caused the nation to largely ignore his calls for energy sacrifices.
15. True

II. B.

1. c
2. c
3. d
4. a
5. e
6. b
7. d
8. b

9. c
10. d
11. e
12. b
13. e
14. c
15. e

II. C.

1. Vietnamization
2. Kent State
3. Pentagon Papers
4. My Lai
5. southern strategy
6. Philadelphia Plan
7. Watergate
8. War Powers Act
9. Environmental Protection Agency (EPA)
10. détente
11. Helsinki accords
12. Equal Rights Amendment (ERA)
13. *Roe* v. *Wade*
14. "malaise speech"
15. (Iranian) hostage crisis

II. D.

1. l
2. d
3. h
4. k
5. e
6. c
7. i
8. n
9. b
10. m

11. j
12. a
13. g
14. o
15. f

II. E.

6

4

2

1

3

5

II. F.

1. c
2. g
3. h
4. d
5. f
6. a
7. j
8. i
9. b
10. e

II. G.

1. Nixon's diplomacy involved a delicate and dangerous effort to deal with both the communist powers. His balance bar is a head of wheat—showing his use of American grain sales as a key to his diplomatic effort.
2. Nixon's career as a tough law and order anticrime politician is satirized. The attempt to cover up the Watergate crimes is not very successful, since the burglar's tools and tapes are plainly visible.
3. Nixon is portrayed as only one of the long line of presidents involved in Vietnam.

CHAPTER 40

II. A.

1. True
2. False. Reagan's victory brought many other Republicans into office.

3. False. Reagan kept his conservative promises.
4. False. Reagan's supply-side economic policies did not bog down and actually broke the stalemate in Congress.
5. False. Reagan's policies were strongly supported by British Prime Minister Margaret Thatcher (but not by other European allies).
6. True
7. True
8. True
9. True
10. True
11. True
12. False. The minor restraints on *Roe* v. *Wade* only heightened the political conflict over abortion.
13. False. The rebellions in Eastern Europe came first, followed by the collapse of communism in the Soviet Union.
14. True.
15. True

II. B.

1. e
2. b
3. d
4. a
5. c
6. b
7. e
8. e
9. c
10. b
11. a
12. b
13. c
14. b
15. e

II. C.

1. Neoconservatives
2. Proposition 13

3. supply-side economics
4. yuppies
5. boll weevils
6. Solidarity
7. *Glasnost* and *Perestroika*
8. Sandinistas
9. Contras
10. Iran-Contra Affair
11. Strategic Defense Initiative
12. Moral Majority
13. Berlin Wall
14. Tiananmen Square
15. Operation Desert Storm

II. D.

1. g
2. k
3. o
4. n
5. f
6. c
7. l
8. h
9. e
10. b
11. d
12. i
13. a
14. j
15. m

II. E.

3

6

1

2

4

5

II. F.

1. i
2. e
3. g
4. a
5. c
6. j
7. b
8. f
9. h
10. d
11. o
12. k
13. l
14. m
15. n

II. G.

1. 1983
2. Two years (1985 to 1987)
3. Any three of the following:
   a. 1981: Iran releases American hostages
   b. 1983: U.S. marines killed in Lebanon
   c. 1986: U.S. bombing raid on Libya; Iran-contra scandal revealed
   d. 1987: U.S. naval escorts begin in Persian Gulf
4. Any three of the following:
   a. 1985: U.S.-Soviet arms-control talks resume; Mikhail Gorbachev comes to power in the Soviet Union; First Reagan-Gorbachev summit meeting, in Geneva
   b. 1986: Second Reagan-Gorbachev summit meeting, in Reykjavik, Iceland
   c. 1987: Third Reagan-Gorbachev summit meeting in Washington, D.C.; INF Treaty signed
   d. 1988: Fourth Reagan-Gorbachev summit meeting, in Moscow
   e. 1989: Eastern Europe throws off communist regimes

CHAPTER 41

II. A.

1. False. Clinton endorsed past Democratic traditions on civil rights. He sought to alter Democrats' previous positions on the economy and defense.
2. True
3. False. In the 1994 congressional elections, every incumbent Republican gubernatorial, senatorial, and congressional candidate was reelected. Republicans also picked up eleven new governorships, eight seats in the Senate, and fifty-three seats in the House, giving them control of both chambers of the federal Congress for the first time in forty years.
4. False. Congress took only limited actions on gun control, despite these violent events.
5. False. The strong economy of the 1990s encouraged Clinton to lower international trade barriers and promote free trade.
6. False. The Clinton administration attempted but failed to achieve an Israeli-Palestinian peace agreement.
7. True
8. True
9. True
10. False. Bin Laden was a Saudi Arabian citizen who took refuge in Afghanistan.
11. False. The United Nations authorized the use of force against Iraq in 1991.
12. True
13. False. The proposal was strongly opposed by liberals and senior citizens' groups, and quickly failed.
14. True
15. False. The primary cause was public discontent with the Iraq War.

II. B.

1. c
2. c
3. c
4. c
5. b
6. e
7. a
8. b
9. b
10. c
11. e

12. b
13. b

II. C.

1. Democratic Leadership Council
2. Don't ask, don't tell
3. Branch Davidians
4. Columbine High School
5. Contract with America
6. North American Free Trade Agreement (NAFTA)
7. World Trade Organization (WTO)
8. Haiti
9. Lewinsky Affair
10. Green Party
11. Electoral College
12. Pentagon
13. Al Qaeda
14. USA-Patriot Act
15. Abu Ghraib

II. D.

1. h
2. d
3. j
4. n
5. k
6. m
7. f
8. a
9. o
10. b
11. g
12. c
13. l
14. i
15. e

II. E.

1. 3
2. 2
3. 1
4. 5
5. 4

CHAPTER 42

II. A.

1. True
2. True
3. True
4. False. A majority of mothers with small children worked outside the home.
5. False. The elderly became more affluent through programs like Social Security and Medicare.
6. True
7. True
8. True
9. False. Race still heavily influence the reaction to such events.
10. True
11. False. Immigration reform was opposed by most Republicans.
12. False. Americans in the early twenty-first century were better educated than ever before, and these educated Americans were consumers of high culture.
13. False. Writing about the West increased in quantity and quality
14. False. The art capital was New York City.
15. True

II. B.

1. c
2. c
3. a
4. d
5. a
6. d
7. b
8. e
9. a

10. c
11. a
12. b
13. e
14. c
15. b

II. C.

1. Microsoft Corporation
2. Medicare
3. Immigration Reform and Control Act
4. Hispanics (Latin Americans or Mexican Americans OK)
5. United Farm Workers
6. Los Angeles
7. the West (Northwest or Pacific Northwest is also acceptable)
8. National Endowment for the Arts (NEA)
9. Abstract expressionism
10. *Exxon Valdez*

II. D.

1. g
2. c
3. j
4. i
5. l
6. k
7. h
8. a
9. f
10. e
11. b
12. d

II. E.

3

2

1

4

5

II. F.

1. d
2. j
3. b
4. e
5. a
6. f
7. h
8. i
9. c
10. g